An AUTHOR'S GUIDE TO

SCHOLARLY PUBLISHING

An Author's Guide to Scholarly Publishing

≡ ≡ ≡ ≡ ≡ ≡ ≡ ≡ ≡ ≡

Robin Derricourt

PRINCETON UNIVERSITY PRESS · PRINCETON, NEW JERSEY

Library of Congress Cataloging-in-Publication Data

Derricourt, Robin M.
An author's guide to scholarly publishing / Robin Derricourt.
p. cm.
Includes bibliographical references and index.
ISBN 0-691-03710-8 (cloth : alk. paper).
ISBN 0-691-03709-4 (pbk. : alk. paper)
1. Scholarly publishing.   I. Title.
Z286.S37D46   1996
070.5—dc20   95-36849 CIP

This book has been composed in Palatino

Princeton University Press books are
printed on acid-free paper and meet the guidelines
for permanence and durability of the Committee
on Production Guidelines for Book Longevity
of the Council on Library Resources

Printed in the United States of America by Princeton Academic Press

1 3 5 7 9 10 8 6 4 2

1 3 5 7 9 10 8 6 4 2
(Pbk.)

TO MY PARENTS

Stanley Derricourt and Edith Derricourt

CONTENTS

ACKNOWLEDGEMENTS   xi

INTRODUCTION   3

PLANNING AND WRITING
  1 *Audience*   7
  2 *Style*   10
  3 *Structure*   12

PREPARATION OF MANUSCRIPT
  4 *Length*   16
  5 *Layout*   18
  6 *Word processing the manuscript*   20
  7 *Word processing for the typesetter*   23
  8 *Desktop publishing and camera-ready copy* 24
  9 *Notes*   28
 10 *Bibliographies*   30
 11 *Tables*   33
 12 *Illustrations*   35

APPROACHING A PUBLISHER
 13 *Selecting a publisher*   41
 14 *In-house publishing*   43
 15 *Multiple submissions*   46
 16 *Complete manuscripts*   48
 17 *The formal proposal*   51
     Checklist for submitting a proposal 54
 18 *Peer review*   55
 19 *Visit*   58
 20 *Literary agents*   59
 21 *No reply*   61

CATEGORY OF BOOK
 22 *Scholarly book*   63
 23 *Technical monograph*   65
 24 *Thesis/dissertation*   67
 25 *Conference volume*   70
 26 *Edited volume*   73
 27 *Festschrift*   75

28 *Collected papers*   76
29 *Across the disciplines*   77
30 *Trade book*   81
31 *Textbook*   83
32 *New journals*   84
33 *The non-academic author*   88

THE PUBLISHING DECISION
34 *No—why?*   91
35 *Revise and resubmit*   93
36 *Yes—but revise*   94
37 *Yes*   95

DEALING WITH PRODUCTION
38 *Contract*   97
39 *Late delivery*   100
40 *Delivery of the manuscript*   104
      Checklist for delivery of the manuscript for production   109
41 *Book title*   110
42 *Copyediting*   112
43 *Updating the disk*   116
44 *Design of the pages*   117
45 *Typesetting*   120
46 *Proofreading and alterations in proof*   124
47 *Illustrations in production*   127
48 *Providing camera-ready copy*   129
49 *Preparing the index*   131
50 *Jacket and cover design*   136
51 *Printing*   139
52 *Errata slips*   140
53 *Don't assume all is well*   141

MARKETING THE BOOK
54 *The cost of books*   143
55 *Pricing a book*   146
56 *Changing the pricing variables*   153
57 *Paperbacking*   157
58 *Help with marketing*   160
59 *The book launch*   163
60 *Getting reviews and publishing reviews*   165
61 *Newspapers and magazines*   169
62 *Radio and television coverage*   171
63 *Bookshop sales*   174
64 *Library sales*   176

65 *Direct sales*   178
66 *Prizes*   180
67 *Subsidiary rights*   181
68 *Translations*   185
69 *Getting your book into the developing world*   187
70 *Reprints and new editions*   192
71 *Keeping in touch*   195

PUBLISHING AND THE ACADEMY
72 *Research grants—inputs and outputs*   197
73 *Who sets the agenda?*   200
74 *Books and the appointments committee*   203
75 *Subsidies*   207
76 *Book exhibits and the academic conference*   211
77 *Anthologies*   215
78 *Is too much published?*   217
79 *The electronic library and the end of the book*   221

80 *Conclusion*   226

BIBLIOGRAPHY   229

INDEX   231

ACKNOWLEDGEMENTS

A book such as this is built upon the support, advice and experience of many people—authors, publishing colleagues, readers and more. Some friends will recognize their ideas or questions, and though unnamed they bear my thanks.

I would particularly like to thank those who have commented on parts of the manuscript, including Colin Day, John Patrick Diggins, Daryl Feil, Hari Ho, Linda Hollick, Richard Hollick, Andrew MacLennan, Peter McDonough, Lauren Oppenheim and Peter Warwick, as well as other colleagues. My greatest thanks go to my copyeditors, Eric Van Tassel and Jane Van Tassel. The author knows what the reader can only guess—the weighty contribution made by their commitment of professionalism, insight and care.

My enthusiasm for the publishing craft is due to the commitment of many to high standards combined with creative enthusiasm: among those with whom I have worked I might single out the example and enthusiasm of Julian Rea at Longman Group and Judith Butcher, Jeremy Mynott and John Trevitt at Cambridge University Press. For encouragement to complete this writing I would thank Peter Dougherty, Jane Richardson, Robert Sessions, Bruce Sims; above all Frances Derricourt, Timothy Derricourt and especially Marguerite Derricourt, who made sure it was started, written and finished.

I grew up in a house where the writer was the hero and the publisher or editor not always the ally: I dedicate the book to my parents.

AN AUTHOR'S GUIDE TO

SCHOLARLY PUBLISHING

INTRODUCTION

Imagine a common scene in an academic office or home. Dr. Abelard has been working for some years on his scholarly book, to the encouragement of his departmental colleagues and the despair of his family. He has presented some chapters to seminars at his own or other institutions, or in abridged form at scholarly conferences in warm American hotels or cold British universities. Other chapters he has shown to colleagues, so that he feels reassured he is doing something of quality, in line with his brief to be a research scholar as well as a teacher and (increasingly) a departmental administrator.

After some delays with the word processing and a final delay with a temperamental photocopier, he decides to send the complete finished manuscript off to a publishing house whom he respects for their contribution to his field over the years. He feels sure they will be glad to publish it. He packages the manuscript in firm cardboard and encloses a very brief, modest letter introducing himself and the manuscript to the publisher's office. He knows they will need time to review the manuscript and determine its worth, so he sits back with his relieved family and admiring colleagues.

Dr. Abelard is astonished to receive a letter two weeks later which reads:

Dear Dr. Abelard,

We are grateful to you for allowing us to consider your manuscript *Conflict and Change*. Unfortunately, we have to be very selective in our current publishing programme, and we are unable to offer you publication. This particular work would not suit our list. We are sure you will be successful in finding the right publisher for it in due course, and we wish you every success.   *Yours truly, Editorial Department*

Dr. Abelard feels a mixture of anger and puzzlement. If his book really is no good, have the years of work been in vain? He knows (as do his colleagues, and his family) that he has reached a career barrier. The publication of a book by a reputable publisher is obligatory if he is to get promotion. But as a trained scholar he examines the letter carefully to deconstruct its real significance. They were grateful—a positive sign. The selection, though—why select the books they do publish, and not his? And who is doing the selecting? Did they want to publish but found themselves unable to do so—what were the inhibiting factors? Perhaps the publisher is about to be taken over by some money-grabbing entrepreneur of foreign origins? Yes, they are confident that the manuscript will find a publisher—but if it has given them this confidence, why not enough to publish it themselves? Perhaps it really is no good. For the first time in some years, Dr. Abelard takes up an invitation to join the veteran bachelors in the happy hour at the staff club bar, and is still there when closing time arrives.

Fortunately, Dr. Abelard has not seen another letter, from the same publisher to another author. This is in response to a strange manuscript, a prose poem created in a rather isolated rural setting under distinctly chemical influences, and mailed off (with inadequate postage, and before the chemical traces are fully erased) to an address located under "publishing" in the telephone directory. This is returned to the post office box of its author with a letter which reads:

Dear Mr. Zwingli,

We are grateful to you for allowing us to consider your manuscript *Kerpow: The Expanding Universe of the Mind*. Unfortunately, we have to be very selective in our current publishing programme, and we are unable to offer you publication. This particular work would not suit our list. We are sure you will be successful in finding the right publisher for it in due course, and we wish you every success.

Yours truly, Editorial Department

Authors often forget, and publishing editors forget at least as often, that there are really only two answers to the question "Do you want to publish this manuscript?"

One of them is Yes.

The other is No.

This is not altered by editorial rationalization: about how near to suitable, or how conditionally interesting, the manuscript is, or how in better times . . . Nor is it altered by how the publisher responds—helpfully and with encouragement, or harshly with a standard letter. At the end of the day, either manuscript X is signed up by publisher Z or it is not.

People sometimes believe themselves to be in an in-between position because of letters expressing cautious interest, an invitation to submit a proposal or a manuscript, an editor's suggestion, a conversation that encourages both parties to believe they are in business. But that is of little value compared to the Yes that is formalized only by the signing of a publisher's contract. Nothing else is Yes.

The reasons Dr. Abelard's manuscript received the answer No might be one or more of the following:

- it is too short
- it is too long
- it is too controversial
- it is too boring
- it appears to be academically unsound
- it is reputable, but we are taking only the outstanding
- we cannot identify the market for it
- it is so interdisciplinary it might fall between markets
- we no longer publish in this field
- we do not publish at this level
- we have a quota for new titles which is full this year
- we have a quota for this subject area which is full this year
- we are under a budget squeeze
- the editor for this subject left recently and will not be replaced immediately
- overwork means I do not have time to consider a long manuscript without a detailed synopsis
- the company has just been sold and is being turned into something different
- I am clearing my desk before going on long leave

Getting published

Publishers of scholarly books and authors of scholarly books need each other. Despite the scholar's illusion that the publishers have the upper hand, without good books they will cease to be publishers. No editor who says No (or Yes!) to all comers holds a job long. The academic, scientific and professional worlds are full of authors looking for a publisher and publishers looking for authors.

The purpose of this book is to help bring them together. Specifically, it aims to help the scholarly author to find the right publisher, in the right way, with the right book and at the right time, with the minimum anguish. Once the author and publisher have found each other, this book provides some perspective on the relationship and stages of editing, production, marketing and beyond. There are many misunderstandings between authors (or would-be authors) and their publishers (or would-be publishers), and this book makes an attempt at reducing these, in the hope that it will simplify the path to and through publication.

Inevitably it reflects a publisher's personal perspective and experience (some on the author's side of the relationship). But it is astonishing how much similarity there is across the range of scholarly publishers in the English-speaking world. Because much of this publishing is international, and the authors are working in international fields, a common culture of academic publishing has emerged. The similarities are greater than the differences between academic publishing in the United States and Britain, Australia and Canada, Ireland and New Zealand. Writers from other areas where English is the medium of academic communication share much of the same culture. There are differences, but not dramatic ones, between disciplines of study. And while one useful study (Paul Parsons, *Getting Published: The Acquisition Process at University Presses*, Knoxville: University of Tennessee Press, 1989) showed the similarities across American university presses (but essentially no different from UK or Australian university presses), another (Walter W. Powell, *Getting into Print: The Decision Making Process in Scholarly Publishing*, Chicago: University of Chicago Press, 1985) showed how similar commercial academic imprints are to university presses.

The latter point is perhaps worth emphasizing. University presses (most of them) operate in the same real world of commerce as do privately owned presses—they have to generate cash and avoid losing money in order to continue to publish, even if some universities give their presses some subsidy. All publishers have to achieve sales and pay royalties to attract authors, and reward staff in order to keep them. Privately owned imprints which publish academic books—and there are many—sell the same kinds of books to the same market at the same range of prices, and their overall criteria for selection must in general be similar; otherwise they do not find a market or attract authors. The university presses impose a formal review process for manuscripts which the commercial presses may abbreviate. The main difference, I would argue, is that university presses retain all their surplus for reinvestment; commercial presses retain only part of their surplus and distribute the rest as profit—but unlike university presses they are subject to taxation.

This book, then, should have something to say to scholarly authors in a wide range of disciplines and in all parts of the English-speaking world. If it provokes dissent, or surprise, or disagreement, then it will have achieved some of what publishers are looking for in the books they publish.

$\mathscr{P}$LANNING AND WRITING

≡ ≡ ≡ ≡ ≡ ≡ ≡ ≡ ≡ ≡ ≡ ≡

« 1 » *Audience*

Dear Ms. Construe,

On the telephone you said you would be sending us details of your new book. You say this would be suitable for everyone—for students, for academics and professionals in your field, and for the general reader. You were surprised when we said we preferred books for a narrower band. Let me try to explain.

First, I suppose, publishers have got used to a world in which far too many books are published. Of course, it is always another publisher whose books are the superfluous ones! But in most subjects, at most levels, and for most needs, one or more books exist already. There are perhaps 67,000 new books published every year in the USA, for example, to add to over a million already in print from 41,000 publishers. In Britain around 68,000 are published each year (including, of course, many of the same titles), with 573,000 titles available from 21,250 publishers. And Australia not only has the US and UK titles to sell but publishes over 5000 new books or new editions of its own each year, to join 53,000 already in print. Canadian publications are of the same order. *International Books in Print* adds another 236,000 titles in English from outside the USA and the UK.

So in reality it sometimes seems that bookshops, librarians and others in the book world are looking for a good reason not to buy a new title. Hard-pressed teachers, professors and research workers probably take the same view. Can they do without the new book whose review they have just read, or which has been advertised to them? And most students would certainly rather spend their limited cash on something other than a new book.

Our aim is to publish books they can't do without. Is your book one of those?

Most people can do without most books. Even highly literate bookworms with enormous appetites for new books manage to do without most of the new books that are published. Otherwise they would neither eat nor sleep—nor think.

Of course you are right: there are some key issues which every intelligent reader needs and wants to know about. But that is why people read newspapers and weekly magazines, and sometimes general periodicals of greater depth. Not many people want to read 100,000 words about an issue, because there are so many issues. People need to have a special reason for reading a whole book about a topic, other than for entertainment.

So it does not help to say the book is for the general reader. As publishers we need a specific readership that can be defined—and reached.

What kinds of special reasons are needed for a sale? Well, being a student is a good reason. A student in high school, or at a college or university, devours words and ideas—whether from teachers' handouts, snippets of chapters and articles photocopied or read in the library, or books. Some books for students are designed consciously as textbooks for a specific course. Is your book one of these?

Please pause before you say, Yes, you are writing a textbook. Do you mean that a lecturer or teacher will say to their students that this book covers all or most of their course, and they must each purchase a personal copy and absorb it if they are to understand the subject, follow the course and pass the examinations? Of course textbooks do vary from discipline to discipline and country to country. Many textbooks are planned for use by the teacher as a main crutch: one chapter, one topic, one week, with highlights marked and questions at the end. Other textbooks are expected to complement the teacher, give greater depth or wider perspective. A good teacher may set three textbooks with different perspectives—but not 20 textbooks, all tangential to the course. Those come into the category of "further reading."

Certainly not all the books a student reads for a course are textbooks. But all textbooks are books which correspond to the scope commonly taught in a subject, are didactic, have an appropriate length and level of illustration, assume the right level of knowledge and background, and are written at a language level appropriate for the student. To be economic for a publisher to issue, they must correspond to courses as they exist (or are emerging), perspectives the teachers hold, and approaches that interest the student, and they must correspond to enough courses to make the book viable. If the textbook corresponds to a course taught at only one institution or taken only as a small postgraduate option at a few centres, it probably won't be viable. And if it is too far ahead of its time, it may fail too. On the other hand, if it is dull, too traditionalist and staid in a changing field, it deserves to fail.

So your book is not really a textbook, even though you would expect a lot of students to look at the library copy and read parts of it (or, more likely, photocopy a chapter).

Is it aimed at the academic reader? Yes, you say, and across many disciplines, and so of wide appeal. To be honest, most academic readers, when they read for relaxation, probably read the same as everyone else—a range of books such as adorn the shelves of a good public library or trade bookstore. Within a discipline, academics are hard pressed to keep up with the journals and reviews in their own field or even sub-field. They read the books that they can't do without—those that make a major contribution to their field, or explain at a more basic level an ancillary field they need to keep up with.

Academics buy books of this kind at certain times—either when they are young, eager and unattached, forging the start of their research and teaching; or when they are old, prosperous and successful, and if there is room on their bookshelves. The average scholar is not sitting in a booklined study looking for excuses to spend money (though a gratifying number do so!), but is maintaining a family and a mortgage and an aging motor vehicle while the kids go through school. Scholars are glad to have books to review for journals, willing to purchase essential tools of the trade and keep up with their colleagues and ahead of their students, but books of marginal interest or cross-disciplinary concern they are just as likely to leave—though the opportunity might arise to borrow a copy from the library.

So your book is for the library market, you say. But many academic libraries wait for a book to be recommended (many public libraries will do the same). In universities and colleges, libraries have a basic commitment to renew subscriptions to their journals and a high commitment to staff salaries, services and costly new technologies to access their collections. The balance can go on a small proportion of the important books published every year. If there is a limited budget for a subject area (and there usually is), the members of one academic department will probably agree to recommend that the library acquire books central to their subject—leaving the interdisciplinary books to someone else. Such books may well fall into the troughs between subjects: everyone agrees interdisciplinary studies are a good thing, but on someone else's budget. Even some of those fields deliberately developed as cross-disciplinary, like area studies, have suffered as hard-pressed scholars retreat behind their disciplinary boundary walls. Of course some academic institutions have dissolved their departments into broad schools of study. But maturity sometimes erodes the appeal of this, and those who wish to move on in their careers find the more conventional disciplinary limits taking on a strange new attraction.

As for your book, you mention that the people who have to have it and cannot do without it are professional ecologists hired to do environmental impact statements under contract, and postgraduates on courses which train them for that role. There is a specific, real, identifiable and probably reachable market in an expanding field. We could well be in business. Send us the manuscript.   *Yours truly, R.M.D.*

« 2 » *Style*

Dear Dr. Sinclair,

The submission of your manuscript brought a warm glow—and the more I read, the greater the pleasure. It was not so much the content, but rather the style which attracted me to it, made me want to read on, page after page. For a serious manuscript, a piece of academic scientific writing, the open style and sympathetic approach of the book are sure to put it head and shoulders above a hundred other manuscripts jostling for publication and competing for the attention of busy readers.

To receive such a well-written manuscript was a pleasure and, sadly, a rarity. While general trade publishers are troubled by stylish writers who lack confidence and up-to-date knowledge in their subject, most scientific and academic publishers complain regularly about the opposite—experts who do not easily communicate.

Why is good style so rare in scholarly writing? Why do so many academics, highly educated, sensitive people, create barriers in their text? Even good clear teachers in the classroom, who write accessible pieces for the golf club newsletter, can turn their ideas into inaccessible prose when it comes to a book manuscript.

Why is style important? Perhaps because it is the compliment an author pays to a reader, saying "This piece of prose is written for you, because I want you to read it, understand it and appreciate it, because you—the reader—matter." If the text says, "I don't much care about you as a reader," the consumer is unlikely to care much about the author—or the author's ideas and arguments.

Style does not necessarily mean flourish. Good style in scholarly and scientific writing is often invisible, as are good editing and good page design. The flaws are visible, not the quality. Poor style is tangible, good style often not. Mannered style, which wears its qualities like a slogan on a T-shirt, is not required. The distinguished (and the metropolitan French) can perhaps get away with it, and some may even make a reputation for it, but it is not for all. You have avoided it in your welcome manuscript.

Good style is primarily clarity. It reflects clarity of ideas—an open, lucid, even luminous presentation. It is also clarity of structure, the ease with which the reader sees not only what is being said, but how the book is organized to present the argument. And within this clear structure, style is clarity of expression: sentence structure, phrasing, vocabulary all intended to convey the explanation or argument or description to an audience or to a range of readers.

Clarity—and the sense of communication—is all that really matters. Beyond that, every reader, every author, and certainly every editor will have preferences in style. And many have preferences in the style guides they refer to, or the model authors they seek to follow. These subjectivities are fine. Some like to follow prescriptive guides on correct English style. Some are influenced by informal descriptive reference works which demonstrate the range of actual usage in details of style matters. Some writers always seek to use the active voice; others can weave a seductive web with passive voice and subordinate clauses in an elegant construction. But clarity remains the test. Too often the adoption of Latinate over Anglo-Saxon English, or of passive over active voice, disguises half-baked ideas and unresolved formulations.

What good style does *not* mean is "talking down." Some of the proponents of good, plain English risk the use of patronizing language that jars as much as the complex variety. Sophisticated ideas may demand sophisticated (but not obscure) expression. Not all ideas need or can use simplified language. Those ideas that can be expressed plainly and simply surely should be, but they account for only part of the academic spectrum.

In my view, good expression does not mean the total removal of jargon. Each form of scholarly discourse has its language, understood by those in the field and mystifying to those outside it. One woman's jargon is another man's core intellectual framework. I suspect the trouble comes in the "softer studies"—the social sciences and humanities. Technical terms are accepted as the language of the discipline in pure mathematics, laser particle physics, estuarine ecology, ophthalmology, palaeolithic archaeology. In philosophy, theology, music it is the same—there are terms which have a technical meaning. But in social theory, sociology, literary theory, economics, social history, suddenly it is a case not of disciplinary terms of art, but of jargon. Why so?

Perhaps it is a compliment to those disciplines—that some readers from outside the disciplines want to read and understand their writing, though they might not so happily delve into professional-level microbiology or structural engineering. If that is so, it is an argument for introducing unfamiliar terms gently, defining them the first time they are used, perhaps even repeating the definitions in an appendix or in the index to help the cross-disciplinary reader along. That is part of the welcoming embrace. Rather than avoid intra-disciplinary terms, why not define them clearly when used?

There is less excuse for numerous and obscure acronyms and abbreviations. If they are used only once or twice, why not spell them out in full? If they are used frequently, do they need to be? And if they do have to be abbreviated, an easily accessible reference list avoids giving the reader a feeling of being an ignorant outsider. If you find it too tedious to type them out in full each time, why not use your word processor's search-and-replace facility to substitute the full form for the abbreviation after typing is complete?

With good ideas, good structure, good expression and explanation of terms, a book wins the hearts and minds of readers. Why would anyone aim lower? Is it a matter of ability, or is it a matter of time? Or is it actually the desire to impress rather than express, to demonstrate boldly that one is not frightened of complexity, that one is up there with the best of them?

This possibility is reinforced by the demographic distribution of less graceful writing. If we look at the student dissertation or the first papers of a young scientist or scholar, the language is often obscure. If we look at the writing of a senior scientist or scholar we particularly admire, it usually is not. Most respected senior scholars and scientists in the English-speaking world are admired for the clarity of their writing; they no longer have to write to daunt their readers. Are we accepting the wrong models, or expecting the wrong level of writing as proof of competence in a discipline?

But in your manuscript you know what you want to say, and have given the book the best organization to say it. You have carefully controlled the language you use, and explained terms which may not be familiar to some of your readers. You write for an audience, not just for yourself or to impress. For avoiding so many of these problems—for writing a book that is designed to be read and is a pleasure to read— thank you. We look forward to publishing it, and we hope that readers and reviewers appreciate the effort you have gone to in using the writing craft to its best advantage.   *Yours truly, R.M.D.*

« 3 » *Structure*

Dear Professor Nile,

As we are very interested in your idea for a book, it was useful to have the chance to comment on its proposed structure.

All publishers and publishers' editors have their own individual prejudices and preferences, of course. If every book was organized in the same way, scholarly publishing would be very dull. And different disciplines have their own expectations too—on what appears in the text and what in appendices, on how much data you publish and how much background you give.

But if we are to advise on your book, here are some thoughts. First, remember that your book, unlike a thesis or a commissioned report, is not obligatory reading for anyone. And unlike the audience for a seminar or conference paper, readers can get up and run away at any point. You have to win them one by one. You have to ensnare them, hold their attention, leave them feeling satisfied at the end of the experience of your book.

The other thing to remember is sometimes hard to believe: that many—probably most—of your readers will not read the whole book but will dip into it at a point of concern or relevance to them. You need to help them find what they want—and maybe then you will attract them to read the rest of the book.

So the first thing to say about structure is that it must be clear. In other words, the contents list should, ideally, make it plain how the argument of the book is organized. For a scholarly book, chapter titles which are not too enigmatic may help. And if the chapters fall into discrete blocks, grouping them into (named) "parts" is a further help.

But beyond that, it is a courtesy to the reader in many types of book to divide your chapters with subheadings, and sometimes to list those subheadings in the contents list. That helps to summarize the book's organization and identify the parts of most interest to a reader. We do not favour numbering the subheadings except in a book with a very formal structure—a description of geological or biological data, perhaps, or a very technical argument in philosophy or economics. This numbering of a complex argument often makes it easier to cross-reference than the troublesome insertion of page references late in the proof stage of book production.

An alternative to formal subheadings, for some books, will be to present a continuous analytical breakdown in the contents list, guiding the reader through the arguments of the book, with the number of the page where each topic or argument begins. This echoes a style once common in narrative non-fiction.

A guide for your readers to the structure of the book can be included in the Introduction. Some readers may get lost in your argument; a return to the Introduction will help them place the chapter within the overall structure.

And the organization of the book itself? Well, having not too obscure a structure helps the reader concentrate on the content. A Preface is usually best restricted to formalities—the necessary acknowledgements, perhaps something on the funding of the research or writing and the context in which it was done. Consider leaving the intellectual heart of the book for the Introduction. If you want people to read this (and they should), think of numbering it as Chapter 1—even giving it a title or subtitle.

In the Introduction readers want to know what questions you are asking and how you are seeking to answer them; what is the book's structure (as discussed above) but also, to some extent, the conclusions you reach. You may fear that if you give away all your secrets at the start, no one will read the book. But if you do not suggest where the book has led, no one may read the book that far! I would vote for including something of your overall conclusions of the book in the Introduction, but perhaps with sufficient left hanging to keep the reader in tow, inspired to follow through to the Conclusion. And do not be tempted to try and make your Introduction too grandiose in style; if anything, make it simpler and more open than the core of the book.

A common structure of students' dissertations, and a common mistake in some academic books, is to say the book is about a particular topic and then vanish into two or three lengthy chapters on something else as background. If you abandon your main topic for the first fifty pages, your readers might just abandon you altogether. So do consider giving either a long introductory chapter or enough material from the main thrust of the book before indulging in a lengthy excursus on historical background, or ideological framework, or data handling techniques.

There is some information that the readers need to make sense of the argument, particularly if they are unfamiliar with your field. If you include a basic map, a chronological chart, a genealogy or a list of essential acronyms, no one who is familiar with this material will mind the additional pages, and many who are less familiar will be in your debt. It is not enough to say that so-and-so appears in the text—your book will have uses beyond being read through at one sitting. By including this information prominently at the front of the book you emphasize its value; only if this material is very long (like a chronological list beyond a couple of pages) will the end of the book be a better position for it.

Endpapers look like a useful place to slip in a map or something similar, but they can be expensive for a book whose costing is already tight—and librarians love to use these for sticking labels. If you want to use the endpapers, repeat the same illustration on front and back endpapers. But if you go into paperback, then you may be done for!

Do not be afraid of breaking into the overall style of the book with something unpredictable. If a boxed-off two-page table is essential background for Part 2 of your book, put it in there. Perhaps each chapter of your book deals with a different city, and you want to record some basic historical facts on each city before your text begins. Then it might be much better to box this off as a separate feature before each chapter, rather than go through paragraphs of descriptive text which are not really part of your argument.

A Conclusion to your book, whether relatively brief or a full-length chapter, is usually appropriate. In some complex books, it may be suitable to say in the Introduction what you are going to say, and how; say it in the core of the book; and review in the Conclusion what you have said, and how. But in most cases you will want to use the Conclusion both to look back at what your book has meant and to look forward at what it implies for the discipline, or future research, or the world at large.

An appendix provides a place to present essential material that is not part of the core of the argument. But it is still part of the book; it still has to be paid for in typesetting and printing, and in fact a well-organized book of reasonable length may find itself priced beyond its readership (or ignored by reviewers or uncommitted readers) because of a self-indulgent deposit of appendices.

If data, lists, methodological background, laboratory technical results or detailed commentary on sources have to be within the same covers as the main book to make it a valid contribution to knowledge (the reader's knowledge), then include them as appendices. But if you just want to include them to show they exist, or to boast of the hard labour that went into the book, resist the temptation. It is usually much better to prepare a technical paper, available through your institution or some technical and data series, and include a note (it can be a prominent note!) in the book about the availability of this material for the minority of readers who will need and want it.

Conclude with your bibliography, or Further Reading, as appropriate. And don't even worry about the index at this stage. You could have a good long holiday before any work on that will be needed.

Yours truly, R.M.D.

ᏢREPARATION OF MANUSCRIPT

≣   ≣   ≣   ≣   ≣   ≣   ≣   ≣   ≣   ≣   ≣   ≣

« 4 » *Length*

Dear Dr. Terminus,

You asked how long your book should be. It is a difficult question on which to generalize, and one of the more important questions to review with your publisher.

If you have an offer of a contract from a publisher, it is essential to agree on the length (usually a maximum length) and include this in the contract so there is no misunderstanding.

If you are writing the book without a contract, the length has to be guided by the level and the discipline in which you are writing. But most books lie best under 300 pages and over 200 printed (not word processed) pages in a single-column format. Allowing for preliminary pages and index, that means an overall length between 70,000 and 120,000 words, inclusive of all notes, bibliography, appendices and tables. It is worth emphasizing this inclusiveness. It does not help the book's costing to cut material from the main text but have a lengthy section of notes or appendices. Discussions of length usually mean everything except the contents pages and the index.

Literary studies may be towards the shorter end of this spectrum, historical monographs towards the longer. You should deduct at least 200 words from this total for each half-page of illustration; so with 50 pieces of artwork at least 10,000 words (and probably more) should be subtracted from the total words available.

Publishers often say, "Write 80,000 words": that is in fact quite short for an academic book, but they know people will add on extras. A target length of 100,000 words is typical for a one-topic monograph in most disciplines of the humanities.

Textbooks can be as long or as short as the publisher perceives the costing and the subject demand; there is less of a problem with the length of a comprehensive text in a factually based subject like accountancy or engineering. Reference works, too, can be as long as the publisher agrees they should be.

Other lengthy books tend to be the occasional major work, or edition of a text, or detailed descriptive work. It is rarely appropriate for the first scholarly book by an academic author to be of exceptional length; that would demand exceptional enthusiasm from an audience not yet won.

Short books—say, under 60,000 words or 160 pages—often work best in a series, where one-topic books support each other in a common size, price and market.

Publishers find it difficult to price long books. The overhead costs of the commissioning and production control departments of the publisher, and the design, binding and marketing costs, are constant. In a longer book most of the variables increase—editing time, typesetting, printing and paper. The increased costs push up the likely price of the book; the higher price pushes down the likely sales, and therefore the print run. The lower print run means a higher cost for each copy of the book, since most of the production costs for an academic book are fixed costs, not a function of the print run; that in turn pushes the price up, and the cycle begins again. So a book of 500 pages may have to be sold for significantly more than twice the price of a book of 250 pages on the same topic—and will certainly be read by fewer people.

But short academic books have difficulties too. These difficulties do not arise in short general books or short textbooks, where the print runs are large. But any book has to spread its fixed costs over the print run. The costs of commissioning, design, binding and especially promotion and marketing are the same for a large or small title. In setting a price on a very short monograph, they have to be recovered and may place a heavy burden on the price of the book. These costs are reduced if there is a series of identical books—say, a group of topic books commissioned to be 128 pages each, designed and promoted together. But the solitary short scholarly book may find itself carrying a high price— a 120-page book will normally be significantly more than half the cost of a 240-page book, and readers will justifiably complain. So an author is not necessarily helping the book by making it very short.

A clear discussion between the author and the eventual publisher is needed, and some compromise may be called for. Do not be surprised if your publisher asks you to cut your book to a more "normal" length, but do not be astounded if you are told that a 45,000-word essay is too short for book publication and you are asked to expand it.

Yours truly, R.M.D.

« 5 » *Layout*

Dear Mr. Vermaat,

Like most editors, I am happy to advise you on the format for preparing your manuscript. It is better to be clear now rather than complete it in an unsuitable format.

There are of course writers' and editors' guides which give more help and suggestions on these points. A wise author will bypass artificial boundaries and read the guides for editors as well as those for authors.

Two separate sets of suggestions should be made—one for the majority of writers preparing their manuscripts on word processors, the other for writers who insist on using typewriters. Many traditional sources of advice are aimed at typists and for that reason are only partly applicable today.

The best advice for the academic book author working on a typewriter is: Sell it and buy a word processor. Typing may be acceptable for letters, short articles and the like. It can just about get by for works of fiction, which will often be considered by publishers only as a complete manuscript and which will not be reorganized substantially before publication.

An academic manuscript will almost always be revised at least once, and perhaps several times, between first writing and delivery to its copyeditor. The author may want to update, or revise for style. The publisher may require revisions or restructuring, or the publisher's reader may suggest improvements and changes the author would like to incorporate. A word processor is what makes this easier.

The cheapest word processor is more convenient for all this than the most expensive typewriter. There is no need to emulate the fancy equipment in the departmental office. But there is an argument in favour of the more common hardware—PC (IBM-compatible) or Macintosh—combined with a widely used word processing program. That makes it easier to change machines and to generate a disk of the computer files that can be used in typesetting.

There is no need, either, to own an expensive printer. A very modest printer can be used at all draft stages, and a better-quality printer borrowed to print out the version submitted to a publisher.

However, for the author who is doggedly preparing a manuscript by typewriter, it is necessary to prepare the script in the format required by the final copyeditor who marks it up for the printer (a format which can be imposed at a later stage if the author uses a word processor). That means substantial amounts of space—a good left-hand margin and a lesser one at the right, reasonable space at the top of the page and some space below the main text. The whole text must be double-spaced—the whole text, *including* quoted matter and the notes and bibliography.

The reason for this is not readability, but to provide space in which the publisher's staff can mark up the typescript. The editor needs space between the lines to make clear and unambiguous additions, deletions and substitutions, and to add codes for the typesetter (marking indents, italics and punctuation, distinguishing hyphens from long and short dashes, spelling out abbreviations). Marginal space is needed for coding of headings and special setting and for drawing attention to special sorts; and the designer and typesetter may also mark the typescript.

Notes should not be placed at the bottom of the typescript page, even if they are to appear as footnotes on the final printed page. They should be typed together on separate pages with a new page for the notes of each new chapter, and—all-important—they should be double-spaced.

When making changes on a typescript, do not make marginal marks such as are required in proof correction. Marginal proof corrections draw the typesetter's attention to individual changes to be made, and invite the typesetter to ignore everything not marked in the margin. The typescript is the copy for the typesetter and should read as continuous text. Additions should be inserted above the line, where they are required. Deletions should be simple, but firm, scoring through.

All your pages must be numbered, as is done automatically by a word processor. On a typewriter script, pencil in numbers as you go, and when the manuscript is complete number the pages with a rubber-stamp numbering machine or in ink, in the upper right-hand corner.

Where a significant textual addition is needed after this stage, it does not help to asterisk its position and write it at the bottom of the page. It is better to retype, or to cut the page, paste it up with the new text in position, and photocopy to paper of the same size as the original, adding the necessary page number (147a) with a note on the preceding page ("147a follows"). While typing looks best for these additional words or phrases, it will not always be necessary in revising an accepted manuscript for publication. Loose additions stapled or stuck over a page will not be appropriate, though—the typescript page is held in the typesetter's copyholder with the work position marked by a moving line, and a loose or small section can get torn or lost.

All this shows why it is such a boon to the author of the academic book to use a word processor, which can effortlessly produce a correctly paged final printout incorporating all the author's revisions.

Finally, the format of the finished manuscript. A block of loose pages is likely to get scuffed, and the second publisher you show it to will know they are not the first to review it. But complex binding of a manuscript for review is equally annoying, with each chapter separately packaged. It is worth securing the manuscript with some clearly labelled (and brightly coloured—for recognition) covers of the same size as the script, but in a removable form, so that if you or the publisher want to feed the manuscript through a photocopier this can be done with ease.   *Yours truly, R.M.D.*

« 6 » *Word processing the manuscript*

Dear Ms. Matrix,

Preparing your manuscript using a word processor will certainly make your task easier and will probably ease some of the publisher's tasks, but an explanatory comment may be needed. This has become one of the areas of greatest misunderstanding between authors and their publishers.

Most scholarly authors now choose to prepare their manuscripts on word processors—using stand-alone systems or, now rarely, an institutional mainframe computer. Providing your files on disk may help aspects of the publisher's and typesetter's work. Unfortunately the use of a word processor may also hinder the publisher and typesetter, and raise unrealistic expectations from authors. This letter is to clarify the overall issue and, more important, to make some specific recommendations to authors in word processing their manuscripts.

To an author, the neat and professional-looking output from their office or personal computer printer often represents something close to their concept of a finished book. To the publisher, however, it is one of the stages and elements which will, in due course, lead to the published book. This raw script must still be edited, copyedited and marked up by the copyeditor and further marked up by the designer, and it may be sent to the typesetters (compositors) for estimate. The typesetters will further mark up the typescript and either capture the keystrokes from the author's disk or, if they cannot, keyboard it again. They will then produce a first pass at output for proofing, sometimes as galleys and later in pages, or as page proofs from the start. They will finalize these pages with headlines (running heads) and footnotes, with correction stages to these.

The same procedure will be followed for the index, which cannot begin to go through these stages until later, when the main text is in corrected page proof. Once approved, the illustrations, as sized by the designer, will be scanned or reduced by camera, with screening and proofing of half-tones, before being included in the final pages which are then photographed for imposition. Alternatively, a book may move directly from the typesetter's disk, with illustrations scanned in, to the printer's film. From the imposed film can begin the preparation of printing plates which the printer uses for creating the printed sheets. This stage is still only the raw material for the binder to create a folded, gathered and sewn book block for the addition of the limp cover or the hardback case and, where applicable, for jacketing, each of which has its own design stage.

The most important part of this is producing the manuscript; but it is only one stage. Use of the word processor files may save keyboarding but in most cases will not save the other stages. The saving of keyboarding (assuming no problems arise from the word processing input) means a reduction in time on the typesetting, the need for a different kind of proofreading in the eventual proof, and some discount by the typesetter (compositor) which will ease the publisher's costs and may therefore be reflected in the eventual price of the book. However, incorrect preparation of the word processor output by the author, or its incorrect use by the typesetter, will add delays and push costs above the level which would have been achieved by conventional typesetting.

There are several ways in which word processor output can be used in publication, each one requiring from the author more input and work than was involved in the traditional approach to typesetting.

The first is manuscript preparation. Most authors use word processors to revise, update, change and finalize the manuscript they deliver to the publisher as hard copy. If prepared carefully, this will provide a good basis for the publisher and the typesetter to work from.

Layout of the word processor manuscript can be quite different, initially, from the product of a typewriter, because changes in format are easy to achieve. The well-spaced script which the copyeditor requires is not what the publisher and the publisher's reader require to review and decide whether to publish. Unless you are quite certain no revision will be required, it is acceptable to print the manuscript out in 1½-spacing or (if clearly readable with the typeface and size you have chosen) single-spacing, and not be too generous with margins. This reduces the overall physical size of the manuscript, reduces your cost in printing or photocopying it, and incidentally serves to discourage the reader from scribbling critical comments in the margin of your precious work. If your word processing program allows you to move footnotes easily, you might even include them (for readability) on the relevant page of the copy which you submit for a publisher to consider, numbered by chapter, with the understanding that they will have to be stripped out and transferred to separate pages before final revision of the manuscript for publication.

So in layout, think of context and future plans. If this is the definitive copy for the copyeditor, space and plan it accordingly. If it is a draft version for the publisher and reader, consider reducing its physical size to make it more readable and portable.

When you are delivering a text which will be used in copyediting and publication, however, some strict rules apply. The "hard copy" from your computer printer delivered to the publisher should be prepared to resemble a conventional typescript—not a printed page, nor a thesis or conference paper.

Everything should be printed out double-spaced, as in a conventional typescript. It is safest not to use italic or bold typefaces; underline in the conventional way to signify what is to appear as italic in the final book, and you need to introduce clear codes (wavy underline or computer-related coding) if you need bold.

The right-hand margin should not be justified. Word processing programs do not justify by dividing words at line endings (as printing does), but adjust only the spaces between words, and this can confuse the copyediting and design of a manuscript.

As with a typescript, number the notes consecutively throughout each chapter; print them out separately from the text (not at the foot of each page), grouped at the end of the manuscript (i.e. following the bibliography). Number pages consecutively throughout the manuscript (even if this is done by hand).

Make sure accents are legible—if your printer cannot provide these, do them by hand, and make it clear that the accents are not part of the computer file. Quotation marks may be unclear on your printout—clearly identify them by hand.

Computer codes should not appear in the printed manuscript, unless agreed in advance with your editor—otherwise they will confuse the copyeditor.

If you find you have to make changes to your book after submitting your typescript to the publisher for setting and printing, it is essential to be clear what stage of preparation it is at. If copyediting has not begun, it may be acceptable to send a revised disk of text files with a printout of all pages affected by the change, or a new printout of the whole text. But if copyediting has begun, a new disk cannot be substituted. Any new text must be advised clearly and separately to the copyeditor with a hard-copy version of each of the changes. To avoid error, the copyeditor will add these changes individually to the version of the manuscript being copyedited—whether this is done on hard copy or on disk—and the changes will be taken into the manuscript for typesetting with other amendments arising from the copyediting stage.   *Yours truly, R.M.D.*

« 7 » *Word processing for the typesetter*

Dear Ms. Matrix,

A further note on the use of word processor files in the typesetting stage of publication.

An author's disk can be used to help in the typesetting. The majority of typesetters (compositors) can capture data from the author's files—keystrokes from most word processing systems—on condition that these are prepared following guidelines such as those given above. The typesetters will then code the script, or translate computer codes into typesetting codes, in line with the designer's instructions, and go through all the subsequent stages of typesetting.

There are different levels of coding manuscripts to aid in typesetting. Opinions differ between individuals, production departments, publishers and typesetters on how much an author should do. Any author's word processing files will already include some codes—e.g. for paragraph breaks, or for words underlined so that they will finally be printed in italics. All electronic manuscripts will require some final coding by the typesetter. In between is a wide spectrum.

By the time the author's neat hard-copy printout is used for typesetting, it will be festooned with handwritten notes added at successive stages by the editor, the copyeditor, the designer and the typesetter. All these annotations, which contribute to producing an accurate, well-edited and well-designed text proof, have to be taken up into the electronic text files at different stages.

Copyediting—which includes incorporating the author's responses to numerous queries on points of fact or matters of style—may be done on hard copy or directly on the computer. If the copyeditor has worked on screen, they will have made changes to the word processing files as they go; if they have worked on hard copy, their changes must be added to the disk files afterwards. The same is true of markings added by the designer and the typesetter.

A new hard-copy printout is often produced after the copyediting stage; but whether or not this is thought necessary, at each stage in the markup process changes will be made to the latest versions of both the hard copy and the electronic files, so that at all times the electronic version agrees precisely with the hard copy.

If the copyeditor has worked on screen, the designer and the typesetter will be given disk files that already include the changes made in copyediting. If the copyeditor has worked on the hard copy, there are several options for transferring the copyediting and other changes to the final computer file for typesetting.

The changes to the disk may have been made by the copyeditor or by someone else employed by the publisher. Or the typesetter may be given the copyedited hard copy and an unaltered disk, to incorporate the changes. This will especially be true if there are only a modest number of changes.

Some publishers may ask you, as the author, to incorporate the changes, updating your own files. This is a purely technical exercise, and you will be reminded not to make any new changes at this point. Although having the author do much of the coding can save time and money, serious delays and costs can be incurred by quite minor errors in coding; for this reason, many publishers ask their authors to do little or no coding. They take the view that there is little point in giving to an inexperienced author or an insecure typist tasks normally carried out by a skilled typesetter working with familiar programs.

Publishers and typesetters are still developing the best routines for converting good word processing copy into good printed pages.

Yours truly, R.M.D.

« 8 » *Desktop publishing and camera-ready copy*

Dear Professor Dimmage,

It was kind of you to offer us "camera-ready copy"—the finished and complete typeset image—for your book, from the desktop publishing system your university department has bought for producing its own in-house journal and monograph series.

We do sometimes use an author's output, but we would prefer not to in the case of your new book. Why? What makes publishers trouble to typeset a book again instead of using laser-printed pages provided by the author?

There have been major advances in computer software packages to allow individuals to create well-designed pages, including tables and charts. Familiar packages like QuarkXPress, Aldus PageMaker or Ventura allow the author or the operator substantial control over the appearance of a final page. More complex programs using TₑX codes give the user control over layouts for tables, statistics and formulae.

There are indeed some academic books where the publisher can and will use the author's printed output for reproduction directly and exactly on the printed page. This is especially true of books with too small a print run to be economic for publication under the normal criteria. It is also true of those books—such as a "special" on a current topic—where time does not allow for the normal procedures of editing, design and typesetting. And finally there are books so complicated that it is in everyone's interest to keep them in the exact, carefully checked format presented by the author. This is true of some works in economics or the hard sciences. It is also true of complex dictionaries, grammars or linguistic studies, which may include language and special characters unfamiliar to the typesetter. Use of the author's camera-ready copy avoids the long process of error checking and correction.

If you agree in advance with your publisher that you will provide "camera-ready copy"—ready for the printer without involving a typesetter—it must be done in close collaboration with the publisher from the start. There are many technical, design and editing subtleties which can go wrong in author-generated camera-ready copy. A design needs to be created by the publisher or shown to the publisher's designer for comment and, if necessary, amendment. A routine for copyediting, checking that changes are made correctly to the computer files, and proofreading the final output should not be bypassed just because the camera-ready copy is coming through an unconventional route.

Many authors prepare and design their work on an A4 (or 8½ × 11) page. But the output on an A4 page cannot be used by the printer for an A4 book, for an area larger than the typed area must be marked with key-lines which are suppressed in the imposition of text for the film-making process. Because these key-lines must lie outside the visible area, an author's carefully designed A4 page must be given to the publisher on a larger than A4 sheet—and this is not easily done on most in-house computer set-ups. Alternatively, a smaller than A4 area of camera-ready copy can be prepared on an A4 sheet. The difference between "American Quarto" (8½ × 11) pages and printing pages is even greater. Early definition of the print area is needed before the page design is under way.

And all parties need to be sure of the ability of the typesetting (composition) system (and its operators) to provide output to book publication standards. What may look very smart as an in-house publication may appear below expectations when found within the covers of a formally published and often expensive book. Many page make-up files from an author's computer can be output on a departmental laser printer but can also be given to an outside service bureau for a more professional, higher-resolution output. This will have an image close to that of professional typesetting and is appropriate to much technical publication and in-house material.

So why do publishers not ask for and use authors' camera-ready copy every time?

The addition of a publisher's imprint to a publication is a statement of a certain standard. The standard may differ with different imprints, but in commercial terms the publisher's imprint imparts not just scholarly value but commercial value to a book. A publisher of high status in a particular field is held to particular expectations of quality. The publisher adds not just marketing and distribution, but quality aspects to an author's work. These aspects are the difference between the output of the author's typescript—however well prepared—and the final image given to the printer to prepare first film and then printing plates.

It is for these reasons that most publishers will not take an author's output as the final image for printing. They want their own input to add value to the final product.

The first contribution is in the overall structure of the book. A good publisher's editor will be involved in constructive discussions with you, the author, about the length and contents of the book, its overall structure, and the arrangement of its elements to best convey the contents and the argument. The publisher's editor will also discuss division into parts and chapters and subheadings; the nature of any preface, introduction, appendices, notes and bibliography; and the selection and placing of tables and illustrations.

A good book from a good publisher also deserves the best of copyediting. Copyeditors (also called subeditors) are the unsung heroes (more often heroines) of the publishing industry. A good copyeditor keeps the author from erecting inadvertent barriers to communication with the reader. The copyeditor ensures straightforward expression; grammar, spelling and punctuation that follow norms of expression; amplification of obscure allusions; consistency and completeness of notes and references, bibliography and cross-references; even accuracy of tables and information. Many authors have been saved from embarrassment by the gentle wisdom of the copyeditor; perhaps this is one reason why their role is not always acknowledged in print by the author.

The book designer, too, is a skilled craftsperson whose contribution is rarely recognized. Bad design is obvious (though the reasons why it is bad design may be difficult for the untrained eye to name). If a book is difficult to use and read, irritating to the eye, bad design may be the cause. Good design is less obvious to the reader than bad design, precisely because it permits effortless, trouble-free reading.

The copyedited manuscript, marked up with a detailed designer's brief, needs a professional typesetter to transform it into an acceptable and accurate page. Many agencies can transform author's manuscript into an image; far fewer are the proficient, experienced and professional book typesetters. They can ensure that the final image omits those horrors of the printed page—the orphans and widows and rivers of white, poor kerning of letters and insufficient or inappropriate word-breaks which mark the inexperienced typesetter and the word processor output.

Finally, a good publisher will provide professional proofreading as a double-check on the author's own proof-checking, which is still essential. If the manuscript has been keyed in from hard copy, the proofreader is checking the accuracy of the printout. If (as is more common now in academic publishing) an author's word processing files have been read into a typesetter's system, the text is likely to correspond more closely to the author's text. The proofreader is here double-checking the copyeditor's work, but also identifying those oddities in typesetting from disk which tend to be major problems—such as whole sections omitted or set in the wrong font—rather than minor typographical errors.

In the end, the publisher's camera-ready copy is an image acceptable—perhaps after several stages of correction—to the publisher's editor, copyeditor, designer and proofreader as well as to the author.

The distance between this and the author's proposed camera-ready copy is, too often, quite substantial. It is a difference which helps to give a work the stamp of a publisher's imprint, giving booksellers and librarians and readers a certain guarantee of quality and assurance of value for money.

If that sounds too pious, let us admit that in the next few years the barriers between authors' camera-ready copy and publishers' professionally processed material will further erode. The word processing systems and page layout systems of personal computers will increase in sophistication. The interface between author's disk and typesetting system will improve. As authors become more confident and competent in making changes to book files on disk, so will copyeditors and designer be more confident in working on the files on screen.

A good publisher will not bypass any of the stages required to transform an author's book into a printed object of quality: professional editing, copyediting, design, typesetting and proofreading. The transitions between successive stages will, however, become smoother, swifter and less fraught with the anxieties and problems which still permeate the creative process from idea to printed book.   *Yours truly, R.M.D.*

« 9 » *Notes*

Dear Dr. Assad,

Your first draft looks fine, but I am rather worried about the proportion of space given to notes, references and bibliography. Do you think this will please or annoy your readers? It will certainly push up the length and price of the book—and make it look heavier in content than it actually is.

Some books, of course, demand extensive annotation of every statement; indeed, some books (editions of texts, for example) are seen to be valuable in proportion to the quality and profusion of their notes.

But for most books that is not so.

Notes can be in three basic positions, each with implications for the bibliography, and this must be discussed with the publisher's editor for any book.

For many scientific and some social science topics the in-text system works fine. (This is also referred to as the author-date system or the Harvard system.) This starts to look awful if a lot of references have to be run together, or if references are made in succession to different pages of the same work. The author-date system is least appealing when sources include many manuscripts or personal communications, reference to which becomes clumsy and unfriendly. The system is also inappropriate for books which are intended to attract the general reader. In effect, it is useful where the authority for a statement needs to be included as part of the statement: hence the emphasis on scientific usage.

The text reference is simply the bracketed surname and date; all the bibliographical data is in a single alphabetical list at the end of the book.

Notes are the traditional form for references in most humanities books, but changing technologies in typesetting have moved the favoured position from bottom of page to end of book, and (now) back again. In preparing the manuscript for the publisher's copyeditor and typesetter, however, you must never present the notes at the bottom of your own pages, but always in a list of notes for each chapter. Manuscript pages will not correspond to pages of the printed book. If the notes are on the existing manuscript pages, please type them additionally on a separate list.

When footnotes were moved for technical reasons to the end of the book, many people found they preferred the full uncluttered page and are now reluctant to take advantage of new page make-up technologies to move back!

It is true that notes at the bottom of the page are distracting to most readers. But they are very convenient to readers who want to check the source or reference for a statement immediately, and perhaps find a comment on that source. What does jar with most readers and most editors is an author's habit of making tangential remarks in footnotes: at best, this looks mannered and dated, except where the note is commenting on the source itself. At worst, it constantly interrupts the flow of the sense, as the reader leaves the main text to see if something important is being said in the note, and then returns to try and pick up the main flow of the argument.

A good rule for footnotes is that it should be possible to read the book happily at two levels: either ignoring all the notes, or glancing quickly down the page to take in the source and easily back to the reading line. In neither case does there seem a good excuse for indulging in a further paragraph of text, subsidiary to the main text. Many editors take the view: if it is worth saying, put it in the text; if it is not worth saying in the text, don't say it at all, even in a footnote.

The need for a quick glance down and up favours a shortened form of bibliographical reference in the note—a short title for a book, a recognizable abbreviation for a journal, a consistent convention for a manuscript source. The full information can then appear in a bibliography as in the author-date system.

For a large proportion of scholarly books, though, the text stands on its own, and the notes serve the needs of only a minority of readers who may wish to check the sources and read further on a topic. Information for that purpose can happily be hidden away in endnotes. For books with chapters by different authors, the notes are often placed at the end of each chapter (a concession to the photocopier). But equally often the flow of the book is helped if the notes are grouped after the end of the text, just before the bibliography. In this case, the publisher's editor will sometimes adopt the excellent practice whereby the pages to which the notes refer—not just the chapter title or number—appear at the top of each page of endnotes.

The use of endnotes makes it easier to add commentaries on sources which would look overlong at the bottom of the text page. But it gives even less excuse for self-indulgent asides on other matters in the text, since no one will know they are hiding there.

The physical properties of endnotes mean a reader has to search from the text to the page of notes. It is little joy to be given only minimal information on a book and be sent to a bibliography elsewhere for the details. If there is real pressure on space, endnotes with detailed bibliographic data—especially if each source is referred to only once or twice—may provide an excuse for giving only a select bibliography, or none at all. But each academic book is a special case and must be organized to meet its own needs, as agreed with the publisher. The keynote should always be to identify the needs of the readers and design a system of notes, references and bibliography to suit them—not to indulge oneself or impress readers with the thoroughness of one's scholarship.   *Yours truly, R.M.D.*

« 10 » *Bibliographies*

Dear Billy Weil,

As you say in your note, the bibliography of a book can cause an author anguish. Its completion is left to the last: suddenly its shortcomings become visible, and if they do not, the publisher's editor soon reveals problems and doggedly insists on answers.

The secret of a successful bibliography is creating a complete reference system early in a research project. Although it is easily said, there is no substitute for keeping a complete and detailed record of materials consulted—including books, journal articles, conference volumes, unpublished papers or manuscripts. And the researcher looking for an easy life will make such a record include all possible details of interest. It is far easier to cut out irrelevant information in a published bibliography than to recover a journal part number, or the exact name of the institutional publisher of a monograph consulted once on a flying visit to the Charles University Library in Prague.

Regardless of whether, during research, you keep a card index or a computerized data base, an inclusive approach to each listing will make it relatively easy to create a bibliography for your final manuscript. Record the author's (or each co-author's) surname and first name or initials; whether each person is author, translator or editor; the work's full title and subtitle; number of edition, if not the first; publication date of edition used; primary place of publication; publisher. For a chapter within a multi-author book, include full author details, chapter title, pages of the whole chapter, and the full book details as above. For a journal article, record the full article title, full author details, journal title, volume number, part number, first and last page numbers, year for which the volume applies (and, if different, the actual year of publication). Make a note of the library or context in which you consulted the work, or the source of the bibliographical reference, in case you have to chase up some missing information later.

You must decide whether you can limit your references to the footnotes, or whether you will present one or more alphabetical bibliographies at the end of your book. You will also have decided if you need a bibliography for each chapter or will have the more usual consolidated one. Manuscript sources and oral sources often look better listed separately in distinct parts of the bibliography.

If certain sources—a journal, an archive, a series—appear repeatedly in your bibliography, you may decide to use an abridged version of the title or name. It is usually best to give this list of abbreviations at the beginning of the bibliography for ready reference.

Some publishers, some monograph series and almost all journals have a house style for bibliographies. They expect authors to follow this without exception. But where a book publisher has no house style, the dominant principle becomes internal consistency.

This means consistency of content and consistency of presentation. If you are including the place of publication, as is normally expected, be consistent. If you include the publisher, as is common, include all publishers. If you give the part number as well as volume for a journal reference, do so in all cases.

Because a bibliography is compiled over a long period of research and writing, it is usually typed up with inconsistencies in style and presentation. A tight editing job by you, as author, is needed before the manuscript can be delivered to a publisher.

If in doubt you should follow the style guide of a journal in your field, or a publisher's style guide. This will suggest how to list and present authors' names, and the format (capitalization, italics, quotation marks, punctuation) for titles of books, journal articles, contributors to a multi-author book, and series data. Very detailed guidance is included in the *Chicago Manual of Style*. Remember that if you want the typeset version to have words in italics, the convention is for you to underline them, not italicize them, in the typescript or printout, no matter what the powers of your word processor and printer.

What should you include in your bibliography? That depends on its role. It is important to make clear if it is a list of references or a guide to further reading. If your references use the author-date system, in the text or in notes, the bibliography must give full details of each of those citations. If your endnotes or footnotes have only partial details on the article or book, the bibliography must present the complete details. If this is the nature of the bibliography, it will be large enough already; do not pad it out with references which you have dropped from the final draft of the text, or other books you have consulted. You are not trying to impress, and space is always at a premium. Limit your bibliography to details of works actually referred to in text or notes.

There is a temptation to cite unpublished works as sources, and this requires care. A citation is either a source of authority or an acknowledgement. If a manuscript has not been published in any form, it cannot be used by colleagues in your field as an authority: it cannot be checked to confirm or amplify your claim. Is it then an acknowledgement—a demonstration of your reliance on another person's information? If so, have you permission to use that person's material? I suggest it is important to be clear. It is at best frustrating, and at worst unacceptable to scholarly discourse, to cite as a fact some point which cannot be checked because its source is inaccessible. Hearing Smith read a draft paper at a conference or seminar, having a casual chat over a drink with Von Klinkeren at a meeting, or hearing Bronsky's work described at second hand in someone else's paper do not constitute authority to cite "Smith forthcoming," "Von Klinkeren pers. comm." or "Bronsky n.d."

More spurious still is to cite as the definitive authority work by yourself which has not been published, and may not be. Many emerging scholarly authors include in their first book's bibliography reference to everything they have written, published or not, and cite it as if it were the basis for an argument, when it may be only an extension of that argument. Be modest and self-disciplined.

If you have decided to give full details of citations in the notes themselves, the full bibliography is optional. It may be more appropriate to use a bibliography instead to suggest and guide further reading. You might list items for the reader's further attention under topics, or by chapter. Or you might extend to a bibliographical essay, commenting on the nature and value of each source indicated. Even in this case, give full bibliographical details to help the reader find the source.

With this approach, you should have created a bibliography no longer than is needed and no shorter than is required. Every aspect of it will be purposeful, and the purpose will be to serve the real needs of some or all of your readers. It will equip them to confirm or follow up your statements and arguments, with enough information to do so readily. It may take up a significant amount of space in the book, but if no entry is redundant and the structure is logical, that use of space is well worth while.   *Yours truly, R.M.D.*

« 11 » *Tables*

Dear Professor Lister,

You mentioned that your manuscript would have a number of tables in which you would present your data. Thank you for asking about how to present these. If we can agree at an early stage how your tables will be organized, it will save you and us a lot of work later on.

We do not have a standard style guide for tables, because expectations are so varied. The level and the format for presenting data in economics are quite separate from those in astronomy. The appropriate amount of detail in a first-year textbook is very far from the lengthy appendices of data in an economic history monograph.

So you must be guided, primarily, not by your publisher but by the norms of your subject field. But, having said that, let us emphasize that the audience is all-important: it makes a big difference to what you include, and how you include it.

In a book of reference or for specialists, you can present all the data necessary to back up your argument, or for readers to refer to and use in their own research. The data is not there to impress: it is in print for the purpose of availability. Depending on your discipline, there will be another level of information which cannot be represented fully in print. This may be available as hard-copy records in your research institution, or it may be available as computer data on disk or tape, or on line. Or it may be implicit in the material, so that interested researchers can replicate it themselves. There is almost always a cut-off line between what can and should be included in print in the published volume, and what cannot appear there and must be sought elsewhere by the reader interested in pursuing your research work. You are the best initial judge of this line, but as publishers we are likely to take advice from our reviewers if it appears to be a problem.

Even for this technical level of data, presentation is important. You must signal the contents of tables, labelling them to ease their use by the reader. A quick reference—not a laboured disentanglement of the structure of your data set—may be all that a particular reader needs. Think of signposts, guidelines, simplicity and access. (For this reason as well as for economy, a table should if possible fit on the printed page without making the reader turn the book sideways.) When in doubt, try the table on colleagues, to see if they can use it or if the presentation can be improved.

For a student textbook or a book for the more general reader, self-discipline becomes the key. If your tabular presentation helps explain and amplify the argument, include it. If it is a core part of the argument, include it, in a clear and simple form, and explain it in the adjacent text. But if the table is merely there to impress, to daunt, to prove how serious you are, be abstemious and remove or simplify it.

There are many ways simpler than tables to present data for such a readership. Text descriptions, graphs, pie-charts, and more imaginative graphic representations may successfully represent trends, relationships, quantities, issues. The bare numbers may obscure rather than amplify your argument. If they are not needed in the context of a textbook or a book for the more general reader, then replace them with a friendlier form of presentation.

It should then be clear both to you, as author, and to your publisher what is the appropriate number and format of tables. It should also be clear whether they need to appear embedded in the continuous text of your argument or adjacent to an area of discussion (like an illustration), or whether some or all can be grouped as appendices at the end of the book or a chapter.

As with illustrations, you should prepare captions to accompany each table, and a list of tables to be part of the front matter (prelims) of the book, and you should indicate in your text where each should be placed.

If you are preparing your manuscript in a word processing package, we need to know how you will present the tables. You may include them as basic word processor files. That is fine, but please keep the layout simple. To space columns, use tabulation, not typed spaces or a word processor's "column" option, which could disappear or be typeset wrongly in the eventual text. Keep the tabulation consistent—for instance, as to whether a column is right-hand justified or aligned on a decimal point. And be consistent in dealing with empty "cells" (nil entries): decide whether to use a zero or a blank or a long dash (em-rule) or a code like "n/a" for empty or zero-sum columns. Check that you have a consistent and meaningful style across all tables.

All that is fine for the initial preparation of a manuscript and submission to publishers. It may be decided, however, that the tables should be presented not as word processing text for design and typesetting, but as camera-ready art. You will probably do this on a desktop publishing system, with high-quality output on a laser printer or similar, after consultation with your publisher and editor. This effectively means that you are the designer, creating a piece of illustration out of your tables. But be clear which route you will follow. If you expect the publisher to typeset the tables from your version supplied on disk, do

not present these in a complex desktop publishing layout with formatting details which may be lost in the transfer of data to the typesetter's
system. Go for the simple route.

Simplicity in approach, design and presentation can convert a table
from a typesetting problem which never seems to come right into a
straightforward and invaluable piece of well-designed text in the body
of the book, a joy to behold and use.   *Yours truly, R.M.D.*

« 12 » *Illustrations*

Dear Dr. Pincture,

You have raised some important questions about the illustrations for
your book. The level of illustration must be assessed first for any book,
before tackling the technical aspects of presentation.

Some scholarly books which demand or would benefit from illustrations do not have them simply because the author has a completely
non-visual approach to the subject. This is unfortunate, and for such
books a publisher should suggest adding illustrations to suit the topic
and the budget for the book.

But in other cases an author may suggest a lavish level of illustration
that is inappropriate for that particular kind of book. A book on a historical topic or a literary assessment for a general lay audience may
demand far more pictures than a book for an academic readership or
even a textbook. This is not normally a question only of cost, but of
what is relevant for the subject and the readership of each book.

Every academic author will know what is appropriate to their discipline. A philosophical study may have no illustrations; a history book
with a picture on every other "spread" (two-page opening) may look
more unscholarly than intended. But a book in zoology or geomorphol-
ogy may be criticized if it is minimally illustrated and uses words too
much to describe material better presented in graphic or pictorial form.

Guidelines for some subjects—not just for authors but for uncertain
publishers straying into unfamiliar fields—may come from looking at
the professional journals of quality. Journals of the same level and subject as the book will suggest an appropriate level of illustration.

A journal's style guide may include instructions on the presentation
of illustrations more appropriate to that discipline than any general
statements. The most valid generalization is that early consultation between author and publisher's editor will avoid misunderstandings or
wasted efforts or last-minute panic.

In the old letterpress method of printing, illustrations were expensive because each required the printer to create a "block" (cut). But in turn blocks from photographs ("half-tones") were commonly printed on a special coated or art paper, and quality was good. In modern printing, the half-tone (photographic) illustrations are normally placed where they most logically figure in the text, and so are printed on the same paper as the text with the possibility of a corresponding drop in quality. The cost of reproducing photographs is less than before; it does still cost, but the typesetting of an equivalent area of text also costs. Most publishers do not find the good-quality reproduction of a relevant line drawing prohibitively expensive.

Black-and-white photographs must be of good contrast and quality to reproduce adequately on the text paper. Sometimes the inclusion of photographic half-tones, particularly if there are some of less than perfect contrast and quality, means that the whole book must be printed on a more costly coated paper than a book with only text and line illustrations. This additional cost, together with the expense of providing the photographs, permissions to use them, and screening them for print, will add to the total costs of the book, either as a charge to the author or as costs which the publisher can recover only by increasing the price of the book (which may reduce the sales numbers).

If submitting a manuscript for a publisher to consider, it is inadvisable to include original prints; only copies of drawings or other "line" artwork should be sent until the originals are requested.

So there are several areas to clarify between author and publisher, and perhaps to include in the formal contract.

The first is the number of illustrations to appear, and their appropriate distribution through the book.

The second is the division between line artwork and photographs, and whether any illustrations are to be in colour.

The question of permission and preparation costs must be tackled. There are different categories of permission. For a photograph, a print must be acquired, and permission to reproduce in a defined context must be obtained separately. A line drawing—such as a map, chart or newspaper cartoon—can normally be copied from a published source, if an original cannot be obtained, but permission to reproduce is still required. If an illustration is redrawn with modifications, most publishers take the view that an acknowledgement of the source is needed but not the permission of the owner of the original, unless many illustrations are redrawn from the same owner or source. It must be established clearly—and normally in the book contract—who is to obtain these materials and permissions, and who is to pay for them. It is common in contracts for academic books for the author—probably as a charge against royalties—to carry these costs in part or even in whole. It is usually advisable to obtain permission to reproduce once the publisher is known, the number of illustrations is finalized, and it is clear whether the book is to be sold worldwide or just in one region; permission fees often vary according to the territories in which a book will be sold.

Photographs for use in books should be original prints—reproductions of printed versions are normally unusable. The printed versions have already been screened (broken into black dots of varying size) for printing. Rather than try to reproduce each dot of an earlier printing, a much better quality will be obtained from an original photograph by scanning or photographing with a new screen to break it into dots for the printing process. Black-and-white photographs should be supplied unmounted, preferably larger than required in the printed book. They need to be of as good a contrast as possible—which means that subtleties and details are clear as well as overall contrasts between dark and shade.

Photographs must be supplied to the publisher with care. If the total number to be included is unambiguous and non-negotiable, you can write the figure number and the author or book title on an adhesive label and stick it firmly on the back. Otherwise a brief caption can be attached with tape. If a condition of providing the print is that it be returned to the owner, it is useful to say this on the label on the back. You should not write on the back of a photograph, unless in very soft crayon—pencil or hard pen can dent the surface of a print and affect its reproduction, and the ink from even a soft pen can rub off on other photographs in the same folder.

Good protective covering for your illustrations will ensure their safe passage through the many hands that receive them before the final book is printed. Paperclips are very likely to damage your prints: do not use them.

If there are very many photographs, do not use a separate envelope for each one: it would probably only increase the handling they receive.

Finally, the way the photograph is to be printed. The top of the picture may have to be indicated by an arrow on the back in soft crayon. The photograph may include areas not required in the book: a designer will need to know what parts of a picture can and cannot be omitted (masked) to fit the page layout of the book (such cropping will not damage the original print). An area of sky might be cropped without loss, but equally there might be some essential details at the edge of a photograph. Alternatively, it is easy to enclose a photocopy of a photograph and indicate on this what should, or should not, be masked in the camera work. This is the easiest way to show any additions, such as labelling, which have to be drawn or typeset and overlaid on the photograph on the printed page.

Sometimes authors, in agreement with their publishers, provide roughs for their line illustrations, which are then drawn up professionally. This often happens with a humanities or social science book in which there are only a few diagrams or maps. The roughs should be clear, unambiguous and large enough for editing annotation—the roughs should be larger than the expected size of the printed page, though not *too* large. Ideally, the rough would come in three parts—the author's idea of how the finished artwork would look; a list of words to be edited and typeset (e.g. in a map); and any notes for the designer or draftsperson to follow. The draftsperson is briefed to convert your idea into finished artwork, not to interpret content or reposition inaccurately placed information.

Line drawings should ideally be prepared with the knowledge of the final page size. Making originals oversize—preferably half as large again as required in the printed book—allows careful consideration of the size of lettering required. One error, though, which many authors make is to assume that a line drawing has to be printed larger than is really necessary to convey the required information. In general a line drawing will be reduced to as small a unit (column width or page width) as is consonant with its detail. The size of the lettering must be appropriate for this reduction, so that it can easily be read without being so large that it obscures details in the diagram.

A conscientious copyeditor will edit the illustrations as fully as the text and may suggest changes to wording or typography within the figure. There may therefore be some advantage in preparing the labelling as a separate overlay sheet, for incorporation in the final artwork. Occasionally your publisher may agree to typeset the labels and apply them in the design studio; in that case, a clear handwritten overlay to show position should be accompanied by a typewritten list of names for design mark-up and setting.

Labelling of axes of graphs is normally needed on the artwork. Wide graphs ("landscape" format), which make the reader turn the book sideways, are even more to be avoided than wide tables: the vertical axis in a graph may actually end up upside down.

Do not be tempted to give too much descriptive text within an illustration; such information looks better in the printed caption. But it is advisable to include a linear scale within a map or diagram, rather than state the information in a caption. Your assumption that a plan will be reproduced 1 : 10,000 may not be reflected in reality. A visual scale in the artwork will be correct whatever the reduction of the illustrations for print, and will remain accurate if a reprint changes the page size, as can happen.

A scholar working in a mainly non-visual discipline may prepare ink roughs and have them redrawn. In many disciplines, graphs, tables, maps and other illustrations will be prepared on computer graphics programs, and a disk of the relevant files will be delivered to the publisher with a printed copy. This raises the same issues as in taking a word processing disk or camera-ready copy from an author's desktop publishing system.

Discuss procedures with your publisher. It may prove more trouble than it is worth to give computer graphics files for conversion in a typesetter's system. Instead, the publisher may prefer you to deliver printed copies of the artwork in final form, and it does not matter to the publisher whether you created these with a state-of-the-art computer drafting program or a nib pen and indian ink. What matters is the quality of the design and the quality of the output. A draft should be submitted with the manuscript for copyediting. After copyediting, a final version should be prepared with the relevant computer program and output on a very high-definition printer or plotter. If your institution does not have the facility to output illustrations to print-quality definition, the publisher may arrange, or ask you to arrange, to use a service bureau to provide final art of the required quality from your computer files. There is little point in presenting excellent visual data in a well-typeset book in illustrations with shaky graph lines or crude tinting and shading.

Colour illustrations are often requested by authors of scholarly books and are equally often resisted by publishers. Colour is expensive—it involves scanning for separations, creating four printing plates and using four inks instead of one in the printing process. Colour is more frequently used in books with a large print run or books which can bear an unusually high cost. This excludes the great majority of academic books.

There are different levels of resistance and difficulty, though. The publisher may decide that a colour jacket or cover is appropriate. A colour jacket for the book is attractive if a suitable transparency is available. A jacket is primarily an advertising tool—the illustration must have obvious and immediate visual impact, not a meaning that has to be explained. And the jacket may be discarded quickly on library copies. Colour jackets are most appropriate on books which will attract bookstore displays or some spontaneous purchase—the trade end of the spectrum—and are most easily afforded on books with long print runs. Maps on endpapers are printed separately from the book. If the book requires a two-colour map, this may be an appropriate place to have it—and repeating the illustration on front and back endpapers may avoid the frustrations caused when librarians attach labels or wrappers to the inside covers.

A frontispiece in colour is the next most costly item: this usually has to be "tipped in"—gummed and inserted by hand—and does add a significant cost to the book. But a whole section of colour illustrations will be more costly: it must be on a better-quality paper than the rest of the book, involves the costs of colour separation and colour printing too, and yet does not present illustrations adjacent to the relevant part of the text. It is a route followed only where the colour illustrations are an essential part of the book (as in an art book, or in some scientific monographs) or a valuable adjunct (some history books, for example).

Most costly of all is scattering colour through the book. Not only must each colour picture be separated into the four process colours used for printing it, but every page of that sheet must be passed through a four-colour printing press, with four separate printing plates, three of which will be mostly blank unless there is colour on almost every page. If a book does have a large amount of colour illustration—as some science or art titles demand—it may still be possible to limit the colour to one side of the printed sheets only, reducing the number of printing plates and inking, and resulting in the availability of colour on alternate spreads.

Maps and diagrams often look attractive and informative in two colours. But the same effect may be achieved without the cost of colour printing by the use of a fine screen over black—thus using grey, or a range of greys, to represent the second colour.

Illustration, therefore, demands consideration by the publisher, in consultation with the author, in the light of readership and level, subject, production costs and selling price. While these questions have different answers for every book, the technical limitations of the process are much less variable.   *Yours truly, R.M.D.*

≣   ≣   ≣   ≣   ≣   ≣   ≣   ≣   ≣   ≣   ≣   ≣

« 13 » *Selecting a publisher*

Dear Mr. Chance,

You said on the phone that I was the first editor you had reached, as you had not got past the switchboard on the calls earlier in your *A–Z* list of publishers. I did say I would try to explain how to find the right publisher for your particular book. Telephoning them all in turn is not the best way!

There are reference books which list publishers and describe the kinds of books they publish and are seeking. I am rather doubtful about relying on these. They are not going to distinguish for you the reliable and secure from the insecure, the expansionist from the contracting, or the big from the small. A smaller publisher really looking for new material—for whatever reason—may be prominent in these lists. On the other hand, a well-established publisher might pay little attention to their entry in a list of publishers. They may already have enough books to consider without encouraging more; they may publish in too many fields to list them all; or they might be such a large organization that no one bothers to update their entry in line with the firm's current directions.

If you want to take reference sources seriously, it might be just as useful to look through trade publications such as *Publishers Weekly* in the USA, *The Bookseller* in the UK, *Australian Publisher and Bookseller* in Australia, and so on. These journals emphasize more general publishing over scholarly and professional imprints. They report as news items the establishment of new imprints, new breakaway publishing houses and new initiatives, which will often be imprints at that early stage of development when they are very keen to consider a range of new manuscripts—but, of course, only in the fields they have chosen.

It is worth paying attention to promising new imprints, especially those which are started with a clear commercial imperative and therefore a need to succeed. They are likely to be more committed than an amateur publishing enterprise started by a colleague in your field as a hobby. The new publisher has to find good books to publish, and make sure they will reach their audience fully and quickly. They cannot rest on their laurels, or on their backlist. Be aware of what imprints are new and impress you.

Any publisher has a limited range in which they publish—limited in subject areas but also in level. The academic publisher in life sciences may not publish personal health books; the publisher of show-business biographies may not take historical biographies; the college textbook publisher may have no interest in postgraduate philosophy; the fiction house may do no poetry.

The way to identify publishers worth approaching with a book is much the same in scholarly, educational or general publishing. It is to see who is doing similar books—in subject and level. If you are not already in touch with all the new publications in your field, a serious survey of some specialist bookshop shelves will show who is publishing actively in a particular field and at a particular level. Advertisements in relevant journals will give an even clearer view, as will a survey of recent reviews in the same journals. But beware of those academic journals which might take years to publish their reviews. In their reviews, their paid advertisements and their editorial comment it is the most lively and current journals that may give the best image of who is publishing what. Once you have identified a possible publishing house active in that area, there is no harm in calling up the switchboard and asking to confirm the name and postal address of the relevant editor. That will be more productive than a call to ask, "Do you publish history?"

Of course you might say that no one is publishing books of the kind you have written; yours is unique. That is probably untrue, given the number of titles published annually, though you might find that the best publisher is in fact overseas! You might just be ahead of your time with a new kind of book. Or you might be writing something for which there is no market at all. Unless it is a family or local history, suitable for self-publication, that may be a warning that the world is not yet ready for your work.   *Yours truly, R.M.D.*

« 14 » *In-house publishing*

Dear Dr. Youssef,

On my editorial visit to your research unit and department you showed me several book-length projects you were writing or editing, but you felt they could most readily be published "in house," without need of an outside publisher.

I admire your energies, demonstrated in the in-house publications you showed me—the newsletter, the journal, the paperbound monograph series and the one-off short publications. You are fortunate in having secretarial help to work on these, graduate students you can pay to do editorial work, and a part-time distribution assistant, as well as substantial storage space where you showed me your large stock of books and journal back issues.

There is, I am sure, a future for such in-house publishing, and a future for private or university-owned academic publishers as well. There is a difference in the way they operate; there is a difference, too, in what they can and should publish. Therefore I do not agree that all your projects are most suitable for your in-house programme.

As you rightly say, within your research centre you can undertake a lot of the same tasks a full-blown publisher does. Your editorial board insists on full peer review for a text of any length before it is published, using readers from other institutions, and this is a guarantee against poor-quality material or nepotism. You have access to the services of a couple of graduate students with an editorial background, who will undertake the necessary professional editing. As you point out, there is an advantage in having an editor in the same building as the author— queries can be raised without delay, changes can be made readily, misunderstandings can be minimized. And there is an advantage if the final image, the typesetting, can also be done in house by one of the secretaries on a desktop publishing program.

You are fortunate to have someone who knows their way around these programs with confidence—I hope you retain their services. There are many areas where an unwarranted confidence in a desktop publishing program on a personal computer can lead to basic errors in design, typesetting and page make-up. If you have access to advice from typographic designers on the university staff, I suggest you consult them regularly and willingly about your publications—not just ask them to design a fancy cover.

You are budgeting for a higher-quality laser printer for the publications programme, and this seems a good investment. But equally I think you are right not to try and acquire, even together with other departments, printing machinery, or be satisfied with the university's own equipment, which is designed for other kinds of documents. If you keep in touch with two or three different commercial printers, of good quality and reliability, I am sure the final product will justify all the work you have put into the programme. You want something that is well printed and well bound with good-quality materials, and the optimal combination of quality, reliability and price; the cheapest bid may not always be the best, and you might do best to retain some flexibility of control beyond your university's normal tendering procedures.

So in the end, as you showed me in your storeroom, you can create a very professional-looking monograph or journal issue. You can then sell this at a quarter or a third of what you think a commercial publisher selling through a bookshop would charge, and at a price which recovers the cost of printing and binding and postage and packing, adds a contribution towards advertising costs, and still leaves a small margin over on each sale.

So why would you and your colleagues need a privately owned publisher or a university press to handle your material?

For certain categories of publication, the answer is that you wouldn't. If you can make the sums work, and all parties are happy with the outcome, that is fine. On the journey home I did some rough calculations about your centre's publishing. Based on the figures you kindly gave me, your real publishing costs are very many times the figure used as the production cost of the book. You may have a cheap local printer. But what if you had to cost in the time of your graduate editor, your secretarial typesetter, their offices and equipment, the offices used for postage and packing, the salary and overheads of your part-time publications officer who deals with sales and distribution? By my reckoning you actually use a third of the overhead costs we do for a twelfth of the output; in other words, your efficiency is one-quarter of ours, and we feel hard pressed with the resources we have.

This is all fine and good. It is appropriate for institutions to subsidize their publications, and it is appropriate for departments to disguise these costs under other headings. Many essential research publications could not appear if it were not for these acknowledged or hidden subsidies. It may not please the scholarly world to see numerous in-house publications of questionable value. But for specialist work, work in progress, discussion papers, technical reports both short and long, urgent documentation, hard copy of data, reference materials—for all these, the in-house programme is a vital part of the scientific, professional and scholarly world.

What disturbed me about your programme was one of the things you are most proud of: your full storeroom. If you want to boast about your programme to a publisher, show them an *empty* storeroom! Because you are pricing your books so close to your perceived outlay of costs, you cannot really afford to be printing and storing books which are not going to sell. Some of the books in your publications storeroom date back many years, some of the journal parts even longer; and these will never sell. If you are pricing your books at, say, 25 per cent above production cost but are selling only 60 per cent of the print run, you are clearly losing income on each publication—and this will affect your ability to fund new publications in the future.

That is why investment of thought, people, time and money in marketing, promotion and sales activity is all-important, for a small institutional publisher as much as for a large self-funding publisher. Such publishers can expect to spend as much on marketing and distributing the book to its readership as they do on producing the book in the first place. Many institutional self-publishers and in-house publishing programmes emulate commercial publishers admirably up to the point of bringing the book into stock (even if in overprinted quantities), but collapse thereafter.

This is unnecessary, especially because in-house publishers could be better than commercial publishers and university presses at niche marketing. For it is in niche publishing that institutions thrive. In a specialist area, a research centre like yours is ideally placed to construct a cost-effective mailing list of international and local libraries, research centres and professional bodies, and individual specialists. You will be best placed to maintain this mailing list with amendments, additions and updates. You will have awareness of the journals which merit review copies, of the best places to advertise the book, of the conferences at which it should be displayed and the bibliographic sources which should be advised of it. As long as you do not spread the scope of your publishing too wide, this should be your forte. But it needs resources, and these resources usually have to be recovered in the selling price of the book.

So with all these positive statements, why are we not urging you to self-publish all your projects? The answer is that we believe one, perhaps two, of the books you mentioned have greater potential. These are book-length manuscripts whose likely market and readership is wider than the specialist libraries, institutions and individuals on your mailing list. For one of your projects we believe there is an international potential across several disciplines and in a wide range of libraries, deserving a considerable promotion and marketing effort. It would not be cost-effective for you to undertake this. For us, adding this one title to our mailings, advertisements, and conference exhibits would be relatively easy and productive.

And, to be realistic, the fact that a book appears under a recognized independent imprint does make a difference. In-house publishing is often—too often—perceived as vanity publishing, despite the important role it plays and despite the protection of peer review. Publication by a reputable private commercial imprint or university press is seen as a mark of quality, an independent judgement on the worth and importance of a book. The worst of commercial publication is often seen by academic peers, or host institutions, as more desirable than the best of in-house publishing.

Another of your titles clearly has real potential in bookshops—admittedly in upmarket and university bookshops, but nevertheless it demands subscription to bookshops who serve a wide audience which cannot be identified in mailings or targeted advertising. And, frankly, bookshops cannot usually be bothered to deal with institutions selling one-off products. They prefer to see publishers' representatives, and to stock titles on the basis of already established discount terms, credit accounts and credit payments, and arrangements for returns or restocking. We can reach such bookshops; you cannot.

So for your two projects with the widest potential, we believe you and your audience need a commercial imprint or a university press to be involved as the publisher; for the others, you do not. There is a place for both kinds of publishing, and they need not be anything but complementary. Good luck with your in-house publishing; as for the projects with the widest potential, send them along!

Yours truly, R.M.D.

« 15 » *Multiple submissions*

Dear Prof. Ligate,

I phoned you up to say we would not consider your complete manuscript further at this stage, because we discovered you had also submitted it to other publishers. You expressed surprise that we knew this, and even greater surprise at our attitude, so let me explain our viewpoint. Not all publishers would accept it, and many scholarly publishers recognize the need to consider multiple submissions, as long as they know the situation.

If you had told us you were approaching other publishers, at least we would have known where we stood. To act as if the option was ours was misleading. There are increasingly authors—usually well-established authors with a strong track record—who will advise several publishers that their book is on offer and say that they have approached more than one publisher.

We found out easily enough that you had approached other publishers. We phoned a leading expert in your field to ask if she would report on the manuscript for us. She said she had just agreed to do so for a rival publisher. (She also said that, since you were approaching several publishers, her report might be a waste of time for everyone and therefore for her—so she is sending the manuscript back to the other publisher without reading it.)

Publishers, if they are conscientious, say No fairly promptly to manuscripts that are clearly unsuitable for their list. For the other manuscripts they tend to take external advice, usually from scholars in the field, on whom they rely for judgement and help. The fees paid by publishers are never adequate compensation for the time, judgement and help of an expert reader. Readers oblige out of interest in new work and as a contribution to their field—to ensure that the right books get published and the right decisions are made in declining the inadequate.

Putting more than one publisher at a time through the review process is a waste of the publisher's time, a waste of the publisher's reading fee and, perhaps most important, a waste of the scholarly reader's time. Readers are unlikely to be pleased if they are told, after burning the midnight or weekend oil to review and report on a manuscript, that their report is no longer needed as the manuscript has been taken by another publisher.

Authors sometimes make multiple submissions because they fear their manuscript is unpublishable, but they hope that if they fire enough shots at random one will somehow hit a live target. Others do this because of ignorance of the way publishers work.

But to be realistic, many authors send their manuscript off simultaneously to different publishers because they do not trust publishers to consider their book conscientiously or promptly. One answer to the latter problem is to follow up on your proposal by courteously and systematically reminding the publisher with a request for news. If a publisher fails to respond to letters, or cannot explain the delay in reaching a decision, then you have the right to first hint that you will approach another publisher and then quietly do so.

In my view, though, the best answer is to approach publishers one at a time, in order of preference. Early in the development of a manuscript, well before it is complete, submit a synopsis and sample material. If the first publisher expresses genuine interest, they can be given first option on a final manuscript. If they appear lukewarm, there is plenty of time to approach a second or subsequent publisher before the manuscript is finished, so no time will have been lost.

Also, while a rejection from a publisher demands patience, it can produce constructive advice. The reasons a publisher declines a manuscript—along with the comments from a publisher's reader—can be useful to you; if the publisher has commissioned a report, ask to see it. The reasons one publisher says No may suggest that you should approach a different type of publisher, not just a clone. A reader's comments should suggest weaknesses in the manuscript which you need to confront and, at least in part, modify before resubmission.

At least you have avoided sending a photocopied letter to publishers asking if we would like to publish your book. That does happen. Publishers of course receive many more proposals than an author writes books. If an author is not sufficiently interested to select us specifically and write to tell us why a book is suited to our own particular list, we are probably better advised to spend our time on authors who do address their letters to us by choice.

We like to feel that we are being offered first choice of a manuscript. And if the contact is early enough in the development of a manuscript, we can avoid wasting our own time dealing with a multiple submission, and an author can avoid wasting time with a publisher who fails to respond.   *Yours truly, R.M.D.*

« 16 » *Complete manuscripts*

Dear Dr. Domuch,

When we met, you expressed surprise that we did not need your full manuscript in final form before we could make a decision on publication. There are some institutional presses that do have this rule, but it is the exception among academic imprints.

If you were the author of a first novel, a publisher probably would want to see the whole script. It is difficult to judge a novel from a proposal or a sample—a description may be fancy, samples may conceal an inability to structure or resolve the plot.

Of course the same may be true, in a sense, of academic non-fiction. But we live in a different world. First, we physically do not want a large uninvited manuscript in the office. Publishers' offices are small, and so are their desks. A bulky manuscript is only too likely to be relegated to some convenient corner than to haunt us from our desk.

Second, manuscripts are expensive things to move about. They are costly to package up and send back. Nor can we afford to photocopy them, on the off chance, to show to a colleague in another department, or fax them to an associate office overseas, or pass them across the desk of a sharp but busy adviser. With a proper outline we can do all this.

If you submit a complete manuscript, make it a good copy but not your only copy. Yes, I know the writers' guides used to say send a top copy of your manuscript for consideration, and that is still best if you use a word processor. But the rare experience of receiving the top copy of a manually typed script to consider actually makes us nervous. We have to send it out to readers. We could photocopy it to send—but then so could you. It might get lost in the mail; our readers are not perfect (some are downright disorganized). In the case of some publishers it might even get lost in the office, since publishers receive many manuscripts and you as author have just the one. As our disclaimer notes, we take no responsibility for loss of original material. And if we say No after exhaustive refereeing, reviewing and mailing about the country, the manuscript returned to you will show the next publisher that it has lost its virginal status. Our advice is: Invest in an electric typewriter with a carbon ribbon, if you do not want to invest in a word processor, and then make a photocopy for submission. Conceal from publishers the fact that it may not be the only copy in existence, and thus conceal from the next publisher to whom you submit it that they may not be the only publisher in existence.

It takes longer to look at a manuscript than at a good, well-constructed synopsis. So a synopsis will get earlier attention, because there is never enough time for all the tasks waiting to be done. If we look at a manuscript which does not have an accompanying synopsis, all we are trying to do is construct a provisional synopsis for our own sake— one that we cannot transmit to others except inaccurately. True, we may be interested in length, writing style, balance of text, illustrations, notes and tables, but even those things can be judged from a synopsis supported by sample chapters as easily as from all the chapters. We can also use this material to project the tentative length of the book.

The synopsis, properly prepared, with sample chapters where appropriate, will help us to help you by moving us towards an earlier decision. That may be a quick realization that yours is not a book in a category in which we publish; or that its length is inappropriate for our list; or that it should better be considered by someone else in our publishing house, perhaps based in another city or even overseas. In that case we shall want a synopsis to show them, not a weighty manuscript. If we think it is a possibility for us, we shall probably want to take advice from other academics, and the best advisers are busy people. We in turn will get a quick reply if we show them an outline, not a manuscript, and they can guide our decision and may suggest a suitable reader. The reader too will want to see an outline before deciding whether or not to report on the manuscript.

It is true that we may want to look over the finished manuscript in house before taking outside advice, but we can always reserve the option to ask you to send it along. And with many publishers, many books and many authors, it will be sufficient either to see sample chapters or to see a late draft without the final polish. Publishers differ over this, of course.

From the academic author's point of view, too, it is better to negotiate with a publisher before a manuscript is complete. The publisher may make an expression of interest contingent upon seeing the final version. But even then a publisher can say from an outline whether or not they are interested in the book and give guidelines on length, number of illustrations and so on. Review of a publishing proposal—in house, and by outside readers—will take time if it is done thoroughly and conscientiously; while publishers may be able to say No immediately, it may take anything from six weeks to six months to say Yes. If the discussions begin early, they can continue while you, the author, are still writing. If the manuscript is completed before a discussion with a publisher begins, this is lost time and indeed adds to the datedness of the final product. If—as is more than likely—the publisher requests changes, these may well be changes which could equally have been made at an earlier stage in the book's planning: length, structure, organization, level and so on.

If we were to be cynical, we could suggest that it is easier to have a synopsis accepted than a manuscript. Synopses are full of hope and promise. Manuscripts are often full of disappointment.

Be aware, though, that different publishers operate in different ways. All publishers have established procedures by which an acquisitions (or sponsoring or commissioning) editor has a proposal for contract approved. There is a key point at which this individual editor's support for a project is transformed into the publishing imprint's formal commitment, which is then signalled by the issuing of a contract. In a private commercial house, this commitment is of course an internal staff decision and may be relatively speedy, although the higher the quality of the imprint, the more careful the quality of advice and assessment should be. The decision will involve a route towards approval which may include a formal meeting and will certainly involve the circulation of a written proposal. The editor's peers may have a voice, the editorial director will have to support it, and the marketing department will certainly have a say before the final commitment is made.

University presses in the English-speaking world operate differently. In just a few, staff editors have authority to make the final decision. In others, the academic board approves the offer of a contract at any stage, after receiving a recommendation from a staff editor. This recommendation is normally supported by peer reviews of the proposal or manuscript from scholars in the relevant field. The academic board is appointed by the university. Depending on the size and tradition of the organization, members of the academic board may be closely involved in the consideration of a publishing proposal, or theirs may be the final formal endorsement of a judgement effectively made on their behalf by editorial professionals. But at some university presses any offer of contract before the completion of a full and final manuscript is only conditional, and the binding authority to publish follows positive review of the complete manuscript when delivered.

Yours truly, R.M.D.

« 17 » *The formal proposal*

Dear Mr. Auchermuchty,

We discussed very briefly your writing plans and you asked the best way to approach a publisher, in view of problems you had experienced and conflicting advice you had been given.

It is difficult to give absolute rules, because different publishers, and different editors, operate rather differently. But I suggest that the initial approach to a publisher should give them enough information to judge whether the book is suitable to be considered for their list, but not so much material (or the wrong material) so that this judgement is difficult to make or too time-consuming to make.

What we find least useful is a complete manuscript, a brief covering letter, and nothing else. This tends to wait until there is time to look at it, which puts it at the bottom of the pile.

Other things we find unhelpful, unless we ask for them, are lengthy testimonials, an overlong curriculum vitae, exaggerated projections of the likely market, bulky photocopies of conference papers and articles to show how productive the author is, and other material that is more form than content.

A lengthy curriculum vitae is not essential—some publishers like them more than others. It is surely better to include a brief statement of your professional qualifications to write this book, and details of other related publications of yours, rather than hand over pages of personal and irrelevant detail.

The essential parts of a submission I would consider to be the following.

First, a relatively brief letter explaining the context of the approach. Is the book being offered to us for a series, or for our list in general? Is the manuscript just in planning, or are several chapters available for us to review? Or is the manuscript complete? If not, what is your schedule for completing it?

This letter might include some brief information on the author: other books published or under contract, current appointment and so forth.

Finally, feel free to give the names of scholars who have read the manuscript and might be available to advise the publisher; or to suggest possible readers.

There should then be a descriptive synopsis of the book, perhaps three pages long. Under separate subheadings this would initially summarize the argument of the book and show where this argument fits into the discipline. Something should be said about the audience for the book: the disciplinary framework, the level at which it is written and the geographical interest in the subject. Included in this should be the readership for whom you are writing it: from the publisher's point of view, the market. This means the discipline or disciplines it will appeal to, the level at which it can realistically be expected to find a use, the countries where it will be suitable, and so on. A final note about "competition"—other books in the field—will be useful.

This should be followed by a structural synopsis or a fully annotated list of contents, also two to three pages long. This will show the organization of the book, by parts and chapters and apparatus; what will go into each chapter; and what is the word count, number of illustrations, and length of appendices or other matter.

And that is all.

These six pages—one page of letter, two to three pages of description, two to three pages of structure—are, I suggest, all the publisher needs initially. This is short enough to photocopy or fax to a colleague, another office, a series editor or an adviser, with the question "Does this look interesting to you?"

Material organized in the way described answers most of the questions a publisher asks of a proposal. These questions include the following, the answers to which will raise or dampen the publisher's interest in the book:

- Is it an edited collection?
- Is it a revamped Ph.D. thesis?
- Is it a technical or very specialized report?
- Is it a trade book in search of a trade and general publisher?
- Is it a textbook for adoption for a specific course?
- Is it in a subject in which we publish?
- Is it at a level at which we publish?
- Is it up to date within the discipline?
- Is it for a real, identifiable and reachable readership, of adequate size, in the regions where we publish?
- Is there a prima facie case that the author is competent—other publications, academic position, etc.?
- Is it of a reasonable length?
- Do the relationships between text, illustrations and apparatus seem reasonable?
- Is the topic of the book an interesting and current one?
- Is the structure of the book a logical one?
- Can the author write good English?
- How does it compare with the competition—other books in print at the same level and on the same subject?

If the answers to all these questions seem the right ones, can we follow it up by requesting enough sample material (chapters now, or a full manuscript shortly) to make a definitive judgement?

Thus, by producing the right kind of approach, an author can help the publisher and help themselves to a productive outcome.

One side issue. Most guides for writers advise authors to submit material with return postage or a stamped addressed envelope, to ensure safe and speedy return. I believe this is appropriate to trade, general and (especially) fiction publishing, as well as to magazines and literary journals, which receive numerous submissions in which they have no interest. A rapid return in the same post is the pattern.

For academic books a different and quite acceptable pattern has emerged. The photocopier means there is no need to send an original document of any text, and an author would be ill advised to send unsolicited and uninvited the top copy of any artwork, testimonials or other document.

If the first approach is either a letter or a letter plus photocopies of sample material, these copies should—from your viewpoint—be disposable copies. Most publishers will probably do you the courtesy of returning them (even if by second-class mail). If the publisher cannot even afford the cost of a stamp for the letter that says, "No, thank you," they are probably not worth the risk of handling your manuscript in the first place.

I fear that the inclusion of a stamped self-addressed envelope with a submission of a scholarly book to a suitable scholarly publisher suggests either "This is really a trade book going the rounds" or "I expect you to turn this down, so here is the envelope to send it back." If you send only a modest amount of material in the form of a good photocopy, and in a quantity that you can spare, and if you follow up any silence with a firm but courteous enquiry, the old rule about the stamped self-addressed envelope can probably be dropped.

There are exceptions, and in authors' guides some publishers will specifically say, "SAE please for return." But others may say, "No responsibility taken for manuscripts submitted"—another argument for being careful what you send.   *Yours truly, R.M.D.*

CHECKLIST FOR SUBMITTING A PROPOSAL

❐ Covering letter
❐ Some details of professional standing, previous books, and other relevant publications
❐ Description of project, with: argument of the book; length; current status and completion date; level of readership; areas/countries of readership; disciplines of readership; contrast with comparable/competing titles
❐ List of chapters, with (for each chapter) details of contents, length, number/type of illustrations and tables, appendices and other matter
❐ Readers' names—those who may already have read the manuscript; others who might be suitable referees (optional)
❐ Note on the availability of sample chapters, or whole manuscript, for review
❐ And something original, non-formulaic and interesting . . .

« 18 » *Peer review*

Dear Judy Cation,

We are still considering your manuscript—or, rather, it is with a couple of our advisers for their expert assessment. I know you think all this decision-making takes longer than it should. You said your work was well known and your previous writing was highly regarded, and you thought that there was no doubt we would want to offer you a contract. So you are mystified by the delays.

We too believe it very likely, in view of your previous work and high reputation, that we shall want to publish your book. In fact, that is why we approached you for it in the first place. But we still think that you and we will benefit from the process of peer review.

In fact, your letter arrived just as we were going to ask you to review for us another manuscript we are considering, so I had better explain what peer review is for, and what it is not for. A lot of academics give a lot of time to various forms of assessment: masters' and doctoral theses; research grant applications; manuscripts submitted to scientific and scholarly journals; manuscripts and proposals submitted for book publication. With the theses, it may be the ordained judging who is suitable to become ordained in the academic priesthood; but the rest of these evaluations are forms of peer review, where scholars evaluate each other's work. Why do they do it, and why is it so important?

Certainly they do not do it for financial reward. The value of an examiner's fee or a book publisher's honorarium is not likely to reward at a professional rate the time required, and reviews of journal submissions commonly attract no fee at all. If publishers paid academics at an hourly rate commensurate with their talents and professional abilities, the same publishers would turn down far more manuscripts without being able to give them any consideration. Scholars undertake these roles as part of their professional work, as active participants in their field of study, and as a way of staying on the cutting edge of the field. Any lively and conscientious scholar seeks to keep up with the literature which has been published in their field, and the most lively and conscientious among them are, generally, glad of an opportunity to keep up with the new writing and research which will form the publications of tomorrow—if their evaluation is positive.

Peer review in scientific and scholarly journals is the norm, and indeed some of the career evaluations in place in universities require papers in "refereed journals" to be distinguished from papers contributed

APPROACHING A PUBLISHER

to popular or in-house journals, or unrefereed papers presented at conferences. There is a lot of discussion of the role and value of such reviewing. Its success depends upon the judgement and authority of a journal editor or editorial board. Only the journal editors can know the audience for whom the journal is intended. They have to make the first judgement whether a paper fits their profile; only then can a decision be made if the paper should be reviewed—with the implication of publication if the review is favourable.

But what of the *Brain and Behavioral Sciences* study? This classic study in the United States (S. Harnad, ed., *Peer Commentary on Peer Review*, Cambridge: Cambridge University Press, 1983) showed that when the successfully published articles from scholars in high-reputation institutions were resubmitted for peer review with the authors' affiliations changed, the response differed. When the Ivy League laboratory's paper was resubmitted as from an unknown small college, the assessment of its scientific value suddenly changed.

A journal has its readership already lined up. The journal editor's main duty is to give the readership the best papers in the field. This and other studies do clearly suggest that anonymity for journal articles and papers should be provided to both parties; that a paper should be reviewed on its merits alone. This would avoid the initial doubts about a paper from an unknown source or scholar which may prove excellent, or the natural enthusiasm for a paper from a respected source which may not live up to expectations.

Publishers' readers are usually kept anonymous—unsung heroes of the scholarly publishing world. But should the authors of books also be kept anonymous when their proposals or manuscripts go out for review? That is more difficult. It would be useful to have your views, since we are asking you to review a manuscript for us.

In favour of anonymity is the objectivity this brings. Only the book is being assessed, not the past record or lack of reputation or affiliation of the author, nor the context in which the book was written or the author's mentors and guides.

But unfortunately, unlike the journal editor whose audience already exists, the book publisher does not have a waiting audience. Each new book has to find its audience—if there is one—singly from a base figure of zero. And the question "Will this book find an audience?" is influenced by the name and reputation and affiliation of the author and even by the context in which it was written.

So if a publisher is asking peer reviewers, "Will this book find an audience? Will it sell?" and not just, "Is it reputable?" then the publisher probably does have to reveal the author's identity.

On the other hand, if the publisher has a clear view on these matters, then it is the intrinsic quality of the manuscript that is of primary interest. There will be a rare occasion when a manuscript by a very saleable author, perhaps even a book commissioned on the basis of an outline, does not seem up to standard. An objective assessment, uninfluenced by the authorship, may be needed to save both publisher and author from an embarrassing gaffe. Great scholars do sometimes produce third-rate manuscripts; it takes the use and anonymity of the peer review process to guard against this.

In a manuscript as long as a book, too, there are usually clues to the pedigree and identity of the author that are hard to disguise. The bibliography often includes unpublished papers by the author. So perhaps the anonymous book manuscript is an impossibility anyway.

And there are particular problems in smaller subject areas. Scholars know, or believe they know, most of what is happening in a small field of research. If a manuscript is anonymous, they may guess or already know who is working on this subject. But if it not anonymous, they may, consciously or not, already have an attitude to the author, or to the author's institution or network. If they do not know the author, they may consider that fact already a black mark. This makes for difficulties in scholarly objectivity. But the publisher must persist.

Where practical, perhaps this is an argument for using readers at some geographical distance from the author. For our books, where we are asking not "Is this person reputable?" but "Is this manuscript first-class?" we may need input from outside the regional or national network.

So is it all worth while? Should the publishers just bypass the peer review process in scholarly publishing and take a punt on hunches?

There are two good reasons to answer No. The first is from the publisher's viewpoint. There have always been some imprints which do publish almost anything and everything in their field, without much evaluation, in cheap formats (though not always at cheap prices). They may well have a commercial argument for doing many books in a narrow range of fields just as long as the authors are card-carrying academics, without worrying too much about the results—most will sell enough to recover basic costs. But given this, other publishers (the majority of professional, scholarly and scientific imprints, I hope) need to distance themselves from the "catchall" imprints by demonstrating a commitment to selectivity and quality.

The other argument is from the author's standpoint. Peer review, with the protection of anonymity, permits an honest assessment of the unpublished manuscript which will be seen initially only by the publisher. In most cases the publisher will show or paraphrase the report to the author, concealing the reviewer's identity. Although colleagues, family and friends will have made subjective comments on the project, this may be the first independent assessment ever. If there are things wrong with the overall project, or improvements that can and should be made, or if there are errors of fact or detail or interpretation, it is better to have these before publication. Otherwise, the first published review will draw them to the attention of thousands of one's peers, and it will be too late to correct them.

So we hope you will be willing to review for us the manuscript we are showing you. We will respect your anonymity (unless you request otherwise). We will tell you who the author is but ask you to address the manuscript before you on its merits, and not to be too influenced by what you know or do not know of the author. We shall be taking the publishing decision, not you. We are asking your scholarly advice on the quality and importance of the book; you are not examining a thesis for a university. You will receive a fee below what your work deserves, but we shall still be pressing you to give us a report as soon as possible. You will be helping determine what is to form the next generation of scholarly output and discourse in your field. That is why I describe publishers' readers as the unsung heroes of the scholarly world.

And for your own manuscript? Please be patient; our readers are working to a timetable for their reports, and they have another week to go. Whatever their assessment, and whatever our publishing decision, we hope that their comments will be useful to you as a fair and independent assessment of your manuscript.   *Yours truly, R.M.D.*

« 19 » *Visit*

Dear Mr. Point,

Your request to visit us and talk about the book you are writing is one we shall have to decline—or at least postpone—but we hope you will not take offence. Let me explain frankly.

I can do this on two levels. The negative side is that publishers are very busy people, and they consider a large number of proposals, the majority of which are unsuitable for their particular list (though they may well suit someone else, publishing in a different area). Thus—statistically—the likelihood is that any particular book will not suit us.

If you come to explain and discuss your book but we find it is not appropriate for us, we will have wasted your time and ours. We shall be the essence of politeness, which means we shall be taking up more of your time than is useful to you and us if your book is not suitable.

If you send in a synopsis, we can tell directly if it is clearly unsuitable for us, and perhaps suggest a publisher you might better approach.

But on a positive note, if your manuscript is a possibility for us, it will be much more useful for us to see a detailed outline first, perhaps with some sample material. We can then look through it and assess it, and if we think it might suit us, then a visit to our office to talk about it will be useful. That will be a better use of our time and yours.

All this suggests that, from any viewpoint, if you are planning a visit to our city you should submit a synopsis well in advance. That will have saved you time if we cannot go ahead with it. And a later meeting will be far more useful, less bland and platitudinous, if we have had material to look at beforehand.

Your invitation to join you for lunch was a generous one. Don't take offence, but on the rare occasions when a unknown would-be author offers an editor lunch, it often turns out to be a prelude to our being offered a no-hope proposal. It is bit embarrassing to say No uncompromisingly into the later part of a sociable meal (worse still to say Yes and have to withdraw later). It is pretty reasonable for a would-be author to decline hospitality from a publisher, on the ground that this puts unfair moral pressure on him or her. (I have never experienced such a decline, but I met a man once who had a previous colleague who said it had once happened.)

So thanks, but let us skip the lunch or other meeting, and agree you will send me a synopsis in the usual way. Then we can get together in an appropriate manner and discuss it.

To be frank, we don't know you—though perhaps we should. It is true that an established author or distinguished name can expect the answer Yes to a request for a meeting or a visit. But even then it is more a courtesy. A written synopsis, with time to consider it, is still much more valuable for all concerned.   *Yours truly, R.M.D.*

« 20 » *Literary agents*

Dear Dr. Supplix,

When we spoke about your book you said you were thinking of putting it in the hands of a literary agent. That decision is certainly yours, and scholarly publishers are not unwilling to deal with authors' agents—at least, with recognized, established literary agents—but you may find our thoughts on this useful.

Agents come into their own in dealing with books for the general trade market—fiction and general non-fiction, some of which of course may be of high scholarly quality. Agents also have a valuable role acting for academics who combine television appearances, documentary films, public lectures and prominent commissioned articles with their own writing. But such academics are in a minority.

Agents may be able to help an academic in checking a publisher's contract, ensuring its clauses are fair, possibly improving the royalty terms and probably helping to secure or increase an advance. Writers' associations can perform the same role. But agents need to be realistic about the limited financial profile of academic publishing. If they hold out for a level of royalties and advances more appropriate to a high-profile trade book, they may find the offer of publication itself disappearing. An author needs to keep pressure on an agent, to make sure negotiations do not get bogged down. And of course for their professional services agents will charge a percentage—and the author needs to know what that percentage will be.

What agents are unlikely to do for a scholarly author is to identify the right scholarly imprint to consider a manuscript. The agent has to be a generalist. The author, as a subject specialist, is much more likely to know who is publishing actively in a particular field and who should be offered the manuscript.

Publishers of fiction trust the literary agent to act as a filter, to send them only work of quality that is appropriate for their particular list. Academic publishers will not have a similar trust in the ability of literary agents to assess academic work; nor should literary agents expect to have this ability, except perhaps in certain marginally general areas such as literary biography.

But consider the agent's viewpoint. An agent has to make a living, maintain an office, secure a cash flow to operate a business. But 10 per cent of not very much is not very much. So an agent—probably even more than a publisher—has to concentrate on what will generate income. That tends to favour books which will secure advances over books which will earn royalties. It certainly favours books that attract substantial royalties over a short time, rather than the slow-selling title of scholarly distinction.

An agented book has to be an earning book. The agent cannot claim 10 per cent of the research grant that allows an author to write a book, or of a salary during a sabbatical, or even of a cash prize a book might receive. And the agent cannot expect a percentage of the salary increase following the promotion that an academic book sometimes leads to. It has to be cash in hand.

And, not least, agents are looking not for books to represent but authors to represent. It is the consistent and trusting relationship between a productive and saleable author and a conscientious agent that is the happiest relationship. So for a single academic book—especially a first book—you are unlikely to attract a literary agent.

They say that wounds heal often; that doctors heal, but less often; that given the choice and the odds, you may be better off with a wound than a doctor. It is difficult to find a publisher for a book; it is difficult to find an agent for a book. But given the odds, it will probably be easier to find a publisher than an agent in most cases; and if you do find and use an agent, the arrangement has to be to the clear financial benefit of both parties.   *Yours truly, R.M.D.*

« 21 » *No reply*

Dear Dr. Fides,

I was very embarrassed to have your letter which cautiously asked if we had completed our review of your manuscript sent to us eight months ago. You had our routine formal acknowledgement but have heard nothing since then.

The truth is that your proposal was filed away and nothing was done with it. This is not common. But it does happen that projects get misfiled, or forgotten, or lost on someone's desk. All publishers are human. Some are efficient and conscientious, some languid and careless.

It is worth finding out, from colleagues and friends, which publishers seem relatively efficient and which are slapdash, before choosing whom to approach with a book manuscript or proposal. But even efficient publishers may have a lapse.

I suggest that you should always make firm but courteous enquiries about the progress of your publishing proposal. You will probably get a more factual, less bland response if you make your enquiry by letter and follow up by telephone a couple of weeks later.

It is reasonable to expect a publisher to acknowledge an initial proposal within two weeks, and to indicate within two months what action they are taking. It may well take four months to secure outside advice and process a proposal through the acquisitions procedure of a publishing house. But the author deserves to be kept informed.

If you receive no acknowledgement of your initial approach after three weeks, send an enquiry letter. If at any stage two months go by with no news of how things stand, a letter of enquiry makes good sense. It will certainly help to move a project to the top of the pile, or prompt a telephone call to a slow adviser, or jog the memory of an

editorial assistant. It may even prompt an editor who is going to say
No eventually to say it now, and release your manuscript so that you
can approach other publishers. It is not worth an aggressive call threat-
ening to withdraw a manuscript (it may be too easy to let you); but a
gentle hint that other though less satisfactory options lie in the background might prompt a little productive jealousy.

So if there is silence from the publisher, don't assume that vigorous
and conscientious activity is under way; recognize that your project
might have fallen into some black hole, and send a gentle prompt to
check.

For a good publisher there is nothing worse than discovering that for
eight months someone has believed in their faultless pursuit of a project that was filed away in error on the day it arrived.

Yours truly, R.M.D.

$\mathcal{C}$ATEGORY OF BOOK

≡ ≡ ≡ ≡ ≡ ≡ ≡ ≡ ≡ ≡ ≡ ≡

« 22 » *Scholarly book*

Dear Dr. Scriptor,

We were very pleased to receive the outline and sample chapters for your proposed scholarly book. We have considered these carefully and consulted with advisers and our marketing colleagues, and we are pleased to accept it for publication. Academic publishers—like all publishing houses—spend much of their time saying No to projects; it is our much greater pleasure to say Yes.

Your outline showed us that you had thought carefully about what your book was trying to say, how you were going to say it, and for whom you were writing. The structure, length and balance of the book demonstrated this.

Your accompanying letter suggested, apologetically, that your book might not be a best seller in many general bookshops. You write that the main audience will be academics, professionals, senior students and serious avocational enthusiasts in your (admittedly growing) field of study, as well as scholars in adjacent disciplines who need to keep up with the trends in your field but do not have the time or facility to follow the more detailed papers in the specialist journals.

This seems an excellent reason to write a book on your subject, and a good time to do so. What matters to us is that you are writing a book for an audience, that you can identify this audience, and that we recognize it as an audience whom we can and do reach. In other words, the good thing about your book is that it is written as a book to be read, not just as a demonstration of academic integrity, the dutiful documentation of a research project or an obligatory stage in an academic career.

If your book is reaching out to readers from other disciplines, please remember not to get caught up in too much intra-discipline jargon. It is worth explaining your terms when you use them—those familiar with the discourse and terminology of the discipline will not resent you for repeating the familiar.

You also apologize for the fact that you do not think the book will be adopted as a course textbook that students must purchase, though you do think students, particularly those in upper-level courses, will read all or part of it—probably in the library. Don't apologize. Scholarly publishers are looking for books of outstanding quality written for the real and solid market they reach through sales to libraries and individuals. Not all books are expected to be textbooks.

You have borne your readership in mind, too, in your style. Some authors consider that their ideas transcend the need for style in presentation; some even get away with it, if their ideas are so important and their reputation already high. But for most authors style is the courtesy they pay those whom they wish to address, and a good, clear English prose style is desirable for any book, however scholarly the intent.

Also, to achieve your intention to communicate, you have kept to a modest length a topic which could have been written about at twice or three times the length. In other words, you have resisted the common academic temptation towards prolixity. This helps the publisher's costing directly, of course, but it does so even more because the shorter the book, within reason, the more people will read it. That may be unfortunate, but with the information explosion all printed matter is competing for time as well as budgets, and even an academic reader needs high motivation to read a book that is not central to their main field. There has to be a very good reason to go over 300 pages.

The balance among the elements of your book, too, shows that you have your readers' needs in mind. Some books try to cram in so many words of text and so many factual assertions that the effect is like sitting through a week of lectures offered at some vast disciplinary annual conference.

In a well-balanced book, the illustrations are relevant, appropriate and well distributed. The tables or other presentations of data are designed to communicate information, not to impress. They sum up in readily accessible format information which would be less accessible within the main text of the book, and they do so in a format appropriate to the readership of the book, whether this is a simple or complex table, or a simple or complex graphic presentation. Appendices give only that material which is superfluous to the flow of the argument. The notes are not used to make too many side remarks, but refer to sources, at the appropriate level. Notes and bibliography are provided to help the reader, not to show off.

What we like about your proposal is not just the clear content and the certainty about the level at which you are writing, but also the way you have structured the book. As an academic you start with some clear ideas, derived from your research and thinking over recent years. But for the book you start with the reader's need to understand, not just your own to expound, so you have created a plan for the book which appears to unfold the argument in a sympathetic, clear and open way. It is a scholarly and learned book, but one written for real readers.

The structure of parts, and of chapters within parts, looks logical. The structure is made clear in chapter titles and therefore in the contents list, which details the few subheadings you have introduced into each chapter to help your readers through the book. Particularly helpful is the use of the introductory chapter to amplify further the structure and contents of the book, and to presage the overall conclusions. The concluding chapter can therefore pull all these strands together.

All this was enough to demonstrate to us that yours was an academic book proposal worth taking on for our list. It was worth our thinking about carefully; it was worth our showing to our regular advisers, who confirmed the importance and merits of the project.

You have planned a real book for a real audience, and it is a great pleasure to accept it for our list.   *Yours truly, R.M.D.*

« 23 » *Technical monograph*

Dear Dr. Leydon,

We have been considering the manuscript you sent us for publication. We cannot fault its professionalism, nor do we doubt that it represents a contribution to learning. The readers to whom we showed it advise that the research you have undertaken is of very high quality, that the data you have collected is quite possibly unique, and that this material deserves formal publication in order to record it in print for future specialist use.

Despite this, we have decided not to offer you publication, so we should explain the context of this decision.

All publishers—whether self-financing commercial and university presses, or subsidized university and institutional imprints—have to make decisions on priorities in the use of their finite resources. Serving scholarly authors is one criterion; serving scholarly readers is another.

The problem with your manuscript is that while many believe it "ought to be available in print," very few libraries and even fewer individuals would buy it. What you are presenting is not a book for readers but a record of data, presented in a competent, professional but specialized format for the record.

This is a kind of specialist or technical report found in many disciplines. The experimental sciences generate substantial amounts of data—most often available as a backup to a series of scientific papers in the journals. The field sciences—environmental and biological, geological and archaeological—create reports with invaluable data records which may not be replicated for a long time, and in some cases are recording evidence which may vanish. Such records are central to a discipline and may be of value long after the arguments and interpretations based on the evidence have been replaced.

In the social sciences and economics detailed data may be collected, processed, refined, analysed and reanalysed, and may be useful to different groups of readers at different levels. At which level will formal book publication be most appropriate?

Even in the humanities there are technical levels of publication. Scholarly editions of texts or detailed catalogues of artistic works may have information of importance to record and retain but be difficult to publish.

What is the attitude of scholarly presses to such technical and specialist works of record? There is no single answer—it differs between imprints, it differs between disciplines. Most academic imprints, certainly most university presses, have some books on their list which are primarily publications of record rather than books of appeal, contributions to knowledge that cannot expect to cover their costs. But how good a use of publishing resources is this?

Books presenting a large amount of "technical" material are often very expensive to edit, design and typeset; they are much more complex than the straightforward narrative text. But their potential sales are smaller than for the normal academic book, so the print run will be smaller, and higher than normal costs must be spread across fewer than normal units. The selling price will be very much higher than the normal cost of an academic book; and the threat of an excessive selling price may make the whole project seem pointless to author as well as publisher, for the distribution will be inhibited.

A subsidy—from the sponsors of the original research or an independent donor—is often seen as the answer. But while you can pay a publisher to produce a book, money cannot force a reader to buy it.

Publishing technical monographs through scholarly publishers therefore tends to lead to misery on all sides: very high prices, very low sales; the publishers thinking they are doing a service to the scholarly community, the community thinking they are being exploited by excessive prices, the authors thinking their work is being suppressed.

Much better outlets are emerging for such technical material, though. The rise of in-house word processing systems means that it is possible for a research worker or a research team to create a well-organized version of their manuscript. Desktop publishing systems make it possible for an institution to generate an acceptable visual layout for presentation of this material. Agencies are available that will transform computer data from desktop publishing programs into high-resolution output for printing. And institutions are able to create or purchase specialist mailing lists which can sell this material direct to the libraries, institutions and individuals who need it, while keeping it bibliographically visible by including it in national bibliographies, cataloguing-in-publication and so on.

The costing pattern of institutional publishing means, too, that institutions will often sell much closer to apparent cost than a publisher can, so that real economies are achieved and the scholarly community is well served.

Why not publish your technical monograph in such an institutional series, using desktop publishing techniques and low-cost distribution?

You might then consider giving wider dissemination to your ideas by writing for us a scholarly book with more argument and less detailed technical data. You can refer to the publication of your data elsewhere in the knowledge that it is readily obtainable through the institutional outlet.   *Yours truly, R.M.D.*

« 24 » *Thesis/dissertation*

Dear Dr. Arduus,

Thank you for your university dissertation, which you sent us with a request that we publish it as a book. This request does, however, raise problems, as does any thesis.

You mention that your examiners were asked by the university, as part of their report, if it should be published—and they said Yes. But they so often do! In our view, this question should never be asked in the context of an examination—it is unfair on you. When examiners are asked both if a book-length work should be granted a higher degree and if it merits publication, they may believe they would appear inconsistent if they said Yes to one question and No to the other. But this raises unfair hopes in you and asks publishers to perform a quite different judgement. After all, publishers are not asked if a book's author should be granted a higher degree.

Every year in the English-language academic world, tens of thousands of dissertations are judged suitable to be awarded a higher degree, and we do not challenge that judgement. But those are theses, not books. Graduate students now are at least as numerous as undergraduate students were a couple of generations ago. In the USA and Canada only, over 37,000 doctorates are awarded each year, and the numbers increase annually. The proportion which can be developed into publishable books must necessarily diminish annually.

You say that you know theses are not normally published, but that you wrote yours as a book with publication in mind. We do not want to sound cynical, but everyone says that.

When we say a thesis is not a book, we are normally asked, What is the difference, and how can my thesis be transformed into a book?

The problem is that the two are *supposed* to be different. A thesis is written to be read by two or three examiners, as a demonstration of research capability. A book is written to be read by several thousand people, as a means of communication. That is one difference.

Authors and their advisers vary, of course; but in general, a thesis usually aims to do certain specific and identifiable things. It seeks to make a single contribution to its field of study, setting this contribution within a carefully documented research procedure, and showing full acquaintance with the literature and research that has preceded it and with the norms of the discipline. If approved in an examination, it licenses the writer, the researcher, to practise as a professional in the field—hence the degree. It is thus part of being certified to do the real thing; it is not itself the real thing.

So a thesis or dissertation summarizes its argument carefully to avoid seeming too daring or innovative, which might frighten the examiners. It exhaustively reviews the previous work in the field and the literature that reflects this, including previous theses (so theses do get read, even if they do not get published). It sets out with care and decorum the questions being investigated by the research (even though the reader and the author know that these questions have been reformulated in the light of the answers). It then lays out with care the research methodology employed, to show that no stone has been left unturned, no tenet of the tried and tested approaches of the field has been ignored, no logical jumps made or testing procedures bypassed. We then get to the results, expressed definitively but with some caution lest the innovative appear too unprofessional, the insights too tentative, the methodology too untested, or the project too ambitious. If there are no results the dissertation may be failed; but if the results are too far away from the mainstream of the field the risk of failure is higher, or is perceived to be higher.

The thesis commonly has a careful apparatus of abstract, lengthy acknowledgements (that list of librarians is there for a purpose, isn't it, not just to impress?) and several introductory chapters before the main text. It has a modest conclusion, many long appendices and an immense bibliography; and its evidence is arrayed for the eyes in a feast

of tables, lists, graphs or whatever. And then, justly, the licence to practise is granted by the two or three readers for whom it was written.

Is this something a publisher can sell to hundreds or thousands of
readers and to the libraries that serve them?

Put another way, what would the solemn university-appointed examiners say if a thesis came their way in a different format? If it began
with a declaration of its ideas, its discovery, the breakthrough in
knowledge it represented? If it grasped the reader with a set of deci-
sive, even incautious statements, and then dealt with these in more
detail in successive chapters, starting with the most important and
gradually working down to the ground floor of the argument? If the
methodology that led to this innovative work were hidden subtly away
in a short endnote on research methodology, in some footnotes, in a
brief appendix? If the writer's research ability were taken more on
trust? If the acknowledgements were minimal, to grant-giving bodies
and a loved one? If the bibliography were just a tool to take the reader
direct to some essential information, the illustrations just the essential
ones—or even just the beautiful ones? If in place of a carefully worded
abstract there were a bold, dynamic blurb demanding the reader's attention? Would it not be failed as a thesis, referred back for reworking?
But that, of course, would not be a thesis; that would be a book.

So how to transform a thesis into a book, you may ask? If you take it
away and work on it, jolly it up, make it less cautious, trim the notes
and bibliography and apparatus, reorder the chapters so that the argument comes first and the methodology is a subtle subtext, will that then
be a publishable book?

The answer is Maybe. Do it at your own risk, though. Do not do it
because you said the publisher asked you to, and come back in two,
three or five years with a book which might be turned down anyway.
And certainly do not do it if you don't believe in the book as much as
you believed in the thesis, and take a book's potential readers as seriously as you took the examiners.

One criterion, then, will be: is it a good book? But another will be:
does it look like a book that was carved out of a thesis? People in a
specialist field know who has researched what; they know the tricks of
the trade. Is it worth five years' hard work to reformat a thesis into a
book, only to have reviewers—or colleagues—say of the book, "This is
X's thesis of five years ago, now published."

A lot of emotion goes into writing a book. It strains the pocket; it
sorely tests the patience of those who care for the writer, and may cause
some of them to cease doing so. It may be the pinnacle of one's abilities
in the direction of writing. It may burn out one's interest in a particular
subject area, or inspire a move to a much more significant area of writ-

ing or research. The thesis author may be more than tired of the topic: if any of that weariness shows through in a book, the book is doomed. For a thesis starts with two or three people who have to read it—as the appointed examiners. A book starts with no readers and may find none.

There is, then, often a good argument for doing something different with a thesis. Two, three or four good articles in major journals, based on the dissertation, will be read—for journals already have readers, subscribers, library browsers, circulation routes and coverage in bibliographies. Journal articles can refer to each other and build up a corpus of work, whereas a book stands alone and refers only to itself. And if there is technical data which should be made available to a specialist audience, and which backs up the arguments in journal articles, there are departmental, university, informal and institutional series which exist, in modest print runs, exactly at that level and for that purpose.

Publication of your work in such a format will find readers, create interest in you and your work, and draw it to the attention of your peers. You will have fulfilled the examiners' recommendation that you publish your work, in an appropriate format. So your conscience will be clear. You can sit down to an empty desk, never blight your loved ones' lives again with the mention of your thesis topic, and write a real book, designed for publication, and with thousands of readers in mind, on another (if perhaps related!) topic.

When you do so, please send it to us. We look forward to hearing from you.   *Yours truly, R.M.D.*

« 25 » *Conference volume*

Dear Committee of the Biosophical Association,

You wrote asking if we would publish the proceedings of your recent conference—the handsomely produced programme of which you were kind enough to send us.

I have no doubt that it was, as you say, a most successful conference and one of the most memorable you have ever held. I am sure that was not entirely due to the Polynesian Night on the Tuesday, though I am surprised at your mystery tour on the Saturday. I was born in the town where you met, and to me the mystery is how you found anything to tour. But be that as it may . . .

Our serious answer is No, and that deserves an explanation. A conference is an occasion when ideas are floated, work in progress is reported, work long faded is revived, the distinguished pretend to be modest, and the young make a desperate bid for recognition in the search for jobs, grants and position in a difficult and competitive scholarly world.

The papers presented at conferences are sometimes volunteered, sometimes put together by a group, occasionally invited from distinguished guest speakers.

From the visitor's point of view the best papers are often, though not always, the papers invited by a session organizer. Less satisfactory are many of the volunteered papers, though the need for young academics to make an impression is understandable.

The worst papers, too often, are those delivered by academics who cannot get a travel grant to a conference from their institution unless they are speaking. Their provision of a poster paper at a conference—a posted visual presentation rather than a paper delivered orally—often fails to count towards attracting a travel grant.

Publishers sit through more conferences than academics do, and they see some sorry sights along with some high points. They have learnt to judge papers by seeing how many in the audience are studying the periodic table of elements mounted on the walls of the lecture theatre.

You note that your two main guests spoke without a written script—as happens frequently. Your tape recording will have given some permanence to their musings; but are you sure that the excitement of the live presentation will survive in cold print? Did those guest speakers even want their work to appear in print? If, as you suggest, they will be given the opportunity to edit the transcript, have you any reason to believe they will respond with enthusiasm in the time available?

Papers at a conference are not the same as papers in a book or journal, even if they have been handed round in advance and the audience pretends to have read them the night before instead of taking advantage of the extended opening hours at the bar.

A book needs, say, a thousand purchasers—several thousand readers. With 300 delegates you may have had your society's biggest conference ever, but that is a small segment of the human race. Where are the thousand?

If we say No to reprinting the conference papers as a book, we are not being negative towards science and scholarship. Any good paper will be revised by its author, illuminated by the discussion at the meeting or warned by the lack of discussion. It will be submitted to a journal in the field, where in the bright light of day it will be judged, assessed, and accepted as important or rejected as less important. That is the procedure of the scholarly world: short-circuiting it with another heavy volume to tax library budgets is usually not a constructive contribution.

You will probably argue that the two editors chosen by the conference will work hard and conscientiously to get a book into first-class order. But they will have arrived on the scene too late. They cannot invite new papers; they will have to be brave indeed to omit the keynote speakers. If they rush their job, they will produce a book that does not match the normal quality of scholarly work. But if they go through the tortuous process of reviewing each paper, getting revisions done and approved, cross-referencing and imposing an editorial structure, the book will not come out until well into the future.

There are two main exceptions to the academic publisher's lack of enthusiasm for conference volumes.

The first is the occasion—often in the pure or applied sciences—where an institution organizes a symposium on a key topic of current intellectual or practical importance. This is not the annual meeting of a learned society; all the papers are invited, probably from an international range of scientists, and commonly are put on the programme only after approval of their abstracts. The meeting is therefore a "state of the question" meeting, and though the topic is narrower than at a typical professional meeting it may lead to a much more publishable volume. As a rule of thumb, the narrower the topic for such a meeting, the more likely it is to lead to a publishable book. But although "state of the question," it still needs the tough assessment of individual papers that would be applied if they were being considered for a scientific journal.

The other exception is where a conference exists for the sole purpose of presenting drafts of chapters previously commissioned for an edited book. Edited books have their own problems, of course; but some of these can be reduced if, during preparation, the contributors meet with selected discussants, present their draft chapters and pre-circulated papers, discuss the drafts, and use the meeting to modify and mould the planned book. This is a conference of the book, not a book of the conference.

I suspect that a conference is most often an event of the moment, not an event for all time, and publication is not the appropriate result. For other conferences, or major sessions of conferences, the interest in the papers might be reflected in a cheap and cheerful publication produced quickly through desktop publishing methods.

If the authors deliver their papers on disk or as a high-quality printout (and if the Polynesian Night generated some profit for conference funds), the conference organizers may be able to produce, fairly quickly, a minimally edited and informally bound monograph in an in-house series. A subscription to this publication could be included in the conference fee, and departmental or institutional mailing lists could be used to sell it.

Production can be done very soon after the conference itself, so that those wanting a permanent record of the meeting, and those unable to attend, can be satisfied. Is this not better than taking the long and painful route of approaching publishers, awaiting the outcome of their refereeing, and going through your own editing, revising, polishing and refinement processes to generate a book of the conference long after the excitement of the face-to-face meeting has faded and the sounds of laughter and applause have ceased to echo around the lecture rooms?   *Yours truly, R.M.D.*

« 26 » *Edited volume*

Dear Dr. Catchall,

We expressed cautious interest in your proposal for an edited volume. Publishers take different approaches to edited volumes. Certainly there are an enormous number on offer, though most betray their original derivation from papers presented at conferences.

Commonly a scholarly publisher may start to look at a book proposal by an individual writer with optimism, while the normal first reaction to an edited volume is fairly negative.

You mention that your proposal is different, because you want to commission a group of articles especially for a book. In that case a publisher is certainly likely to be more interested. But there are some key questions a publisher will ask. Will it be coherent? Will it be balanced? Will it actually happen with the contents as planned, at the intended length and level? And does it have to be an edited volume, or could a single author cover the whole field better?

In most cases a single voice may have strengths in a book which multiple voices cannot have. It may be that there are a dozen specialists who can write better about their own topics. But they will usually have proven this ability in published and citable works. So an individual author may be better able to take what is important, quoting and fully acknowledging the sources, and synthesize it in a coherent way. The result is a unified and readable book, giving the developments and ideas of a field in a consistent style. To achieve the same quality with a team of authors is extremely difficult, if not impossible.

In an edited volume each author is likely to stress the importance of their own topic, and a volume editor must resist and control this tendency. A single author may be better able to balance the claims and significance of different topics.

But if you remain convinced of the value of the collaborative approach, how should you present such a proposal to a publisher? It is ideal to have a complete manuscript, but often a volume editor needs a publisher's contract—or at least expression of interest—to secure the final draft manuscripts.

So the alternative is to ask each contributor for a good synopsis (half a page, say). This serves three roles. It can be used by the volume editor to sell the project to the publisher, and to demonstrate that the most distinguished authors on the list are really committed to the project. It can be used by the volume editor to ensure that authors are writing at the level and on the topic required for the book, and to help guide authors towards links with each other. Finally, the competence, care and promptness with which authors submit their synopses may indicate how they will perform in the final manuscript: an author who is late in delivering a 250-word synopsis may be more disruptively late in delivering an 8000-word chapter.

An editor must have the respect of the contributors since, to forge a good book, it must pass review by the editor and very possibly by outside readers appointed by the publisher. They will suggest final changes to each contribution before it is ready for publication. Worse still, a contributed chapter may not live up to expectations. No matter how distinguished the author, it must be omitted if it is not to spoil the book.

A frequent problem is that a junior editor may hope to gain a publishing contract by securing contributions to a book from senior members of the profession. Until egged on by the publisher, this junior editor may not have the confidence, nerve or clout to get the senior authors to revise where essential.

Unfortunately, publishers are used to editors who assure them that a book is "almost in." An electrical circuit does not work until all components are present and connected. A book cannot be almost in—if it is not complete, it is not a book. So as far as the publisher and reality are concerned, the book does not exist until the final draft from the most dilatory contributor has been approved by the volume editor and handed over to the publisher.

But that certainly does not end the real work. Copyediting queries, bibliographic work, reference apparatus and finally the index are still to come. All these stages are likely to involve the volume editor in giving answers on sections of text they never wrote in the first place.

All this is not to say an edited book cannot be worth the effort. In some expanding fields, it is exciting to seize the moment and commission key authors—thinking along the same lines in different areas, or periods, or sub-fields—to write as a cooperative presentation. Some of these books have continuing value as reference books, and some can even be used for a few years as student textbooks.

But the illusion that it is easier to edit a book than to write one is false. A high-quality edited book, with the right contents, authors, emphasis, level, length and apparatus, is an immense amount of work. It is easier to write the book yourself in most cases. A second-rate edited book, thrown together like a supermarket basket of products, is easier to create; but publishers are proffered such baskets every day. The answer to these must be No, we do not wish to publish.

Sometimes a good alternative to a book is to propose a special issue of a journal. A book starts with no readers. A journal has its subscribers already paid up, eager and waiting. It may be appealing to a journal's editors, and readers, to dedicate one quarterly issue to a special theme, with all the papers commissioned to a length and format to suit the journal. And it is even possible (especially if it is the first part of a volume, numbered from page 1) to discuss with a publisher the reissuing of the material in book form.

Publishers have to think very hard before taking on a multi-author volume. Would-be editors have to think very hard before committing themselves to the substantial effort needed to produce such a volume—effort which might be better spent on writing the single-author book.

Yours truly, R.M.D.

« 27 » *Festschrift*

Dear Dr. Pius,

You asked if we would be willing to consider a "festschrift"—a volume put together in honour of your senior colleague, who is retiring. The tenor of your letter hints that you know how negative publishers can be about such projects.

The word "festschrift" itself is redolent of another age, of ancient Teutonic scholarship, where the peers and followers of a great scholar come together to do homage in the way they know best—by a testimony of their own scholarship in the permanent form of the printed word. Perhaps the genre has lost its power because of the large number of academic retirements—and of academics willing and eager to see their papers in print.

Publishers "owe" debts of gratitude to a vast array of senior scholars who have been their authors, advisers, general editors, readers and supporters over the years. But because they cannot select which of them to honour, they commonly choose to honour none; indeed, some publishers—especially university presses—have taken a policy decision to consider no festschrifts at all, in order to avoid the offence that might arise if they accepted some and turned down others.

But this is rather a narrow view. The imminent retirement, birthday or other celebratory occasion provides an excuse for the creation of an edited book from invited contributors, and perhaps a reason for them to give of their best. But the criteria of quality—and of suitability for publication—are no different from those for any other book. And it may be best for the publisher to disguise the fact that this is a dedicated volume.

So a book may be good despite being a festschrift. But the irony is, of course, that it does not matter to whom it is dedicated. A book created to honour the president of the Academy may have no intrinsic merits; a book in honour of the office janitor may be outstanding.

This all suggests that you might use the "festschrift to honour X" as a way to attract your desired authors, but not as a way to attract a publisher. To secure a readership, and to convince publishers there will be a real readership, you need to confront all the normal demands and problems of an edited book. To create a valuable and coherent book, you may need to include authors who have no special link with the person to be honoured. More awkwardly, it will almost certainly mean omitting some scholars who do have strong ties to the honouree but whose contribution will not help to strengthen the volume.

Yours truly, R.M.D.

« 28 » *Collected papers*

Dear Professor Summers,

Your idea of a collected volume of your papers is an interesting one; as you say, the suggestion was made by your colleagues in view of your distinction in the field.

The attraction of bringing together a scholar's papers in one volume or set of volumes has been rather undermined by the photocopier and by inter-library loan systems, which make it so much easier to obtain copies of an article published in a journal or an edited volume. But as you rightly note, some of your own publications have appeared in very obscure publications and are not readily available.

A library is unlikely to buy the collected papers by any but the most widely read of authors if the works are already available scattered through the library. So the "difficulty of access" test is often the crucial one.

There is an added attraction in bringing together the work of a very distinguished author whose work forms a linked pattern. A theologian, philosopher or social theorist may have written a coherent body of work that has been dispersed in publication, and whose significance is only clear once these papers are collected. The fact that students want—or need—to study them is a better reason than the mere neatness of assembly in one set of covers.

If a publisher is convinced that there is a demand for a volume of collected papers from one author, other criteria still come in. The more coherent the volume, the better: papers around a common theme, rather than varied topics (there may even be merit in having more than one such volume by a single author). Linking material, to give the book more coherence and to put each paper in context, is especially useful, though a general introduction will also be suggested by most publishers, perhaps to be written by another scholar.

It is tempting for an author to "update" previously published articles slightly, but in most cases this is rather subversive of the image of collected papers.

Alternatively, a scholar—especially one who has not yet come to the final stage of a career—may use published papers as a brief and basis for a new book, of the same scope, written as a continuous narrative. To publishers this will be a more appealing idea; to most readers a more accessible format; and to the author a chance to pull thoughts together at one time and with the real benefit of hindsight.

Yours truly, R.M.D.

« 29 » *Across the disciplines*

Dear Prof. Erdfield,

I enjoyed our discussion about your current academic work and how it might be developed into one or more books for our list. I have been looking over both of the synopses you sent me. One is for a book with two overseas colleagues, comparing three national studies. The other is deliberately crossing the boundaries between disciplines, to appeal to a wider scholarly audience and a wider range of student courses. Both are rather different from the norm of a book within a discipline, dealing with a single topic or case study, or with a general theme.

78 CATEGORY OF BOOK

Publishing editors often express admiration at the scholar who is prepared to extend beyond the limits of one narrow discipline, or go beyond the case study of one country. But our marketing colleagues, who actually have to sell the books, remind us of the reality—that broadening the scope of a book in this way may narrow the potential sales and audience for a book, not broaden it. Why the enigma?

Comparative studies can make for wonderful conferences. There is a real buzz in bringing together colleagues from Canada and New Zealand to discuss new literary forms, or from Japan and the USA to compare industry-government relations, or from Australia and Peru to exchange views on mining in the economy, or from China and the UK to discuss environmental impact assessment. The combination of a shared disciplinary background with different national traditions and contrasting data can generate exchanges, both formal and informal, that most participants find productive, and that can lead into new perspectives, new questions and continuing new contacts. But does this experience translate successfully into a book? Almost never. All the normal problems of a volume of conference papers are compounded when the subject of the conference is "Country X and Country Y compared and contrasted."

Is there a significant improvement in the saleability of a book when several authors ask a parallel set of questions about their own country of study? Or when each author's perspective is conscientiously applied to the same sample of countries? The answer, I suspect, is "Sometimes, but rarely."

The reason, perhaps, is that most researchers are basically concerned with their own country or area of study. That will be the primary area in which they buy books for their own use, and to which they give priority when recommending books for library purchase. They may peruse, for comparative purposes, work from another country or area; but then what they seek from a library is a substantive monograph on that area—not necessarily a prepackaged decision, in one set of covers, on what is the sample for comparison. One ecologist may want to make comparisons with humid tropical zones, another with areas of maximum genetic isolation. One literary scholar's comparative framework might be post-colonial literatures in English, another's may be magical realists whatever the language of their writing. One political scientist's natural field for comparison may be industrialized nations with shrinking agricultural sectors, another's may be stable two-party democracies.

So the argument is not against comparative studies, but against the assumption that one book's "x versus y" comparisons will correspond to that of the field as a whole. Each subject will have a few exceptions.

Marsupials of Australia and South America may be a safe topic; comparisons between the three economic blocs of the European Community and Japan and the USA may pass muster. But for the proposed volume on Argentina and South Africa, 50 per cent on each, I am afraid my publishing answer has to be No.

As a better idea, why not consider a book by yourself alone, concentrating on one country but with a chapter which makes wide-ranging contrasts and comparisons across several other areas? The broadsweep comparative chapter—drawing on the work of others as appropriate—can lift and expand the coverage and make it, perhaps, an even more attractive proposal. Could you consider this approach?

Sadly, most individuals are making choices not of what books to buy, but of what they can afford to do without; not what they would like the library to purchase, but what are the clear priorities within a limited budget; not how widely they wish their students to read, but what is a realistic and attainable list of books for them to acquire and of books and articles to read through. The book which is half on one key area and half on another may fall between two priorities and reach half, instead of double, the market.

Curiously, the same phenomenon can also be seen in cross-disciplinary books. In principle, what could be more stimulating than the book which breaks the disciplinary boundaries, which crosses the divide between philosophy and microbiology, between economic geology and economics, between medieval history and modern political science, between linguistics and psychology; the topic which transcends the traditional limitations of the academic disciplines from which the university or scientific research world is constructed; the author prepared to write for a broader audience of intellectual enquiry, and not just for the rigid confines of the subject with its career structure?

We can all name books of this kind which have been a major influence on us: books which reflect the return of grand theory; books which unify two disparate or conflicting fields; books which take a specific important topic and explore all its dimensions in the light of two disciplines—perhaps psychology and political science, or law and ethics, or engineering and public policy, or even theology and theoretical physics.

There are also books, ahead of their time, which create new disciplines or sub-disciplines by linking existing subjects. That is how chaos theory, or artificial intelligence, or cultural studies, or law-and-society, or gender studies came into being. But some of these subjects arise only to disappear: the once-heralded fields of area studies have now mainly retreated back into their subject disciplines.

But, equally, such memorable books are the exception, and indeed they have to be exceptional in quality as well as ambition. Few scholars and scientists can successfully cross disciplinary boundaries; their books must be more exceptional than most to make their mark by doing do, and even more exceptional to allow colleagues to say, Yes, here is a new sub-discipline emerging.

Perhaps your book will prove to be one of these pathfinding, boundary-crossing pioneers. The sample material will suggest, and a complete manuscript will show, whether this is so.

But the average scholarly book stretching beyond boundaries will, in my view and experience, suffer from going against the limitations of the bounded world of academe. We are back to the key question in library or individual purchase: what can I afford to do without? When library budgets are allocated to subjects, each subject area is likely to select books central to that subject. Most students on a course are likely to acquire books central to that course. And the individual academic purchaser (that hard-pressed creature) may also feel that the occasional broad-sweep work of genius must be supplemented, primarily by books central to the individual's primary disciplinary interest. Scientific and academic journals, too, have limited review space, which they may decide to allocate to books central to their field rather than at its margins.

So the book with a foot in two disciplines may find it secures a home in neither. Perhaps this is a curse of the Anglo-Saxon tradition, suspicious of the broad sweep and the over-ambitious ground-breaker. (And, in fact, for every successful neo-Frankfurt School theorist or Rive Gauche deconstructionist who can cross boundaries successfully there are probably a hundred unpublished authors who would be better advised to narrow down.) It is the academic "market," rather than the enthusiasms and whims of the publisher, that guides academic publishing. So if the academic market supports books that stay within formal disciplinary boundaries, accepting only the most excellent and outstanding titles that cross these boundaries, then publishers are bound to follow these patterns. Is your book one of the exceptional few? Or would it be safer to specify, and share with your publisher, a vision of a definable, reachable audience within a disciplinary boundary; an audience who will know that yours is a book essential to their field?

Yours truly, R.M.D.

« 30 » *Trade book*

Dear Professor Populus,

Your suggestion that your book is for "the general reader" is an interesting one, but in this case I am afraid we do not believe it.

There is no reason why a professional academic should not write a trade book on their subject for the general reader, though more often these are written by the non-specialist for the non-specialist. The professional calling of the scholar may, in a minority of the academic population, be combined with the skill of the writer able to explain and interpret at a non-specialist level. There are many books written to explain the author's subject to a lay audience—from popular astronomy or physics or archaeology through to the genuine "trade" biography or piece of public and political interest.

But academics may also write general books outside their discipline. Humorous works, novels and introductions to a hobby may all attract academic authors from quite different specializations.

Within the book trade the distances which separate the academic book, the textbook and the general book seem to be widening. In the USA the general trade book carries a trade discount—a high discount to the bookseller which recognizes the risk taken and the cost of space provided in displaying the book on open shelves. A textbook will typically receive a discount only half as large, since it is stocked by college bookstores not at total risk but to meet course adoptions announced by college professors. The academic book, or a book for specific professional purposes, may be stocked in some specialist stores, especially in paperback, at an intermediate discount; but it is just as likely to sell direct from the publisher to the purchaser as through a bookstore. And the hardback academic monograph will certainly not be stocked by trade bookstores but will be supplied to academic and professional readers direct, and to library suppliers for their clients.

In the United Kingdom these barriers are not so firm, as major chains with university bookshop members seek to serve city and university customers alike. But the truly trade and general sections of the bookselling industry are not likely to stock academic paperbacks or hardbacks for an academic readership.

The boundaries are not quite so firmly drawn in Australia and New Zealand, either, but the same differences obtain. Bookshops limit their stockholding to a conservative estimate of what they can sell—which again excludes from general trade outlets academic books for an academic readership.

Authors tend to think of their books on a continuum from the most specialized to the most general. But books are published at discontinuous points on this range, influenced by the kind of publisher handling a book, the market they think they can reach and its expectations. These expectations touch on format, design, price and discount or supply routes. The publisher thinks of the book as a trade book or an academic book or a professional book or a textbook. The publisher's decision on the category influences everything from the price to the level of editing, the colours on the cover and even the title.

Many authors believe that their book could serve the needs of general readers, and would reach them if only their publisher were not so cautious. Unfortunately, this is generally an illusion. If there were a significantly larger market to be reached than the one being identified and catered for, the publisher would normally go for it. Most academic books deal with a topic—and at a level of writing, presentation, detail, understanding or argument—that will attract mainly professionals and academics and advanced students in the author's field, with a minority of camp followers and a few academics in adjacent disciplines.

It is true that there is a wider audience in many subjects. But the needs of this audience are most often met by articles in periodical publications, rather than a whole book; by library borrowing, rather than a personal purchase. Or—most irritating to some academics—the best of academic thinking may be made accessible to this audience by a popularizing writer whose work rests (though usually with full acknowledgement) on the research and writing of others. Most disciplines and sub-disciplines have such popularizers able to address the more general audience. Indeed, scholars should normally be grateful for these people, who attract students, public interest and even financial sponsors to a subject area.

But of course you may—against the odds—have a true trade book for the general store. If so, you might best be advised not to approach a scholarly press and ask them to make it into a general book; nor, perhaps, should you go to one of those presses who handle both academic and trade books, as their categorization may not be yours. It will probably be best to approach a true trade publisher with a general list, and see if they agree with your perception of the market and role of your book. If you and they are right, and there is a trade book here, you may have taken the first step towards becoming that rarity of rarities, a reputable scholar able to write about their own discipline for a general lay audience, and to attract the attention (and cash) of that audience.

Yours truly, R.M.D.

« 31 » *Textbook*

Dear Don,

We were pleased to hear you are writing a textbook and seek a suitable publisher for it. Are we the right publisher? And is yours the right book?

Models in publishing differ, but there is an increasing distance between the publishing of scholarly books and the publishing of textbooks.

Publishers make a further distinction between recommended reading and the true basic textbook. The real textbook is a volume that covers all or a defined part of an identifiable course, taught commonly across a number of institutions. If a course is not taught in enough institutions, a textbook cannot economically reprint and will disappear.

That does not mean that students will not read widely—or that a textbook must lack intellectual originality. But textbooks are a specific kind of publication, and they tend to have different publishers, or at least different divisions of a publishing house. Many academic publishers, especially university presses, do not publish basic introductory university-level textbooks, while textbook publishers are not, in general, set up to publish books written by academics for their peers. Most textbooks are developed and commissioned by publishers' editorial staff who have researched and identified a market niche.

The increased number of students in colleges and universities throughout the English-speaking world puts pressures on teachers, students and institutions alike. Most teachers would like their students to read widely, but the reality is that students must concentrate on those books that will guide them most cost-effectively through their training. Of course, this is especially so in courses with a lot of practical work—such as engineering, architecture, computer science and laboratory sciences.

So the question to any would-be author of a textbook is, What course is it for, how much of the course does it cover, how many institutions offer the course, and how many students are there annually? Sometimes of real importance, too, is the international dimension. Can the book be used only in your own country, or can it be exported for international use wherever English is a teaching or reading medium in education? What minor adjustments to style, content, reference points or presentation would help the book cross national boundaries?

A textbook—like any other book being considered for publication—must then be compared with the competition. It must be better in style, design, price or comprehensiveness, or more appealing to staff or students in its approach, to make it worth pursuing. If there is no competition for the textbook, there may be a good market reason.

Unfortunately, many scholars think that writing a successful textbook will do nothing for their academic reputation and career—despite the fact that it will have more readers and users than a scholarly work. When authors volunteer that they are writing a book for students, more often they mean that students ought to read the academic book that they are writing. And indeed if it is favoured by lecturers, well written and broad ranging, it is certainly likely to be stocked by libraries—perhaps in multiple copies—and included on reading lists. Some enthusiastic and better-funded students will buy their own copies. But that is different from a textbook that is adopted for courses.

If the two types do overlap, it is on some higher-level "option" courses—specialist areas where smaller numbers of students work on a particular topic. These upper-level courses will be too few or too small to attract the college textbook publishers, and they will use books which have been written for the academic and professional reader. That is a level at which academic and scholarly publishers feel confident about publishing.

So is your book a textbook written for formal course adoption, or is it something rather different?   *Yours truly, R.M.D.*

« 32 » *New journals*

Dear Cyril,

It was useful to talk to you and your colleagues about your ambitious plans for journal publishing. We were impressed by the success of your own association's professional journal and newsletter. I can see why you are encouraged to develop these and consider starting new journals. I can also see why you think it timely to discuss the programme with a professional journal publisher—if your plans develop, you will be busy enough on editorial matters and would be wise to hand over production, marketing and distribution to an outside publisher.

Much of the weight of scientific and scholarly journals falls on their academic editors and on these brave individuals' host institutions. There is a distinguished tradition of journal publishing by professional societies, associations and academies. But the advantages of expert help in the technical areas of production and sales push many institutions to seek collaborative arrangements with publishers. Journal publishers have advantages of scale; by handling the publication of several or many journals, they can negotiate favourable rates with typesetters, printers and mailing houses. Most especially, a publishing company with a significant journals operation can rationalize systems of invoicing and distribution to libraries and can promote journals more cost-effectively than can most institutions—though, to be sure, the cost of these functions is added to the cost of the journals, whereas it is sometimes hidden within the general operations of institutions which handle their own publications.

For publishing companies—whether private or university press—journals are an attractive form of publishing. Once a journal subscription is established, it can generally be expected to see annual renewals. Unlike monographs—even monographs in a series—each issue does not have to be promoted, marketed and sold separately. Except with a brand-new journal, the size of the required print run is normally quite clear in advance.

A journal is commonly sold direct to libraries, or handled by library suppliers against a firm order; or it forms part of the membership fees of a society. So there is less need than in the world of books to deal with an intermediary; the natural caution of the bookshop does not enter the picture. And, not least, journal subscriptions are mainly paid up at the beginning of a subscription year, long before the issues are shipped; income from books, in contrast, arrives months—sometimes many months—after the despatch of copies to a bookshop.

So publishers are enthusiastic about journals; they seek to acquire new journals for their list from institutions or from other publishers, and at times by establishing new journals independently or with institutions.

That is, presumably, why you approached us for discussions. We certainly welcome discussions early in a new project. Successful journal publishing should be a collaboration and should be a long-term relationship.

Academics are remarkably eager to start new journals. Though they may complain about the difficulty of keeping up with the literature, and bemoan their libraries' (and their own!) limited budgets, there seems hardly a sub-field of a sub-field that does not yearn to have a new journal to publish its material. Many societies, research centres and institutions feel that owning and managing a journal is a badge of honour, desirable for its own sake.

Few librarians would agree. The greatest pressure on library resources is perhaps from serials. Exchange-rate variations are unpredictable; publishers' pricing for different territories may also seem unpredictable; what seems predictable is the continuing rise of journal prices. Many scientific and academic libraries will now agree to subscribe to a new journal only if an existing subscription is dropped.

Part of the answer, as seen by libraries, is to share journals. If current contents can easily be perused in on-line data bases, one library can order copies of individual papers from a collaborating institution instead of having its own subscription. But of course if libraries decide to share fewer subscriptions to a journal, the cost of those subscriptions will go up to match, and collectively the libraries will gain nothing.

These pressures mean that publishers of journals are, essentially, looking for journals that libraries need to have, that a subject area of reasonable size cannot do without. This is not too different from the world of books, of course. It is not a question of what journals are attractive and interesting; it is a question of what journals are essential.

This appears to give some preference to scientific, technical and professional fields over many social science and humanities areas. A core scientific journal is the basic vehicle for communicating research results; few arts subjects give such prominence to the journal article. So a scientific journal, more often than its humanities or social science counterpart, may manage to meet the criterion of being "essential."

But there must still be a market of adequate size to make a new scientific journal viable. And the market will mainly be libraries, in most cases, within a framework where library budgets will extend to acquire the essential journal whatever the price, and will balk at acquiring inessential journals however modest the price.

What makes many journals viable in non-scientific areas is their being allied to a scholarly or professional association. It is attractive to a publisher to take on a journal which has a core subscription as a part—normally a compulsory part—of the membership dues. The publisher may be unable to add to the membership directly, although improvements in reliability of production dates and quality may help indirectly. But a publisher can usually take a journal with an institutional subscription and add to its library sales by professional and committed promotion. A publisher will be much less enthusiastic about a journal which is tied to a society but where the individual subscription is voluntary—unless it can be shown that the members already take up this subscription in large numbers and can be expected to go on doing so even if the journal price rises a little to absorb the new costs.

All this favours the successful established journal over new journals. If a new journal proposal is to form part of a large membership subscription, fine. If it is in an important, large or new field (especially in the sciences) and is assured of "must-have" status in many academic libraries, it is in with a chance. But if it cannot be guaranteed to meet either of these criteria, then even a journal that contains quality articles in a lively field is much less likely to meet with encouragement from a publisher.

Now, what about your association's impressive and ambitious ideas? Well, in principle we agree with you that your current journal has potential for wider marketing and distribution through a large and internationally connected publisher. It has a high reputation in its field; it has the solid basis of a subscription's being a compulsory part of your membership fee. You have some subscriptions from libraries and non-members, and we are sure we could increase the library sales and some non-library sales as well. If we took over production and marketing without interfering in your editorial control, allowing you to concentrate on questions of content, we have the basis for a satisfactory long-term partnership.

Your newsletter is produced very inexpensively with volunteer labour, using in-house services. We do not think it would make sense for us to take over production of this, nor do we think it has a potential readership much beyond your association's members. We therefore do not wish to take over its production or try and market it. However, since we will be distributing the main journal to a mailing list of your members using our own professional systems, it would be relatively easy for us to distribute the newsletter at nominal cost to you, and we hope you would find this a useful service. Let us discuss this idea further.

Finally, your proposals for two new journals. Each looked impressive academically, and we could not fault your plans for their scope and editorial development. But, as you said, these would be offered to members at a special rate and not be part of the membership package. We are not convinced that enough members would take up this offer. The projects would therefore rise or fall on their importance to libraries, which would need to prefer them to existing journals, and there we have our doubts. We will take advice on this, but you should be warned that, as with most of the many proposals we receive for brand-new journals, we shall probably decline this idea and discourage the diversion of your resources from current projects into new journals, to supplement the 100,000 already in existence.   *Yours truly, R.M.D.*

« 33 » *The non-academic author*

Dear Mr. Post,

We were embarrassed by your letter, and it is no fault of yours. But it put us on the spot to be asked whether, as scholarly publishers, we consider works by authors who do not have formal academic qualifications or affiliations.

The answer of course ought to be Yes, willingly. It is the book and its ideas that matter, not the nominal status of the author. But we do know that, with the increasing professionalization of the academic industry, mental boundaries are being drawn round academic subjects and academia itself by its inmates. And as operators in the real world we have to confront that.

Many great academic works have come from authors holding no academic appointment. But not every aeronautical engineering student is a Wittgenstein, not every patents office clerk an Einstein. How can we filter out our own and our readers' prejudices to broaden the scope of academic publishing?

There are fewest problems with authors whose background and context is identifiable, even if they do not hold an academic position or a research appointment at some recognized institution. Many fine minds (some suggest, the finest) move from university undergraduate and postgraduate study into professions other than research and teaching. This may be in the professional practice of their field—whether medicine or architecture, law or engineering, business administration or whatever. And many more move into public life, in politics or administration, or into the media—broadcasting, journalism, even publishing. Most academic disciplines recognize work by such writers as being "as if" academic work, as a contribution to the field either from within it or from nearby. And publishers are often more than pleased to have a fresh contribution to a subject area that comes from someone who knows it but is not entirely limited by its daily patterns and networks.

There may be some greater difficulty with the professional writer who has established an expertise in a subject area entirely from outside: the science journalist without a science degree, the politician who turns to writing abstract volumes on political science, the successful business leader who writes about management, the journalist who turns into a regional specialist or economics guru without formal training. Academics may be reluctant to acknowledge the entry of these successful writers into the field, but academic and scientific publishers will usually accept them into a list as readily as they do professionals. In particular, they cannot dismiss books that sell and draw attention to a programme of more specialized or more difficult works.

Yet how do such writers begin? How do we tackle approaches like yours? I wish we were consistent and knew the answer. I think we look for tell-tale signs about the author. To be frank, and at the risk of sounding prejudiced, we need to know a bit more about you and not just about the manuscript.

The problem is that all publishers receive enquiries from hundreds of would-be authors about totally unsuitable projects. Many authors do not research who is an appropriate publisher for their work. Indeed, there may be no suitable publisher for their work. Imprints whose identity is academic and scholarly, scientific or professional are catering for a clear readership base. If a proposal comes from someone in a university or a research institution, from a professional with relevant qualifications and experience, or from a writer with a track record, it is going to be taken seriously.

If, on the other hand, a proposal comes from an unknown name, with no personal details and a private address, it is fighting for attention in a busy editorial office. If there is nothing in the introduction, the outline or the contents list to give the author and the work a context, it may well be given shorter shrift than it deserves. It may find it is turned down with minimal consideration, together with the many book proposals designed to save the world, unfold religious revelations, show how to win the state lottery, rewrite history through the memoirs of an obscure relative, or establish the unity of mind with matter.

In almost every field of academic and scientific research, the non-professional author—even more than the full-time academic—needs to establish some reputation in a field before their book can be published. In some fields—theoretical physics, say, or medicine or philosophy—the struggle for acceptance will be great enough to discourage almost all. But there are subject areas where the talented amateur (probably a professional in a quite different field) makes major contributions. In archaeology, local history or many areas of zoology and botany, for example, contributions to the field from outside the core professionals are probably still essential. In other areas—anthropology, linguistics—those days are probably over.

But if the non-academic author's reputation has been established by lectures, articles, technical papers and personal networking, the book is likely to be more acceptable to readers in the academic field. And if it is acceptable to the market, it is certainly acceptable to the publisher.

The publisher of such work does, however, need further help from the author. A writer who is not a central part of an existing academic network needs to do more to promote their work than the established figure. Again, this is a pity; in an ideal world a book will sell itself. But reviews take a long time to come. Before then an author needs to publish short articles around the topic of the book, give seminars and lectures, and help to counteract the lack of normal networking which dominates so much of the academic world.

If there is an informal prejudice against the unestablished author in academic publishing, an effective bias also shows itself in the financial aspects of publishing. A non-academic author (other than an established full-time writer) is likely to attract no better royalty terms than an academic author with a formal research position. Yet the academic author has received research funding and institutional support, along with a salary, while undertaking the research. And frequently the academic author may win promotion as a result of publishing a major book. All this is additional to the royalties received from the publisher. The author without a base in a research institution or university is more likely to fund their own research, to undertake the writing without pay in their spare time, and to gain no career advantage from publication. Royalties become the only financial recompense. Yet the royalties a publisher can pay relate to the commercial potential of the book—not to the efforts or needs or relative deprivation of the author. This is unlikely to change unless academic authors and publishers agree that writers should give according to their abilities and receive according to their needs. Not even academics writing about the author of that suggestion would willingly concede it in practice.

So please help us to assess not just the merit of your book, but its publishability. Tell us a little about other work you have done and published; tell us if you have, or are likely to create, some reputation in the field of your writing beyond this book; tell us how you would help us promote the book to an academic audience. First be sure that you want to publish with a scholarly press for its own target audience, rather than a more general trade book for a general readership! And accept our shamefaced prejudice against the unannounced manuscript without context from an unknown author. Without such manuscripts in the past, the values and knowledge of Western civilization would be greatly diminished.   *Yours truly, R.M.D.*

$\mathscr{T}$HE PUBLISHING DECISION

« 34 » No—why?

Dear Dick Lyneham,
 I regret that we have to say No to your three book proposals, each for different reasons. The reasons are our own and remain confidential to us.
 Publishers have different ways of saying No, but they all mean the same. The reasons given may be minimal or expansive. They may be accurate or just euphemisms: it is usually hard to tell. If we receive a positive report on your manuscript but have some embarrassing reason why we cannot publish, you are likely to get a bland letter with some empty phrases. We are not likely to explain that the person who initially encouraged you was recently fired, or has gone on six months' rest cure. We may not say that we have run out of money for new books, or that there has been a shift of resources into accountancy textbooks. We are certainly not likely to admit that we did nothing at all about your book, found it on someone's desk after they resigned and were not replaced, and felt the least embarrassing course of action was to say No without delay so that you could approach other publishers quickly and make up lost time.
 All these things do happen.
 You are equally likely to get a fairly bland letter if your book is declined for quite different reasons. Your work may have been very carefully assessed by outside readers, who may have told us that your work was second-rate, that your field was in decline, that you were a hopeless old fraud or that your writing style and intellectual powers were those of a mental cripple. In such cases the readers' reports are usually suppressed or heavily edited.
 You should not worry too much about the exact formulation of a letter which says No. Whatever the reasons, and whatever the justice of those reasons, the outcome is the same.
 The publisher, in declining your manuscript, may choose to show you parts of the readers' reports; and if they feel that the book is good but not suitable for their list they may say so. But the omission of these courtesies should not be overinterpreted.

A decline letter does, inevitably, make an author question the publishability of their work. On the positive side, the period that has elapsed between submitting the proposal and having it declined should have allowed some creative thoughts, and in any case it is common to make some improvements before submitting it to another publisher. If the rejection letter includes readers' reports, or very specific reasons for the decision, it is worth considering whether these are valid.

But—it is important not to consider that one letter from one publisher gives a definitive statement on a book's potential as a publication. If you believe in your book you should proceed to submit it to another suitable publisher.

Three final suggestions in resubmitting, all based on real life.

First, do not wait until the editor has left that publishing house and resubmit it to the same organization. That looks like testing their judgement and consistency.

A second scenario: your book is declined by an editor with a polite letter that says it would be more suited for another press of specified character (a subsidized regional university press, for example). The editor changes jobs and joins such a publisher. Do not be tempted to call his bluff and try him again. If an editor moves publishing houses you should not, in general, approach that editor again unless you know that they fought a battle for your book and lost. If they are keen to publish it, they know you exist.

Third, do not offer your book around with a letter that says, "Ms. Smith of publishing house X said they would like to have published it but were unable to justify its inclusion in their programme on financial grounds," or quote whatever phrases you were given. Publishers recognize other publishers' meaningless phrasing easily and will not be impressed.

"No" means No. Be annoyed, briefly. If the publisher has shown you readers' reports, recognize that these anticipate reactions that might have come to the published work. Consider these carefully, before polishing your strategy to achieve publication from your next approach with the same book, or an improved version of it.

Yours truly, R.M.D.

« 35 » *Revise and resubmit*

Dear Ms. Fortune,

We suggested that you revise the manuscript you submitted to us and resubmit it for us to reconsider. We did not want to say Yes or No at this stage.

Perhaps not surprisingly, you pressed us to explain more and said you knew of a bad experience of a friend. He had revised as suggested by a publisher, without much enthusiasm and while embarking on a demanding new job. When he resubmitted to the publisher, his new manuscript was turned down within a month.

One of the letters we hate to get is that which says, "Five years ago your predecessor showed me readers' reports and suggested I revise my manuscript. I now enclose the manuscript in line with the readers' suggestions; will you now please send me a contract?"

But, in contrast, it can be a pleasure to have a letter thanking us for the reader's comments, and saying that on balance the author agrees with them and that, within a reasonable and stated time, the manuscript will be resubmitted in a fully revised state.

If a publisher likes a manuscript, they will accept it first time round, and work with the author on final polish. If they like its potential but not its current form, they will often offer a contract with a clause which makes publication conditional on satisfactory revision along agreed lines.

Without a contract or the offer of a contract, there is no commitment whatever by the publisher to publish the book, and this must be clearly understood. An individual editor may make encouraging noises in a letter, or give spoken reassurance that a revised manuscript may be offered a contract, but such noises are not enough. The editor may well leave the publishing house, or move on to different responsibilities, before the resubmitted manuscript arrives. There may be a shift of interest or direction which would make a previously promising manuscript unsuitable for the imprint's new profile.

So should an author revise and resubmit if invited to do so? The invitation will be phrased with varying degrees of enthusiasm—in this case, the style of the letter needs to be weighed up. A decline letter that says, "If you wish to resubmit we would be willing to reconsider" is not very enthusiastic. An invitation that is brought personally by the editor, or discussed in detail over the phone or in a lengthy letter, is more encouraging.

In many cases suggestions made by the publisher's reader will be sent to show why the present manuscript was not accepted, and to suggest problems which need to be overcome before it can be published. But it is usually incorrect to believe that a contract will be offered if these criticisms are met. Not only may the publisher's editor change, but the manuscript might be sent next time to quite different readers who will have different views and suggestions.

The best response to the invitation "revise and resubmit" is to see whether you agree with the suggestions and criticisms made. If they strengthen the quality of the book, its structure and argument, they should be done in any case. You still have the option to submit to the original publisher or to go elsewhere. But the book appears under your name and it has to be a book that you are happy with. Without the security of a contract, you should not undertake major revisions and changes in a direction you would rather not take.

If you are happy with the manuscript as it is, and do not wish to revise in the direction suggested, take it to another publisher. It is better to have a marriage based on love than on misunderstanding.

Yours truly, R.M.D.

« 36 » *Yes—but revise*

Dear Anne Exeter,

Let me clarify our answer—Yes, we will publish your manuscript, but we require its revision to our satisfaction.

First, you are right to say that you would like a contract at this stage that will spell out all the other details of the publication. This contract can be finalized like any other. But it will have as one clause (or as an accompanying memorandum) the condition that revision be undertaken.

The suggestion that revision is necessary will usually be a result of the views of the in-house staff of the publishing firm and the external readers whose advice they have taken. If the readers' comments have not been shown to you, ask for them. If you have them, and find them generally sympathetic but want to discuss them further as guidance in your revision, you can ask through your editor if the readers would be willing to talk to you. They may well say No—but it is worth a try.

Certainly, if you have been offered a contract subject to revision, you should ask your editor to spell out as closely as possible the nature of the revisions required. But it is best that you meet with the editor to discuss these points. You and the publisher are now bound by a contract; you are working together; it is in the interests of you both to ensure you are travelling along the same tracks and in the same direction.

If there is some part of the suggested revision you feel would not work—length, or structure, or whatever—a discussion with the editor is the answer. But if your view prevails—for example, if the publisher agrees that the book can retain its illustrations section or be the extra length you require—ensure that this is put in writing, either in the contract or in a letter from the publisher.

Also, be clear what will happen when your manuscript is returned to the publisher in its revised form. Will the decision to go ahead with publication now be in the hands of the publishing house editor, or a board of that publishing house? Will the revised script go to external readers again, and if so can you be reassured they will be the same ones? The earlier questions are asked, the surer you can be that misunderstandings will not emerge later. *Yours truly, R.M.D.*

« 37 » *Yes*

Dear Ms. Nort,

This is one of the most pleasant letters to write. We are pleased to say Yes to your book and offer you a firm contract for its publication.

Of the various letters a would-be author can receive from a publisher, the one saying simply Yes is the only one they really want to receive. The publisher, naturally, hopes the author will then sign the contract, deliver the final manuscript exactly in line with the contract and proceed with publication, and that no further problems will arise.

But in the interest of the author, a few warning notes should be sounded. First, the details of the contract have to be agreed, and must be acceptable to both author and publisher. The statement "Yes, we will publish" can normally be taken at face value, but you need a clear understanding about royalties, any advances or contributions to costs, and all other contractual matters. You have to be sure that publication is not conditional on some subsidy which you hinted would be available, or on some sponsor's agreeing to purchase copies, or on the publisher's selling international rights to another publisher. In most cases these matters will be straightforward—but you need to be sure.

Sometimes an author has made an approach to several publishers, one of whom now says Yes. The author is not obliged to accept the first such offer. Or, indeed, an offer to publish may have come out of the

blue without the author's formal submission of a proposal. Some care
is needed. Publishers come in all shapes, sizes and characters. Some are
very cautious and protective of their imprint, and are conservative in
the decision to offer a contract. Others—perhaps new ones, or publishers who maintain turnover by bulk of titles—carry about a folder of
ready-made standard contracts and will take a large proportion of the
academic books of reasonable length which they are offered in their
chosen disciplines.

So one should not always accept the offer of publication that comes
through the door. It is necessary to be sure that this is an imprint with
which you want to publish; that there are no rumours that they are
about to close or the editor is about to leave. You want to feel sure they
are a reputable imprint and will distribute your book professionally
and well.

Bookselling is a commercial activity, but of course in academic publishing status does enter in. Your academic reputation will be enhanced
if you are published by an established press who seem to take forever
and a day with readers and formal decision-making before saying Yes
to your book. Your reputation will not be damaged if you publish with
a small new imprint that is beginning to establish a high reputation for
quality publishing in your specialized field. But your reputation may
not be helped if you immediately sign with one of that small minority
of publishers who tour academic campuses with a sheaf of pre-signed
contracts in the briefcase, and give near-instant agreement to a barely
considered proposal.

It takes two parties to agree to a contract—author and publisher.
Each party needs to be sure of the other. Then can begin the most positive part of the whole book business: publication.

Yours truly, R.M.D.

DEALING WITH PRODUCTION

« 38 » *Contract*

Dear Dr. Klaus,

I am enclosing the contract for the publication of your book. On the phone you seemed worried about such a legal document and said you might have some queries to raise. Please feel free to do so.

As with any legally binding agreement, it is important that the parties who sign a contract understand both its spirit and its detail. Publishers' contracts do not follow a particular model or standard. Those of different publishers vary, and the terms of any one publisher's contracts vary according to what is agreed with a particular author and what is appropriate to a particular kind of book.

The relationship between a publisher and an author is, essentially, one of trust and mutual respect. The author has a book worth publishing; the publisher has the professional expertise to produce and market it, and the reputation to help launch it into the market. The basic trust needs to be there.

The contract formalizes the trust, and it is an essential document. No matter what pleasant reassurances have taken place on both sides, all authors must have a signed contract before they can be certain their book will be published. And publishers must have a contract signed before they can be certain that they have the right to publish and that the book will not go elsewhere. The contract is the confirmation of these points.

But the contract is equally important for its detail. This is especially important with scholarly books, which are often contracted before the final version of the manuscript is completed for publication. An author's ideas on length or format may evolve away from what the publisher expected. The publisher's commissioning (acquisitions) editor— one bright enough to have chosen your book as a winner—may well be seduced to another publisher's employment. The imprint for which your book is accepted might become part of another publishing house before the book hits the bookshop shelves. The contract is to cover in legal terms all possible eventualities.

Publishers pay copyeditors large amounts of money (well, amounts of money, but they *are* paid) to ensure that every word of the text you write is utterly clear. Yet these editors are rarely let loose on the legal wording of the company's standard contracts, which may be in badly expressed legalisms. So before you sign a contract it is good to make sure you understand what both sides are agreeing to. If something is unclear, ask your editor for clarification. Editors will probably not understand all the phrasing either, but they can find out.

The basic clauses in a publisher's contract tend to be cumulative. That is, a clause has been added on some past occasion to meet some special need, and since no one can remember why it is there no one is prepared to remove it. The right to reproduce an author's illustrations and descriptions on cigarette cards caused an unfortunate disagreement in 1921, so the cigarette-card subsidiary rights clause is there. The CD-ROM subsidiary rights, though, or the licences for on-line access and downloading, may not even be hinted at—publishers are nervous about adding new standard clauses since they do stay in the standard contract for ever once they arrive.

It is a fair assumption that a reputable publisher will have a reputable contract, and that a reputable author will intend to honour its terms. Reputable publishers are unlikely to use the small print of a contract to try to deceive or misuse an author. But an author should feel happy with the details of a contract before they sign.

Contracts are negotiable: that is to say, the terms proposed by the publisher are not, definitively, the only terms that can be agreed to. But equally the room for negotiation has limits. Some of the clauses in the contract are not worth arguing about. If you want to increase the cigarette-card subsidiary licence fee percentage, go for it. Questions of copyright, option clauses on subsequent books, reversion of copyright when the book goes out of print may all be malleable—but an attempt to rewrite every clause of a standard contract may meet with weary resistance.

Authors sometimes ask that a contract include a commitment on the time to be taken in production, or on print run and price. Some publishers will agree to this; most won't. If a book is worth publishing it is worth bringing out as soon as possible, and it is not in a publisher's interest to delay it. A period ("not more than two years") specified in a time clause in the contract should cover the worst case and may seem unacceptably long if misconstrued as an average. Perhaps this point is better covered by an exchange of letters of intent. As for print run and price, these are commercial decisions, not moral ones. The publisher has to be left some options and be given the benefit of the doubt that

they will make a sensible decision. Their decision is unlikely to be finalized for an academic book at the time of contract.

But clauses dealing with real money are the main points of discussion. As you realize, there are limits here. Your research and writing
time is at stake in a publication, but the money at stake is the publisher's. The royalty arrangement does make payments on every copy
sold; the publisher's net margin accrues only after most of the edition
is sold, and in any case may have to be reinvested immediately in a
reprint. There may be some room for negotiation, let us admit, but this
is more likely to take the form of offering to increase royalties after the
sale of so many copies, when the book is clearly established as an economic success. Equally, there is some room for discussion on advances,
especially when the first year's royalties may not be paid until some
point into the second year. But relatively few new academic authors are
likely to attract much in the way of advances before a manuscript is
actually delivered in house, in a form which allows the publication
process to begin. As a writer's reputation increases, negotiating power
may strengthen.

The dread truth is that the contract for an academic book has little of
the force of a legal agreement in other areas. Of course this is a publisher speaking. Why do I say that? Because, alas, many scholarly authors regard the detailed terms of a contract as ballpark figures, expressions of good will rather than statements of fact. The offer of a contract
puts the power in the publisher's hands, but the fulfilment of a contract
gives power entirely to the author.

What do I mean? Well, if a publisher is contracted to pay, say, 10 per
cent royalties but decides to pay 8 per cent, they will rightly be chas-
tised, not only by the author but also by their professional peers. However, if the author proposes to deliver 95,000 words (plus 10 camera-
ready illustrations) by 30 June and actually delivers 105,000 words and
20 roughs some eighteen months late . . . is that not just routine in the
scholarly world?

If the author delivers on time and the publisher decides on a whim
not to honour the contract and publish, an author has a legal claim of
breach of contract. But if the due date comes and no manuscript has
arrived, should the publisher phone your Dean and announce an intention to sue? Perhaps we should. But we don't.

The most that might happen is that, if the delivery date or length or
other details vary significantly from the terms of the contract, the publisher might regard the other details as up for renegotiation, in the light
of changing intellectual or market conditions. The need for books may
be timeless—but not for this particular book.

So it is best for both author and publisher that the terms of a contract should be clearly meant and clearly understood, and should then be honoured. If anything is obscure or unacceptable, say so now. "Seal up the mouth of outrage for a while / Till we can clear these ambiguities" (although by that stage Romeo and Juliet were both dead—best to do it sooner).

Otherwise, please sign the contract and mean what you say, as we shall.   *Yours truly, R.M.D.*

« 39 » *Late delivery*

Dear Professor Dilly,

I am sorry I had to call you by telephone about the non-delivery of your manuscript, which is now well overdue. We agreed a delivery date when we signed the contract. On the phone you mentioned, conversationally, that it was "coming on OK" but was "still some way off," and you expressed surprise at the "intemperate and inappropriate language" of my response.

Intemperate, yes (and I apologize); but inappropriate—really? Publishers' contracts are legal documents agreed between two parties. The publishers, on their side, agree to publish at their own expense, and to pay a royalty of an agreed amount and at agreed times. Publishers seldom depart from this agreement and consider themselves legally bound to honour it or pay compensation if they break it.

The author is an equal party to the agreement, but among scholarly writers there is a frequent breaking of the terms of contract. All academic publishers have authors who deliver overlong manuscripts late and with essential material like illustrations missing. Yet these same scholars would, presumably, not sign a contract for the tenancy of an apartment or the sale of their house, or an agreement to rent a telephone line or to accept permanent employment, without regarding it as a binding agreement. Why are publishers' contracts so often treated differently?

Publishers, in general, want a contract that agrees something seen by both parties as practical, which is meant and adhered to. That includes the delivery date. Contracts usually give a date "on or before" which delivery is expected, so it will have some leeway for early delivery. And most publishers will expect to start work on a manuscript if it comes in early, and avoid delays. But publishers cannot be required to make up lost time when a manuscript arrives late.

Why is it important to agree, and hold to, a delivery date? First, of course, it provides a target for the author to plan writing time. So a delivery date at the end of a period of study leave, at the end of a long vacation, or before taking up a new position makes good sense as a real and necessary target: a date which must be met, not least because the opportunity of writing time then disappears.

But dates—year and month—are important to the publisher too.

As in any business enterprise (or university institution!) a publisher must have forward planning and forward budgets. Part of several months each year are spent in preparing and refining budgets for income and expenditure in the next financial year, with some eye too on the expected pattern in the following and subsequent years. The publisher (and, often, each commissioning or acquisitions editor, each production unit, each marketing manager) must predict what outgoings there will be in the following year and what income these will generate. Budgets for acquisitions are expected to feed back into real manuscripts in house—not just under contract. For manuscripts expected into copyediting and production, funds must be set aside to pay for all the costs of origination and printing. Whether in a small imprint or a single department of a large publisher, these amounts may have to be refined quite carefully, well in advance. Few acquisitions editors can be permitted to commission forty titles without knowing whether twenty or forty will be delivered in the expected year. Marketing departments need to assign a promotion budget ahead of time in the light of books actually expected for publication and the income these are likely to generate.

By signing a contract an author accepts a place in a publishing imprint, but also in a budget of overheads, production expenditure and sales income. The author, by failing to fulfil their role in this financial relationship, is undermining the publisher and may be denying a place to another book of quality.

Delivery dates are not important just for the annual budget. They are also important for work loads. These fluctuate in the copyediting, design and production departments. If all the manuscripts come in together, they cannot all be processed together and all get equal priority. In some ways, a book which arrives on time ought to take priority over a book that arrives late. Too often an author will expect the lost months to be retrieved in house, which means at the expense of other books.

There are seasonal patterns of publishing, and a wise publisher will commission a time-sensitive book so as to ensure that it fits the season. A book for the general reader has to come out for Father's Day, or for Christmas, or perhaps for summer reading. It cannot be published on

15 December, when the bookshops' Christmas rush is on, or in the middle of the summer vacation. So the manuscript is needed in house early enough to achieve production by a suitable date.

Books which will be adopted for classes, as student textbooks, need to be available as inspection copies some months before the end of the academic year. The teaching staff can read them, evaluate them and decide whether to assign them for a course, in good time to announce this decision in course booklets and advise college bookstores. Again, delivery date for these final manuscripts is required well ahead of the required seasonal publication date to allow for the processes of copyediting and production. If such a textbook misses delivery date by two or three months, it may well find that adoptions (and therefore sales, reviews and royalties) are postponed for a whole year.

Books which may be bought by senior students to supplement their courses, or by academics for themselves or for their institutional libraries may better be announced early in the academic year to give them maximum bookshop exposure and access to library budgets. There is little point in mailing details of new books at the end of the academic year when staff and students are just disappearing for the summer.

So seasonality of publication is all-important to scholarly books in many categories. And the publishing seasons determine the seasons when manuscripts must be delivered. Some books can be produced by an express route, usually at the expense of other titles. But it is best for all parties to assume an efficient, methodical route through production, neither lethargic nor panicked into a rush, and with some time allowed for at least one major problem to arise somewhere in the production process. This seasonality has to take account of the "down time" when freelance copyeditors may be occupied with school children on holidays, or when in-house staff are on annual leave, or when printing works are closed for their annual holiday.

This serves, I hope, to show why an agreed and honoured delivery date is important for the author's interest as well as the publisher's.

But it is also essential for author and publisher to be clear what is meant by delivery. Is this to be the delivery of the final manuscript, to go straight into production, or is this the delivery of an author's final draft for external review? If the contract does not make this clear, then discussion is needed in advance. It is frustrating for an author to think that all the writing is complete if the publisher is expecting to send the draft off to two readers for a two- to three-month review process, and only then feed back comments together with those of the in-house editor, for the author to get back to work and do a final revision. If the delivery date for the draft is at the very end of a "window of opportunity" in the author's schedule, then the chance to do final revision may have gone and there may be very substantial delays before publication. It is best to agree, either in the contract or less formally, three delivery dates: author's draft to the publisher; publisher's comments to the author; and final revised version of the manuscript to the publisher for production.

It is equally important to be clear what is to be delivered when. "The typescript" is only part of what is required. It may be quite appropriate for a draft for review to lack a few tables and notes and some bibliographical data, and to have only photocopies of draft or final artwork. But the final manuscript will need all these and more.

Delivery for production will normally require delivery of text, illustrations, permissions, notes on style, computer disk and other information. At production stage, partial delivery may be as big a problem as non-delivery.

So clarity of understanding between author and publisher is the keynote: agreement on a date which is realistic both for writing (and revision) and for the production cycle and the intended season of publication.

There are occasions when a writing schedule goes awry, not through an author's poor judgement or a lackadaisical attitude to contract terms, but through external circumstances. An expected study leave may be cancelled, a personal or family illness may intervene, a career change or sudden summons to public office may arrive. In such cases it is important to discuss a revised delivery date as soon as possible. For a textbook, whose season of publication is critical, it may actually be better to postpone the delivery date by twelve months than by six. Where an interruption makes a firm revised date difficult, the publisher may be sympathetic but may reserve the right not to publish if circumstances warrant.

This decision not to publish is one which most concerns—and puzzles—academic authors; and it is one on which, traditionally, scholarly publishers have been quite soft. But in tough economic times the publisher should retain the right not to publish if a delivery date is not met. Publishing strategies and priorities in an imprint may change; budgets may fluctuate; a series in which a title is commissioned may close. More likely, the scholarly framework may shift because of changing academic interests. A textbook or general book commissioned to fill a gap may find the gap closed by other publishers' new books.

There are occasional tales of the elderly author who arrives bearing a manuscript and a contract drawn up thirty years earlier and long forgotten by the publisher: the book is then published to acclaim. There are more tales of authors who work hard on their contracted manuscripts, fail to deliver on time, and bring them in two or three years late, only to be told that the publisher's current priorities no longer require this book and the contract to publish it has lapsed.

So you see why I responded rather harshly to your telephone response about your overdue manuscript. Let me assure you that yours is a book we do still want to publish. We need to agree a firm, realistic, unambiguous new date for delivery, which you can and will hold to, and which we can consider as a formal agreement to a legally binding contract which you have already infringed. Please make us a proposal which we can discuss.   *Yours truly, R.M.D.*

« 40 » *Delivery of the manuscript*

Dear Joy,

Great news that you have completed the contracted manuscript—and on time! You phoned to say it would be in the mail within two weeks. We are warming the engine here, ready to move into copyediting and production.

To help us move ahead without delay, may I ask you to re-read the notes we sent you with the contract, specifying the format we need for delivery. Most publishers will provide this information—I hope we remembered to send ours. But I will reiterate in case you have mislaid it. In the excitement of delivering their finished typescript, some authors—not you, I'm sure—overlook some essentials.

The first essential is, of course, to be clear with the publisher whether you are submitting a finalized manuscript for review, for approval or for copyediting. If it were for review, as agreed in the contract or an exchange of letters with your publisher, that means it would go off as the final draft to a reader, whose comments would be fed back to help you finalize the manuscript. Provided the publisher agrees, it may be quite acceptable if the final draft for review is single-spaced rather than double-spaced, is double-sided, lacks a few footnotes or references, and has photocopies only of the illustrations.

If it were just for a fairly routine final approval, whether within the publishing house or by an outside reader, then it would have to be prepared as if for production—fully double-spaced, and so on—though there might be a breathing space in which to collect the final illustrations and complete the required information forms for the publisher.

But you are at the final stage, since we have already reviewed and approved your manuscript in a version with most material present. So what we need from you is a complete manuscript.

For our own purposes (here publishers may differ slightly) we require two identical copies of the manuscript, all pages double-spaced with wide margins (the right margin unjustified), and with footnotes on separate pages at the end, numbered sequentially.

TEXT DETAILS

Some points about the text itself. Are you sure you will have ready for us everything we need? Is there a full text? Are the notes here, printed out separately from the main text, complete and in numerical order, double-spaced? Has the bibliography been checked and rechecked for completeness and consistency, and is it too printed out double-spaced? Have you supplied the tables, suitably numbered, separate from the text (especially if they are long) but with their position clearly marked?

We will also need a title page with author, title and subtitle, a contents list, and lists of tables, figures and illustrations. But do not worry about trying to fabricate any other pages of front matter (prelims) which the publisher may need to introduce. The publisher's editor will usually provide the half-title (a page with a short title on it), a page of series information if your book is in a series, and the imprints (copyright) page with publisher and publication details. You should provide other front matter. The conventional order for this is title page, any dedication and/or epigraph, contents list, list of illustrations (or, if they are numbered separately, lists of line drawings, maps and photographs), list of tables, list of contributors (for a multi-author book), any foreword by another party, author's own preface, acknowledgements (if not included in the preface), list of abbreviations—and then we are ready to go with the main text!

Keep these all simple, double-spaced. Do not try to emulate the book design—you are providing copy for copyediting.

The dedication should probably be kept simple and unpretentious. This is between you and your favoured one(s); it is not an Oscar ceremony. If you wish to include an epigraph—a relevant quote—consider placing it at the beginning of the introduction.

The contents list should, at least at this stage, include all your subheadings as well as chapter and part headings. Even if these are not included in the contents list of the printed book, they will help the copyeditor to work on the manuscript.

The listings of illustrations, tables, etc. are just that—the text which will appear in print at the beginning of the book. It is essentially a reader's guide to what is present and where to find it. For that reason it is usually not necessary to include the whole caption. And therefore, by definition, you need to type up separately, and send us with the manuscript, a complete set of caption copy, showing what should actually be set to accompany each illustration and table. You can include these captions with each table or illustration as well, but continuous copy is needed for the typesetter and should be printed out separately from the manuscript and included as a separate file on the disk.

The preface is an opportunity to give a background to the book. You may decide you do not need a preface. It is often efficient and economical to place acknowledgements at the end of the preface rather than start a new page to list these separately. Consider whom you need to acknowledge—sources of funding, colleagues, research assistants, supportive partners. You do not need to list every library whose staff have helped you (it sounds like boasting). If the publisher's anonymous readers have been both positive and helpful, you can ask permission for them to identify themselves and be acknowledged.

Publishers do not like changes to a manuscript after delivery, for both practical and cost reasons. But if you think the copyeditor, picture researcher or designer has been specifically helpful and beneficial to the text (and they usually are) you can ask to add thanks to them, preferably at the end of copyediting.

Yours is a single-author book. In edited volumes it usually looks best if authors follow a common style in their acknowledgements, or if these are consolidated; and it does jar to see contributors thanking each other or their volume editor. Treat the book as a collective endeavour.

In the case of books with numerous illustrations derived from other sources—art history, for example—it is often more appropriate for the lengthy details of sources and acknowledgements to be presented at the end of the book in small type; and in that form they become a useful reference source.

I see a trend towards making an introduction a substantive—and essential—part of many books. Thus a preface is about the book as an entity—its origin, funding, context—and is paginated with the front matter. The introduction is about the content of the book; it does not include acknowledgements; it is commonly paged as part of the main text of the book and may well be labelled Chapter 1.

Please consider whether a list of abbreviations would be helpful to your reader. If most abbreviations are for subjects mentioned only once, spell them out in full instead. If they are abbreviations used frequently in the text, present a convenient list just before the main text— your copyeditor may suggest additions to it. If your abbreviations relate to the bibliography, move it to just before the bibliography.

There: a complete manuscript with all its apparatus. But that is not all we need you to deliver.

ILLUSTRATIONS . . . AND PERMISSIONS

Apart from the tables, we need the illustrations. Please ensure that each of these is in a final form ready for reproduction (see Letter 12). You have probably numbered the illustrations in the list of contents and the list of captions. Please add the number to a front corner of each line drawing—conventionally, blue pencil is used for this—and to the back of each photograph—attaching a pre-written label rather than writing on the photograph itself, since that might show through to the surface. Packaging is all-important: your manuscript will pass through many hands. If possible, put the illustrations in one or more envelopes, clearly labelled with the author's name, the book title and the chapter(s) to which they belong. Thick card to stiffen the envelope will help avoid damage to this material, and is essential when entrusted to mail or courier service. Label all artwork boldly and clearly—there are stories of envelopes being mistaken for packing material and discarded.

I suggest that you send a set of original illustrations (for the printer to reproduce) and two clearly labelled sets of photocopies, with the two copies of the typescript, for the editor and designer to use. That will avoid risk or damage to the originals as the book passes from hand to hand. There may be an illustration which you will definitely use but which is not yet delivered for production; it may be a photograph on order from a library or museum, paid for but not yet supplied, or you may have a map in draft form that is being finalized for you by a draftsperson. Your set of photocopies can include a version of this, for the copyeditor and designer to work on, until the final version of the illustration arrives.

For some books (textbooks, general trade books, multi-author reference books) the publisher may obtain the illustrations and the permissions to reproduce them. But for most scholarly and scientific works the choice of illustrations lies with the author. The choice is limited by the granting of permission—and the task of obtaining originals and securing permissions is usually left with the author, even if the publisher suggests an appropriate form of words. There is little point in developing an argument in the text, and designing a page layout, around a fine illustration if permission to reproduce that illustration is not forthcoming.

Fortunately, in most cases an academic author approaching peers, journals or even commercial publishers will receive a sympathetic response to the request to reproduce an illustration with full acknowledgement. If a line illustration is completely redrawn (not just traced to identical form) this formal permission is not needed, but only the formal acknowledgement ("after X").

What is often forgotten is the need to request permission to quote words by other authors. If a book is actually discussing those words—if they are the subject of a passage—then this probably falls under "fair use" (USA) or the more limited and strictly assessed "purposes of criticism and review" elsewhere, and is exempt from the need to seek permissions. If you are confident that a usage falls within this definition, and if the length quoted is not excessive (say 400 words in any one passage or 800 words altogether) it is better not to request permission—both to defend this right and to avoid embarrassment if permission for such use is refused or subject to fee.

But if you are using a lengthy passage from another author, because the extract makes a point aptly or illuminates an argument usefully, you need to be careful. A short quote is fine (some publishers may suggest a limit—say, quoting no more than 60 words or so from any single source), but if you are using one or more long slabs of material from another source permission—in advance—is needed.

So we expect to receive with your manuscript full details of permissions for illustrations and text included in the book. Please supply a checklist to show who has granted permission and who has not replied or has not been asked. We do not want to change the page proofs of the book just because permission for one illustration or text passage is refused late in the day. We need for our files photocopies of letters granting permission. Advise us clearly of any special conditions imposed (e.g. approval of a colour separation, or the receipt of a free copy of the book). And then separately we need from you the text to be included in the book to acknowledge these permissions. In some cases, particularly with institutions, there may be a specifically required form of wording for this acknowledgement.

THE DISK

We also require a copy of the computer disk containing the word processed version of the text, identical to the hard-copy printout in every way. This must come with the manuscript. Don't think we don't trust you, but . . . well, no, perhaps we don't. Many authors can't resist adding just a few last little changes to their text files after sending the manuscript in for editing, so the typesetter is confronted with two versions of the book. Freeze your text on page and disk simultaneously, and send them in together; if we want you to make changes to the word processing files, we will advise you. And do, please, remember to label the disk with your name and the book title. It may be the only book you are currently writing, but it is not the only one we have in production.

If your disk label just reads "book manuscript final draft" it may get lost somewhere here, or later.

On the disk please include only the text that is in the book, and only the latest draft. You can present this as several files; label them Chap1, Chap2, Notes1, Notes2, Captions or whatever you like, as long as it is clear.

With the manuscript and the identical disk, please also give us details of how the files (word processing or illustration) were created: we need to know the format (PC, Macintosh or whatever), the operating system, the word processing or illustration program, and the version of the program you are using. If you are unsure of the version, there will usually be an "about" topic on the program menu. Your publisher may also ask (though in this case we have not) that you supply a second version of each text file with the formatting codes stripped out—e.g. a

---

Checklist for delivery of manuscript for production

☐ Manuscript, double-spaced and paginated throughout
☐ Duplicate manuscript (if required)
☐ Supplementary text—notes, bibliography, appendices, acknowledge-ments, tables—in similar format
☐ List of abbreviations
☐ Original illustrations, appropriately labelled
☐ Detailed roughs for line illustrations still to be drawn
☐ Photocopies of illustrations with manuscript
☐ Contents list
☐ Lists of illustrations, tables, etc. (to follow contents page)
☐ Caption copy for illustrations, tables
☐ List of permissions received for text or illustrations (with required acknowledgement or other conditions); details of permissions still being sought
☐ List of any items still missing
☐ Note to editor/copyeditor/designer on any special points
☐ Labelled disk with word processor files, illustrations file, etc.
☐ Details of operating system and software used in creating the disk
☐ Draft blurb
☐ Suggestions for cover illustration (if required)
☐ Marketing information (if required)
☐ Style sheet (if required)
☐ Other information forms requested by the publisher

---

simple "text" or "plain ASCII" version—for the typesetter to use. It also helps to enclose a typed key to the ways you have coded the manuscript, if it is not obvious. If you have a subtle mix of bold, italic and italic bold, explain. If you have decided or agreed to follow a mark-up code (for example, putting ⟨Q⟩ for indented quoted matter), again make this clear in a covering memo.

You are sending us, then, your files on disk with their description, your caption copy, and your information on permissions sought and obtained. We also asked you to complete some of our in-house forms to speed editing; most publishers have these, of different types. They will include notes on any special style decisions you have made in finalizing the text. Our marketing colleagues also ask for information about yourself, your ideas for publicity, and a draft blurb to get us started on creating suitable copy for the jacket flap. Do take time to give us the information that will help us produce and promote the book.

All ready? Congratulations! You can relax for a few weeks until the copyeditor gets in touch with you. Go on holiday if you like, to recover from the final push to completion—but stay in touch!

Yours truly, R.M.D.

« 41 » *Book title*

Dear Professor Tuttle,

Sorry to raise so late in the day the question of your book title. I know that since our first correspondence we have been referring to your book as *Continuity and Change*, but we took this to be the working title only. Now that we are about to produce and market your book, we need a real title.

General trade non-fiction books for the mass market often have trendy, jazzy titles which mean nothing in themselves but give a buzz of recognition. If everyone is talking about a book called *Fatal Impact* or *Savage Nights* or *Oblivion*, you have a convenient shorthand for literary gossip columns and dinner parties, easy for the bookshop customer to remember and for the bookseller's assistant or librarian to recognize.

Such titles are appropriate for part of the general trade. Their brevity and catchiness, and even their enigmatic quality, become positive marketing advantages. And occasionally—just occasionally—a scholar's book will move into general intellectual discourse and into wide readership, and become more than a scholarly work. The near-meaningless title proves acceptable.

With respect, I don't think your book can be sure of making this transition. It is, in our view, an excellent work in its field, of real importance to scholars in your discipline and likely to be read by senior students too. The important thing is to let them know that it is a book on a subject of interest to them.

We are constantly competing for the attention of scholars, book review editors on scholarly journals, booksellers and compilers of specialist booklists, and librarians trying to control the flood of new publications. We need to say to these people not "Here is an interesting new book you might like to consider," but "Here is a book you cannot do without."

An appropriate title is a very important weapon in this competition. Unless yours is a one-in-a-thousand book of wide general interest, I believe it best to give it a title that immediately identifies the discipline and, within that, the time or space or subject limitations. Thus *Continuity and Change* is a bad title. *Aztec Health and Disease* is a good title: it is both informative and memorable. *Motion in Marsupials* is useful; *Remorse and Regret* is not.

A catalogue, a mailing piece or even a journal advertisement from a scholarly or scientific publisher promotes several titles. The librarian, bookseller or academic is likely to take only a quick glance at these. They are unlikely to pause and read further about a vague and insubstantial title. If, however, a title indicates a book in a relevant subject area, their attention will be drawn to it and they will look at further details.

This is the reason why a good title is an informative title. It is also a reason why it should be the main title—not just a subtitle—which is informative. Our clients may only read through a list of the main titles—they may never reach the subtitle.

It is also more honest, and in the long term more productive, to clarify the breadth or narrowness of the book in that main title. It looks deceptive to call a book *Sexual Health and Disease* if the subtitle reveals that it is on *The Impact of Colonialism on Nineteenth-Century Tuvalu*. The bookshop agreeing to stock a book entitled *Poetry and Parody* may be displeased to find it is a study of a little-known sixteenth-century Latvian balladeer.

This does not mean titles (or subtitles) need to be dull or long. It does help if a title is short enough to be memorable. There is no need in main titles for *Essays on . . .* , *A Critique of . . .* , *The Evaluation of . . .* Be direct, informative, exact, unpretentious. And use the subtitle to emphasize the interesting aspects of your study, not to delimit and restrict. So avoid subtitles like *Contributions to . . .* , *Some Thoughts on . . .*

Let us discuss possibilities. Each publisher—and each author—will have personal preferences. I dislike dates in the main title of a social science book and am even cautious about dates in history titles; they look too often like a doctoral dissertation.

One final point. The title is a bibliographical tool. Try to start it with a word which everyone can spell and spells the same way. Don't start it with a numeral or an initial if you can help it. That will discourage *Zschokke's Early Drama* or *Gaol Reform Movements, 50,000 Years of Instability* or *T. S. Eliot as Mannerist*. We want people to need your book; we want people to find your book; we want people to grasp your book gratefully and know from the start "This is for me."

Yours truly, R.M.D.

« 42 » *Copyediting*

Dear Mr. Dittle,

It was very good to have your final manuscript, revised after our review, together with the illustrations, apparatus and information.

We have now sent the manuscript, with copies of the illustrations, to our copyeditor. Some publishers copyedit in house; we use a small panel of tried and tested freelance copyeditors whom we brief carefully. You will be hearing from the copyeditor within a few weeks, and should expect a number of queries.

I know you regard your manuscript, after all this work, as in a final, indeed near-perfect, state. The copyediting stage is routine for all books; it is not an indication that we think there are any unusual problems with your book.

There are many advantages to you, as an author, of a professional copyedit. In fact, the copyeditor is the only person who will have read every word of your book with care—the publisher's acquisitions editor, and our outside readers and advisers, may at best have read quickly or even skimmed parts. But the copyeditor is required to read and weigh every letter, number and punctuation mark.

You can assume they can look at your manuscript from the viewpoint of your future readers, while remaining sympathetic to your goals as author. Their aim is to help you communicate with your readership. In scholarly publishing the copyeditor will usually have some understanding of the subject matter of the book but will not necessarily be a specialist in your field. The copyeditor is not there to convert a hopeless style into golden prose, or to find and amend an erroneous stretch of logic or shabbily compiled tables. These faults would normally lead to a manuscript's being refused or returned to the author for further revision.

For this reason, they are not usually expected to rewrite your arguments, or to advise on content or on the overall structure of the book. If there are major problems with a book, we may ask them to tackle it in more wholesale terms, by agreement with you, but the copyeditorial brief is usually more limited. There is, after all, a budget for the book and a limit to the time and resources for editing. That is why a book designed as a general reference work or a textbook for student use may expect more thorough copyeditorial input than a specialist monograph.

From the publisher's viewpoint, their copyeditor is simultaneously undertaking a number of separate tasks on the manuscript, all directed towards making the manuscript as good as possible for the needs of the eventual reader. That means, particularly, removing barriers that may stand between the author and the reader, between the purpose of the manuscript and the fulfilment of a printed book. That often means that good copyediting is invisible, because it brings the book to an expected standard. Inadequate copyediting, by contrast, can be very visible.

Ideally, we would hope there is some understanding between you, us and our copyeditor about how much they will do—somewhere between a minimal and a maximal approach to your text. We do not want to finance a long editing process if you reject all the changes, nor do we wish to leave undone some task you assumed we would do. You need to know whether minor items will be changed or just referred to you for decision. If there is ambiguity, it is often best for the copyeditor to show the publisher, and you, a sample chapter before copyediting the whole text.

The copyeditor will pay some attention to style. If a phrase is infelicitous or a word misused or overused, the copyeditor will change or query it. Errors in typing, spelling or punctuation (which even the best of us can easily make) will be corrected.

You have written the text at different stages, and have quite likely revised its sections in a different order from the final sequence. The copyeditor can approach the book with a fresh eye. When you refer to some concept or term that is not fully explained, they can flag this and ask you to expand. When you repeat an argument or a phrase, they can pick this up and query if the repetition is intentional. If contradictions appear in your text, these can be spotted by the professional eye of the copyeditor. If the overall sense of a section or chapter is unclear, you may be warned of this.

Most copyeditors have particular quirks, interests and concerns which arise from their experience. Some will ask you to accept their approach to punctuating quotations, or to split infinitives, or to capitalization, and you may find yourself in friendly dispute. Their professional advice should be considered carefully. In matters of style they are quite possibly right; where matters of content are queried, the final decision will normally be yours.

Copyeditors today frequently query the use of gender-specific language where gender-neutral meanings are intended. Many authors feel that querying this carries an implied charge of sexism and become defensive. But to many readers the use of masculine pronouns for ungendered references will be as much of an irritation as poor grammar or misspellings. A copyeditor can identify types and places of such usage. There are different conventions to overcome this, however. An author should feel free to select an appropriate style for gender-neutral language, such as "they"/"their," as there is no general standard. You should not feel compelled to take a copyeditor's preference for, say, "s/he" if you prefer "he or she."

It is often useful to have a readily accessible list of abbreviations, or of technical terms, within a book; the copyeditor may suggest additions (or deletions) in such lists to help the reader.

An important part of copyediting is scrutinizing the apparatus of notes and bibliography. The copyeditor checks that the notes are correctly numbered, in the right place, and relevant. Sometimes a copyeditor may question the nature of your notes (whether footnotes or endnotes or in-text bibliographical references). They might add an explanatory note or bibliographical reference; more often, perhaps, they will question the repetitiveness of a citation, or suggest that a rambling expository comment be taken back into the main text or dropped. The copyeditor will also check your use of cross-references.

The copyeditor will check that each reference in the book appears in the complete bibliography, if there is one. As well as checking for internal consistency and completeness, the copyeditor will regularize the bibliography. They may follow a publisher's house style; at the very least they will ensure that layout, punctuation and factual details (date, place, perhaps publisher) are presented in a uniform style. You should expect our copyeditor to raise a number of queries and ask you to fill in some missing places of publication or missing page numbers for journal articles.

This is all work on the manuscript. The copyeditor will also do two other tasks, however polished and perfect the basic text. First, they will provide or edit the apparatus of front matter (prelims), where the publisher normally imposes a house style and preferred order. The half-title, series information, title page, publisher's imprint page, contents lists and other preliminary pages are part of the copyediting process.

But most important is the mark-up. The most carefully completed text, printed out with the finest computer equipment and designed with loving care, will be covered with marginal and in-text marks after copyediting. The mark-up identifies, for the designer and for the type-setter, the elements which go into final typesetting. As author you may have thought these elements were self-evident, consistent and in need of no further comment, but a glance at the copyedited page will demonstrate differently.

The copyeditor usually codes all headings, grading them so that the designer can design part and chapter titles, several distinct grades of subheading and so on. Indented material is marked up, as are the breaks required between main text and indented or tabulated text. Lists and typeset tables are marked for design requirements. The positions for tables, line drawings and half-tones (photographs) will be noted in the text. The author's keyboard dash will be coded as a character in the typesetter's font—an en-rule or an em-rule. Italic and bold text will be marked, and unusual characters—accented letters, phonetic symbols and so on—may be highlighted as "special sorts." Soon the neat print-out is covered with copyeditor's marks.

When the copyeditor has finished work, they will want to consult the author. There are several different ways of doing this.

They may want to meet and go through each query with you, explaining the problem and asking for an on-the-spot decision. This is fine for stylistic matters, but if there is missing bibliographical information, or issues that require further thought from you, it may not be ideal.

Or the copyeditor may type up and send you a list of specific queries—suggested stylistic improvements, missing data, unclear expressions. A quick response to this will be appropriate, but make sure you give the response you mean to stay with. You are defining the text which will be typeset; changing your mind at proof stage will delay the book and impose additional cost either on the book or on yourself.

Many copyeditors return the whole text to the author with queries "flagged" for attention. You are required to put in the correct answer to copyeditor's queries. This gives you a chance to see the version of the text which will go to the typesetter. If you now spot further things which require changing, advise the copyeditor. If you are in doubt about copyediting changes already made but not the subject of queries to yourself, query the copyeditor in turn. But do not routinely go through and "stet" (reverse) copyediting changes wholesale without first consulting the publisher.

Finally, there is the trend towards editing on screen. The copyeditor may have copyedited your word processor files directly—ideally, using some method that allows you to identify the changes. This copyediting will, as with hard copy, include both routine changes and queries for you to answer: you may be sent a computer disk, or hard copy, or both. Be clear as to what you should and should not do to the text at this stage; above all, avoid the temptation to rewrite and add more material without advance discussion with publisher and copyeditor.

It is not uncommon for an author to want to make some changes during copyediting and production. We would discourage you from making changes on a whim; but if there are real errors which you identify, or updates of data which you can insert, it is essential that you promptly and clearly inform the copyeditor before they complete their task; it is not acceptable practice to wait until proof stage.

Occasionally authors may feel they are in pursuit of goals different from the copyeditor's—that the changes to style or structure or preference are inappropriate or excessive. If you feel this is happening, it is best to discuss your concerns with the publisher as early as possible. It helps no one if, after a complete copyediting, the author asks to restore masculine pronouns everywhere, or recapitalize every reference to the deity, or change back every Chinese name in Pinyin to the Wade-Giles orthography.

At the end of copyediting, the copyeditor should feel that the publisher's high standards have been applied to improving the way the author's message is conveyed. The author should feel, too, that their work has been improved in real if unexpected ways and carries out its original purpose better. The publisher should feel that money and time spent on copyediting has been necessary and constructive. The hard-copy version of the text, with the copyediting amendments, should be finalized with no further queries other than those to designer or typesetter. It then travels with its computer disk to the next stage.

Yours truly, R.M.D.

« 43 » *Updating the disk*

Dear Dr. Vise,

Following the copyediting of the printout (hard-copy) version of your book manuscript, we have decided to ask you to update the word processor files and send us new copies of these. This is not a universal practice; in many cases the publisher will ask the typesetter to undertake the corrections or may even do it themselves.

When you submitted your typescript we asked you to "freeze" the word processor text files at that point and make no further changes.

You were to advise the copyeditor of any further essential changes and updates. The printout which you sent for copyediting was therefore identical to the word processor files on your disk. We now ask you to update these files to correspond exactly to the copyedited hard copy. If we are to use your computer output most cost-effectively in typesetting, it must correspond precisely to the hard copy as modified by copyediting.

The task is, therefore, to make each and every change on the copyedited manuscript, as if you were the typesetter. This is a technical, not an intellectual, task. Make each change without amendment; do not make any additional changes; and, above all, do not introduce new copy (even subheadings!) or delete copy at this stage. Any such changes you wish to make should already have been discussed with your copyeditor: if they were not, discuss them without delay.

When you have completed the revision of the files and copied the corrected versions onto the disk, this will again correspond, in all details except the technical mark-up, to the hard copy, and the typesetter can be given both the new disk and the copyedited manuscript to work from in the knowledge that they are identical. We do, however, wish you also to print out a fresh copy of the text from the disk as a double-check. This version, incorporating copyediting changes, should be sent with the copyedited manuscript and the revised disk back to the copyeditor.

This sounds complex and wearisome. That is why, in many cases, we leave correction to the typesetter, despite the expense. But in your case we have confidence that you can and will change the files to correspond accurately to the copyedited manuscript. We appreciate the assistance. *Yours truly, R.M.D.*

« 44 » *Design of the pages*

Dear Dr. Layard,

Now that your manuscript is through copyediting we are finalizing the design of the book. Our designer has done some preliminary work, to help the copyeditor complete their task. This must now be finalized before the book can move to typesetting.

Authors often express surprise that a book with only text and few illustrations needs design at all. Typesetters (compositors) expect to receive detailed instructions from their client—the publisher—and it can be very expensive if a design is changed after typesetting. The work of the publisher's designer, in imagining and imaging the final book, is all-important.

Even a book with only continuous text needs design. The overall page size must be appropriate, and the designer must decide how best to present the typography: the selection and use of typeface and type size, and the layout of text on the page. In part this is a matter of "feel"—the book must look appropriate for its readers, its level, its content. The layout of a reference book will be quite different from a textbook. Recreational reading or fiction will have a more open, spacious design than an academic work. The design that is acceptable for quite a short manuscript will be inappropriate for an unusually lengthy book.

In scholarly publishing, the secret to good design is always that it should be invisible. Scholarly and scientific books rarely gain from having fancy design at chapter openings, lavish artistic whorls and devices on the printed page, or elaborate and mannered layouts for the front matter and appendices and other apparatus.

Just because your book does not need fancy design, do not imagine it needs no design at all. Book design aims to match an appropriate form—both generally and in detail—to the function of a particular book and to the need to appeal to a particular market. Good design in a scholarly book may be invisible, but bad design is immediately visible, though it may be hard for the reader to say just why a bad design fails or is intrusive. A designer must space the page so that lines are of readable length and margins are appropriate in size. The placing and size of page numbers and "running heads" (the headline on each page with the part, chapter or section title) must be clear but unobtrusive. The typeface and type size must be appropriate to the subject, clear and readable; the right amount of space (leading) between lines helps the reader's eye.

Along with the basic page design, the designer must assign a suitable typeface and type size, selection of all-capitals or upper-and lowercase, and position and spacing to all the other elements of the book: part and chapter openings, headings and subheadings. The opening pages have their own needs, as do the notes and bibliography and other apparatus. Finally the index must be designed for readability, and will often have to be adjusted to fit the available space.

Design of tables is a particular challenge; you can assist the designer by working carefully on these with your copyeditor. It will have helped if your word processing disk used tabulation—not spaces—for your table layout. It will also help if you have planned your tables with the printed page in mind. Your tables should convey information clearly and unambiguously. If the designer fails to understand the emphasis, your reader may fail to do so. The structure and arrangement of tables is all-important; the use of rules and boxes may help but cannot fully make up for poor basic structure.

Ideally, all aspects of your proposed illustrations should be discussed at an early stage with your publisher. The publisher's designer will have constructive suggestions to help you with finalizing the form of the illustrations and preparing them for publication.

The designer will size your illustrations, both line artwork and photographs. Authors often expect their line illustrations to be reproduced as large as possible. Publishers like to reduce them to an appropriate size, giving each one no more space than it really requires. The designer will often try to reduce a picture to the width of the page, or to the width of one column in a two-column page. Turning a picture on its side to fit it onto the page is a very poor second-best, to be avoided wherever possible.

It is even less desirable to spread a picture across two pages, and a designer will try to avoid this. Much planning is needed to place a large picture at the centre of a folded section ("signature") of pages—the place where the thread shows in a sewn book; if that cannot be done, putting a picture on any other pair of pages means cutting the picture in half, and assigning it to separate positions in a printed sheet to be reunited after printing. When the pages are gathered, folded and trimmed, the two halves are unlikely to meet exactly: one may be slightly higher than the other; some of the illustration will have disappeared into the gutter of the book.

If the size of a line drawing is a particular concern, it is best to reduce it to size first and show it to you, the author, in this format, so that there are no unpleasant surprises at page proof stage. If detail fails to show in the sized illustration, it can usually be resized. Sometimes a trial reduction shows that the illustration itself needs relettering or redrawing for clarity.

The sizing of photographic half-tones is often a more subjective judgement. Photographs are generally included to convey information. Careful cropping (by masking) of unnecessary detail may be better than presenting a photograph sideways or unattractively large on the page. But in a scholarly book the photographs should be considered as information, not as decoration, and both the author and the designer should have that fact uppermost in their minds.

In all design—even more than in the copyediting stage—any outstanding questions or issues need to be resolved early. Any changes in design at page proof stage would add significant cost and significant delay, and they introduce the risk of further error; such changes at that stage are agreed only in exceptional circumstances. If your text, tables and illustrations have been well prepared and well presented, well copyedited and given a sensible brief from the publisher, the designer's task should be much easier. But if you, as author, have real concerns, then it is best to ask to see sample page layouts as well as sized illustrations. But be warned: publishers consider that they, and their designers, are the experts on typography and page layout. They are unlikely to be influenced much by the views and preferences of authors, especially those offered after the event. The most you might do is suggest that a picture has been inappropriately sized, trimmed or positioned.

We hope you like the final design of the book and that your readers, even if they are unaware of the design elements, will feel at ease with it too. *Yours truly, R.M.D.*

« 45 » *Typesetting*

Dear Mr. Colon,

I can now give you the good news that copyediting and design are complete, and your book is now in the hands of the typesetter (the compositor). We have not yet decided where to print the book, but we are obtaining quotations.

When typesetting was in "hot metal," the printer was the typesetter. The formes of the text (and blocks for the illustrations) would be wheeled across from the typesetting section of the printing works to the machine room and locked into place on the mighty machines. The change is sufficiently recent that most older printers and publishers will have set books in hot metal; they will have learned to set in lead as part of their training.

This old practice is still reflected in some jargon—as when authors say their book is "at the printer's" or proofreaders correct "printer's errors." But in fact the typesetter today is likely to be a room full of computer keyboard operators, distinct from the printer physically and by ownership. Some publishers own their own typesetting departments, which may operate under the same roof; or they may take a manuscript through to finished page in house before conveying a disk or camera-ready copy to the printer.

The remaining difference is between typesetters who use professional-level typesetting systems, and those who use desktop publishing systems or systems derived from small multi-purpose computers. There will continue to be major changes and developments in system hardware and software. A distance still remains between those who are professional typesetters, able to create a book page with all the traditional skills, and typists who lack these skills.

The responsibility of the typesetter/compositor is to create the definitive reproducible image for the book (as computer output, film, bromide or other camera-ready copy) from what they are given. They might be given a computer file (on disk or via modem) already in a format (like PostScript) which can be taken over into the typesetting system, to be output in final quality. They may be given data corrected by the author or the copyeditor, together with a key to formats which they must create within the typesetting system; they may be given uncorrected data with a hard-copy version showing corrections to be input. Or they may be handed a traditional marked-up manuscript to be keyboarded from the start.

The typesetter will estimate to the publisher the cost of setting, of making into pages and of producing the final image. They will allow in their costing for some level of late changes and corrections, and for the work expended either in converting the disk or data into their system or in keyboarding the text. Any changes or corrections requested by the publisher or the author (aside from the typesetter's own errors) will be charged as extras, and the cost of these changes can prove considerable. As electronic procedures in typesetting continue to reduce origination costs, the cost of manual changes after proof becomes an increasing proportion of the total cost.

The easiest method of setting is to take data already coded for format and convert it into the required image for the printed page. This may be done through a typesetting system or other mechanism with output in the quality required by the printer. Little or no further work is needed on the text image itself.

The typesetter will normally translate the author's or copyeditor's codes for formatting features (such as paragraph breaks, subheadings, italics, etc.) into the proprietary codes used in the typesetting system. The hard-copy printout of the manuscript, marked up by copyeditor and designer, gives the typesetter further format instructions. Headings and subheadings have been labelled by the copyeditor, and the designer has assigned a style specification to each of these categories, as well as specifying the overall type size and format of the text itself. Now the typesetters take all this information into their system.

The result is a continuous text file. It might equally have been generated by trained keyboard operators with only the edited manuscript before them. But since a typical academic manuscript might take, say, four days' work to keyboard if there were no electronic file available, well-prepared author text files on disk can save four days. This is not much in the time scale of a book from first conception to the final bound books; but it is a useful saving in cost.

The keyboard operator—no matter whether the basic text comes from disk or from hard copy—undertakes a number of tasks and checks. Very important is the breaking of words at the end of a line. A conventional typewriter leaves a ragged right-hand margin. A word processor can either emulate that appearance or justify the right-hand margin, but only by the limited expedient of varying the spacing between words. Because of this limitation, word processing output may be awkward to read in a typescript and always looks peculiar in a printed book, unless the text measure is very wide.

Typesetting systems break words at the end of the line to overcome this. They do so by following some simple rules and consulting a basic dictionary of acceptable places for word breaks. (Indeed, desktop publishing systems and even many word processing programs do this too, but to a lower standard of precision.) This is not a purely automatic process: the computer dictionary cannot include foreign-language terms, most proper nouns, and other special cases that arise in the text of a book. So good professional typesetters will examine every line for poor word spacing, awkward paragraph or page endings, and bad word breaks caused by the limitations of the computer dictionary. They will interpret the options, and make manual adjustments to improve correctness and readability.

If the book is to be heavily illustrated or has complex page layout because of tables, it may be appropriate to print out the text as galley proofs—in readable lengths, but not yet broken up into final pages. These can be checked before the book goes forward to be made up in pages, either by a designer or directly by the typesetter. If any changes are essential, they are less costly at galley proof stage than after pages have been made up.

Alternatively, the typesetter may check the text at this stage and make it up into pages before sending proofs to publisher and author, with positions and space left for any illustrations or tables still to be added. First proofs, whether galleys or pages, are usually produced on a laser printer, of slightly lower quality but at far less cost than the high-resolution equipment that will be used to generate the final image for printing. The author is usually sent photocopies of these proofs, which are a little less sharp in resolution than the proofs themselves.

Making up pages is a skilled process. Many apparent "design" problems arise from poor page control by the typesetter. Make-up must be planned page by page and spread by spread—that is, visualizing the even-numbered (verso) page on the left together with the facing odd-numbered (recto) page on the right. Even though the initial page make-up may be an automatic procedure on the typesetting system, a good professional typesetter will check, control and adjust what is finally proofed to author and publisher.

Adjustments of the basic text will seek to avoid "widows" and "orphans" where possible. (A widow is a short final line of a paragraph at the top of a page. Less serious, an orphan is the first line of a paragraph isolated at the bottom of a page, especially a right-hand page.) The typesetter will remove these by adjusting word spacing or word breaks, or by allowing an extra line at the bottom of both pages of a spread. If running heads and page numbers align, it is not noticeable if an extra line is added to, or subtracted from, a pair of facing pages.

Page make-up becomes more complex when quoted matter, tables and illustrations are to be included. Quoted matter is often broken across spreads, but may look better kept together if the layout can be adjusted to allow it. Some tables and occasional illustrations must fall in a precise position in the text: this rarely happens naturally, and it requires painstaking layout and often costly adjustment of line breaks and page lengths. Far more often, a table or illustration is needed quite close to a text reference, ideally on the same two-page spread. Though somewhat less taxing for the designer and typesetter, this too may mean juggling the elements to achieve the best result. The designer, or the typesetter (compositor), may have to take duplicates of the sized illustrations and the text and paste up a completed set of pages, in a draft layout.

All this is skilled work and demonstrates that typesetting is far from a simple system of swallowing author's computer files at one end and spitting out camera-ready copy at the other. As with copyediting and design, good typesetting is often invisible. Poor typesetting is highly visible. Too often it comes from a mismatch of people, equipment and skills. A trained typesetter using an unfamiliar system can produce disastrous results; more technologically sophisticated hardware does not necessarily mean better (or, in the long run, cheaper) final output in typesetting. But typists using desktop publishing systems can rarely match the professional skills of a trained typesetter using the right equipment.   *Yours truly, R.M.D.*

« 46 » *Proofreading and alterations in proof*

Dear Ms. Nuthven,

Enclosed is a schedule we have received from the typesetter for the correction of proofs. In this case, as you will see, there will be a stage of galley proofs (we often bypass this stage) and later a set of page proofs, when you will also be required to prepare the index.

The proofs were made on proof paper, not on the paper we will use to print your book, and you will probably receive photocopies of these. So what you see will certainly represent a less sharp image than we should expect in the final product. It may even be reduced in size a little to fit pages convenient for copying—not the final page size of your book.

To keep the book on schedule towards the desired publication date it is essential you hold to these dates for the return of the proofs. This means setting aside enough time to do a thorough and conscientious job.

In practice the typesetter/compositor will look over the proofs, but their proofreading may be comparatively superficial. Ideally, they will either correct and revise before printing the set you see, or else mark some of their own corrections on the proofs. Apart from this possible check, we commonly ask our own proofreader to look over another set of proofs. Although some publishers ask their copyeditor to complement the author as the second reader of proofs, we prefer to have the fresh eye of a new proofreader, who may pick up errors the copyeditor missed at the manuscript editing stage. Our copyeditor will then collate your corrections with those from the independent proofreading, and return them to the typesetter for correction.

When a manuscript has been input into the typesetter's system by their staff, a wide range of typographic errors can occur—missing or misplaced text, wrong fonts, wrong letters or punctuation, even wrong spacing. You need to check the whole proof against the original, word for word and letter for letter.

With your manuscript, we used your own word processor files on disk and asked the typesetter to put in the changes that arose from copyediting. The use of author files reduces the likelihood of misspellings and incorrect punctuation. What may go wrong is more serious. Whole sections of an electronic file may appear in the wrong font, or be missed out altogether, because the data transfer has mistranslated or failed to pick up a formatting code. It is also possible, when a revised piece of text has been taken into a document, that the replaced version appears too, unexpectedly. Proofreading should be easier when a book has been set direct from disk than with a freshly keyboarded text, but it still needs a conscientious reading to pick up the unexpected.

Normally a typesetter is expected not to use their system's capabilities for spellchecking or making global corrections. Most publishers prefer to rely on the check undertaken by the copyeditor; they do not want the typesetter making independent decisions on spelling and style. Occasionally, however, you may find that the built-in checker in a typesetter's system has, in error, overridden the copyedited manuscript: once you pick up a single aspect of this, you need to be wary of the whole manuscript. Equally, you need to note incorrect or misleading end-of-line word breaks or other serious infelicities of layout which could confuse the reader.

What are we asking you to do when you proofread? We are asking you to check that what appears on the typeset page is the same as what appears on the hard-copy printout of the copyedited manuscript. We are not asking you to look at the proofs of the book and suggest further changes and improvements to the contents—the time for that passed before the end of the copyediting stage. The typesetter will charge a significant fee for changes in proof, and this charge will be reflected in a higher price for the book, or a deduction from your royalties, or both.

There are only rare exceptions to the publisher's warning against changes at this stage. If the pagination in these proofs seems final, and if any cross-references remain which require exact page numbers, these should now be inserted (e.g. in text references such as "see p. 000 below"); and you should now insert page numbers in the list of contents, list of illustrations and so on. Second, if you identify actual errors of fact in the text when you read it through, you can ask to change these. The same applies when you see real misspellings or significant grammatical errors not previously noticed in your manuscript. But changes of mind, new preferences in style, and additional text should all be avoided unless absolutely essential—and they rarely are essential. Discuss these with your publisher before marking them for change.

On the other hand, if a change is vital, it is much better to make it now than to record it for insertion in future reprints or editions.

Changes which are really unavoidable are best made at the galley proof stage. This stage is often bypassed, as typesetters output first proofs in made-up pages. But if you do have a galley proof, essential corrections can be a little less costly, since they need not affect page layout or pagination, or disrupt other parts of the book. Mark the correction clearly in the appropriate place.

When you are sent page proofs, they show the designer's and typesetter's carefully considered decisions about where to place the page breaks. If you have seen a previous galley proof, your only task is to ensure that each of the galley proof corrections has been made accurately and without introducing further errors.

While working with page proofs, please make corrections and essential changes in such a way as to minimize the impact on subsequent pages of the book. If text is to be removed, be sure it will not change the number of lines on a full page, unless this is the last page. If text is to be added, try to remove a similar number of words elsewhere on the same page, so that the page overall finishes at the same place. If you are on the last page of a chapter, you can relax; if you are on the next to last page, you may ask that a line be taken over or brought back from that last page. But significant changes earlier in a chapter risk affecting all of its remaining pages. Removal or insertion of a whole paragraph may even add or subtract a full page, affecting the pagination of the rest of the book. So this is just one more good reason to take a cautious and conservative approach to corrections in proof.

When you see page proofs you will see how the tables, illustrations and other material have been sized, designed and placed. If there are serious problems with these decisions, you should query them at this stage. Your proofs may include a scan of an illustration, for information only, or may just show a key-line box to indicate where it is to be placed. Check all the information available to you at each stage—caption setting, picture size and orientation, spacing and so on. The earlier you identify a problem, the easier it will be to fix it.

There are conventional systems for marking proofs. These require a marginal marking to draw the typesetter's attention to the correction and give details of the change needed. Corresponding to this is a mark in the text to show where the correction should be made. These marks are explicit instructions. If you have significant queries, do not write a short essay in the text; flag the place with a sticker and raise the query separately when you send the proofs on.

As your publisher we ask you to assign each correction to the responsible party as honestly as you can, so that the typesetter can allocate costs. We use a colour code for this purpose. Changes of mind and of fact are author's corrections and can be coded in blue. Errors which arise from the copyeditor's or designer's work can be coded in black (but we do not regard it as our fault that we failed to pick up some major error of fact which you have now noticed). Typesetter's errors should be noted in red. You may find the typesetters have themselves used green to mark errors. These conventions may differ among companies and countries—the main thing is to ensure that you are consistent and follow whatever coding instructions you are given with the proofs.

While reading proofs can be a chore, it is a very important stage for conscientious attention. We hope it gives you pleasure to see the real book unfolding, stage by stage. We hope you will find few errors in each stage of proofs; but if there are errors, we hope you will find them! When the page proofs are subject only to corrections that will not affect any of the page numbering, you will be ready to compile the index, which itself has to go through proof stages.   *Yours truly, R.M.D.*

« 47 » *Illustrations in production*

Dear Dr. Ong,

We shall need your assistance to check the illustrations in your book at different stages in the production schedule. A lot can go wrong with illustrations right up to the last moment, and corrections can be more expensive for illustrations than for text.

In your book there are maps, line drawings and photographs, and in this case we have agreed to do some of the work ourselves in preparing these for publication. We shall also want to involve you in each stage. Different books and different publishers have varying needs—some publications will expect much less or much more of the author.

First, the photographs. You submitted some usable prints, provided some detailed references with a request that we obtain photographs, and gave us some copies of photographs in magazines. We have been unable to use the latter, as they have already been screened—broken up into the pattern of black and white dots needed for the printing process. Magazines and newspapers use a coarse screen unsuitable for book use; but in any case it is always better to use an original photographic print and screen it afresh for the book, where we refer to its screened version as a half-tone.

We and you will have obtained photographic prints, in black and white, preferably at a size larger than the eventual reproduction. Our designer will size these for the designed page. This does not just mean establishing a percentage reduction to fit the page design. It also means marking, with a mask, which parts of a photograph are to be used. For reasons of format, but also of relevance, it is often useful to crop (trim) the edges of a photograph to make it most appropriate for its published use. (The cropping is done by masks, not on the print, and the original is unharmed).

We shall expect to show you a version of each cropped and sized half-tone; we want you be sure that we have obtained the right print and that the sizing and trimming do not omit any essential detail in the picture.

You may see page proofs in which a space has been left for the photograph, or in which a rough version has been photocopied in place or scanned as an image for the proof. Even when the page proofs include the full and final version of the half-tone, do not be too concerned about quality—the final quality will come from the printed version, not a proof.

You do need to be sure that all photographs are in the correct position in the book and are not inverted or flipped over; that the correct portion is used; that the right number and caption are associated with a photograph; and that the list of illustrations gives the correct page references.

Sometimes screening and sizing the photographs is left to the printer, with the results shown on the ozalids (dyelines or blues) which are sent to the publisher's production department just before printing. In that case, the first opportunity to check the photographs becomes the last opportunity. There is room here for several errors. Photographs can be mixed up; they can easily be printed upside down or wrong (emulsion) face up. If we have doubts we shall consult you, and at that stage we shall need you to respond very quickly, for the book will be about to print.

More of the work in colour photographic illustration lies in the last stages of production. Therefore, no image of the final colour print will be available until late in the production process. You will see layouts to check generally on sizing, orientation, numbering and captions. We shall see colour proofs shortly before the book goes for printing, to check and correct the colour reproduction and other detail.

When a second colour is used in the text, or when there are two-colour line illustrations (i.e. black and one other colour), proof stages will commonly show up only one colour at a time, and care needs to be taken to ensure that the black-equals-black proof is correctly assigned and that the black-equals-second-colour proof is also correct.

Most line drawings will be black line only. There is no halfway measure between using lines and screening to use dots, since in the final printing the black ink will either be present or absent; there is no gradation. If you need to reproduce, say, a work of art in pen or pencil which has fine shading, wash or other techniques, we may decide not to treat it as line art, but to scan it as a half-tone like a photograph. Otherwise the fine lines in the illustration may disappear or merge.

This means that all preparation of a map or line drawing intended for publication must bear in mind the technical aspects of production. In the case of your book, where you have provided us with detailed roughs, we shall draw up final artwork ourselves, but this procedure is followed only for selected books, when agreed between author and publisher.

First, however, our copyeditor will edit your roughs essentially as if they were part of the text, verifying the spelling of names, the completeness of map information, and the legibility of graphic details. For the maps, the classification of place names—the distinctive typographic styles assigned to peoples, towns, provinces, rivers and so on—will be checked and coded. There are likely to be copyeditorial queries at this stage.

Our draftsperson will then produce final artwork from these briefs to a size agreed by the book designer. This artwork will be larger than required for the book and will bear in mind the reduction factor. We shall show you this artwork—like a proof—but remember that changes to art at this stage are already expensive (though they become even more expensive later). Please correct only inaccuracies in interpreting the edited rough, or major errors in the rough or brief which you identify at this stage (which will probably be charged to you).

Later we will show you sized artwork—if something is wrongly sized for the level of detail, please advise. And finally you will see the illustrations in position on a page proof. We need you to check the numbering, the captions and the pagination in the list of illustrations within the front matter. There may also be cross-references within the text to be completed.

Illustrations are an essential part of many scholarly books. Clarity and accuracy of information are vital; please take time to help us get these processes right. There is no correction more expensive at reprint stage than correction to artwork. *Yours truly, R.M.D.*

« 48 » *Providing camera-ready copy*

Dear Prof. Erpage,

We are glad to have your confirmation that you will soon be sending us camera-ready copy for your book, organized in your own department. The availability of desktop publishing programs for small office computers, along with high-resolution laser printers for output, makes this practical and feasible. As we explained before, this saving in our costs will allow the publication of a book which economically could not otherwise have been brought to press.

We would ask you to make sure that your colleagues handling the program adhere strictly to the page layout which we agreed with you a few months back. Please also look through the notes we gave you about what you would and would not provide—we make different arrangements for different books. In the case of your book, we shall ask you to typeset some of the front matter (the prelim pages), although we shall prepare the title page.

We shall also arrange for the line illustrations to be reduced to size, and for the photographic half-tones to be screened. This puts on you the responsibility to leave adequate space in the appropriate place for these, and to set captions below this space. In all other cases, what you give us will be the final image.

Please therefore undertake a careful final check—*the* final check—of all material.

Because we are not copyediting or proofreading your manuscript, you need to undertake this yourself. You have had editorial assistance from within your department to finalize and polish the manuscript. It would be wise for you also to hire someone who has not previously seen the manuscript to read through the camera-ready printout and proofread for typesetting errors. Remember, we are taking what you give us as final image. It will not be feasible to make corrections at a late production stage or for a reprint.

When the text is correct, we need your typist, word processor operator or desktop designer to ensure that each page works. That means carrying out all the same tasks that a professional typesetter would. Check the line spacing to ensure adequate and appropriate word breaks, in order to correct any poor spacing introduced in achieving a straight (justified) right-hand margin. Ensure that tables are not broken across pages—especially not across two-page spreads—unless this is unavoidable. Equally, try to avoid having the final line of a paragraph at the top of a left-hand page or the initial line at the bottom of a right-hand page.

We shall require you to follow the arrangements for running heads and page numbering agreed when we approved the final design. Do check that any rearrangement leaves all pages numbered correctly and in sequence: it is all too easy to miss or duplicate a page number.

Then, only then, complete the index and type it up so that it accompanies the camera-ready copy for the rest of the book.

We shall move rapidly into production, helped by your efforts, and while the book will lack some of the polish which we believe publishers add to a book, it will nevertheless have the full force of our marketing effort to complement your contribution in seeing it through to this stage.   *Yours truly, R.M.D.*

« 49 » *Preparing the index*

Dear Anna-Louise,

Just when you thought you could relax, having approved the final page proofs as correctly laid out, and having marked the final few corrections—here we are, back again, asking you to produce an index! And worst of all, because the rest of the book is now in page proof and ready to go, we are asking you to do this in a hurry yet to make it a work of excellence.

The index is the last task an author does, and it is often completed in a hurry; yet it is frequently the first part of a book examined by a reader, so it must be a work of high quality and must be user-friendly. Many users of your book will dip into it on library shelves, looking a topic up in the index, and entering the book by that route: if the index suggests that there is nothing on their topic, they abandon the book altogether.

At the other extreme, the most enthusiastic readers and owners of your book will return to it again and again, relying on your index to bring them to the section they wish to use for a particular purpose. It becomes the menu, the road map, the telephone directory for their scholarly or educational purposes.

So a good index is one which starts from the diverse needs of the readers—not from your analysis of your own work. The length, structure, complexity and selectivity of the index must always start from the questions Who will use the index? and What kind of entries (i.e. headwords) will they look up? There is little value in an index which lists every proper name, obscure theme or specific item if these are not identified by words which the enquirer will think to look up. Similarly, the index must open up the text to a wide range of lines of enquiry—subject, place, person, theme, concept—wherever these could realistically be the starting point of an enquiry. You may be interested only in grand themes, but your reader may want to see if a particular individual appears in your narrative. A person of minor importance in your book might be the central character of interest to your index user. A theme to which you give little credence or emphasis may be the one theme which interests your user. What is marginal for one reader is the core issue for another.

It is futile to plan an index by trying to index words only. A word which by itself has no substantive significance in the narrative in one context ("to Hell and back") becomes a meaningful entry in another place ("Dante's description of Hell"). An unimportant personal reference ("Raffles' entrepôt of Singapore") becomes substantive a few pages later ("when Raffles returned from London").

Readers want to be guided to something which leads on from the enquiry word they have chosen: they are not entering a "spot the word" competition. So an entry with five references to discussions of the concept or phenomenon of adaptation is of more use than a list of twenty places where the word "adaptation" is used.

This means there is no short cut to a good index. A computer may help to sort and alphabetize index entries, but for a scholarly book it does not create an index of the quality and form that readers need.

If you are really nervous you can hire a professional indexer to do the job for you, or ask your publisher to hire an indexer—probably at your expense. But this works better in general publishing than in scientific and scholarly publishing. As the author, you understand what themes are important, what terms are synonyms, which apparent synonyms are quite different in technical use, how abstract concepts are related to each other. A professional indexer is unlikely to be a professional in your subject area and so is likely to make mistakes in judgement.

If you are the editor of a multi-author book, then a professional indexer may be an acceptable compromise. But if you are the sole author, no one will be able to understand and analyse the book better than you can. It is well worth allocating the time to create your own index.

Here are some practical suggestions. But there are also a number of authors' guides on indexing; indeed, there are whole books on indexing to assist those for whom this is a full-time activity. If such guides, or your experience and the advice of colleagues, seem to you more helpful, feel free to follow those.

First, decide whether you want one index or several. Depending on the kind of book, and therefore on the kind of user, it may be appropriate to have more than one discrete index. If you are studying fossil flora, readers will be enquiring either under a species or genus name or under some other topic. It is unappealing to have an index which alternates incessantly between the flora and themes and perhaps, therefore, between italic and roman type. And indeed, a separate index of the flora can serve the double function of page reference and complete list of the species under study.

Many scientific works create separate indexes of this kind. It may be appropriate in other topics, too, where a particular class of items belongs together. Examples are linguistic or ethnic groups; the different sections of a writer's literary output; different genres of works of art; places on a voyage; archaeological sites; military units.

But this should not be taken too far. The conventional index mixes people, places, events, specific topics, general themes; these usually belong in a single index. The reader may want to move around among different types of information, and so it may be helpful to include cross-references between people and places and themes within a unified index. Multiple indexes may be a nuisance; think very carefully before you decide to divide your index.

Of course, that question concerns the final form of the index. But you may decide to actually prepare the index entries in separate lists initially, as a working method. Listing people, places and themes separately (planning to integrate them at the end of the exercise) will make it easier for you to find an earlier reference to metaphysics or ergativity or Walt Whitman as the indexing proceeds, rather than working through the whole list.

You also need to decide what kinds of things you will include. If your book mentions a lot of places, will you index them all, or just key places? If there are a great many philosophical themes, where do you make the break between "Index" and "Don't index"? Will all the persons in your narrative be indexed, or only those of historical importance? It is best to include the doubtful ones in case you decide later that they should be in.

More difficult is the inclusion of academic authors. You might argue that the first thing colleagues in your field will do is check the index and bibliography to see if they are mentioned. If they are in the bibliography they will want to see how they are cited. But such a one-time entry, which no one but the author cited will consult, does not justify being indexed. Most publishers would urge you to omit from the index those authors' names who appear only in bibliographical citations. But where you actually discuss an author's work ("Jones' views on the gradualism of this process have met with a critical response"), then they are a topic in the book and merit inclusion. Where the literature in general becomes a subject in the book and not just a formal reference, include it. This would apply in literary works but also, of course, in discussions of the development of a scientific idea or argument.

Depending on your personal preferences, you can make the first draft of an index by writing entries on pages, by making index cards for later sorting and typing, or by generating a word processor document or even a data base file as you go. These are all possible steps in creating the index—use whatever is easiest.

When you are at the initial stage of preparing an index, it is best to over-index. It is much easier to decide to exclude Kelvin from an index because he occurs once in an unimportant reference than it is to decide halfway through indexing that Kelvin is really important, and then to search back to find previously ignored references in pages already indexed.

You should nevertheless start with some idea of what the overall length of the final index will be. This may be determined by the subject of the book, but it will also at times be limited by the available space. The book will print in sections of, say, 16 or 32 pages. If there are 10 pages available for the index and yours is planned for 20 pages, the extra 10 pages will be wastefully expensive and you had better get back to us at the publishing house for a discussion quite quickly!

So you have your cards or paper or word processor file ready. You have an idea of the length of index required, but you plan to index above that length and cut back unnecessary entries later. You have decided to do one comprehensive index, not several. For organizational purposes in creating the index, you are going to index certain categories—people, places, themes, etc.—separately to start with, merging them at the end.

But before you open a page, I suggest you consider what major abstract topics you wish to index—themes, arguments, propositions, theories, analytical modes. These you should list before you find entries for them. And if the book has a major theme—nationalism, for example—plan ahead of time what subdivisions will be useful entries, entries that readers will look up. If your book is on nationalism, the index user does not want a list of 140 page references to nationalism, or a note "Chapters 1–11, passim." Think ahead about what abstractions will make useful headings and subheadings in the index.

Now you are ready to go. Work through the pages of the book in succession, noting down the index word and the printed page reference. Be especially careful to register when you have casually turned the page. Distinguish carefully between references continued across two or more pages (145–47) and those which are separate references but appear on successive pages (145, 146, 147).

Listing personal names, place names and concrete subjects will be reasonably easy, though you will become aware of the need to trim and edit as you progress. The list of themes will be more difficult. As you index, some abstractions and themes will clearly seem to be subdivisions or synonyms of others. Do not try to change such a heading at this stage, but make a marginal note ("? merge with racism and cross-refer").

Other single topics will seem to be too large—as when your references to nationalism start to spill over into two or three lines. If you catch this early, go back and establish better subdivisions. If you realize this too late, make a marginal note to return to each of the entries and find some satisfactory subdivision.

At the end of the task you will be surrounded by words, numbers and empty coffee cups. You will also, probably, feel very bored by your book and wish you could rewrite it. Forget those thoughts. Take a rest; then return to edit and organize the index.

The main task is structuring references. Look through each entry. Are some of them synonyms? Suppose you have used "Radiocarbon" and "Carbon-14" interchangeably. Merge the entries, and add a cross-reference "Carbon-14—*see* Radiocarbon." Many publishers have house styles for indexes, and in any case you should follow consistent style in capitalization, cross-references and spacing.

If some entries are too long, create subdivisions. People can look up "nationalism" but will be helped to use your book by having topics more narrowly defined: "nationalism and race," "Balkan nationalism" and so on.

Add cross-references: at the end of an entry "Russia," add "*see also* Soviet Union." Think of what headwords people will look up, and what other features of the book (specific reference tables, illustrated subjects) they really need to find.

Finally you have a list of your topics and themes, names and other entries, with subdivisions for the larger entries. If they are not yet in a single list, combine them now, and check the alphabetical order carefully.

Now comes the difficult question of length. You have probably created a list of entries greater than is actually needed by users. Edit out those which seem superfluous—entries which, given the overall nature of the book and the index, readers are unlikely to use.

Your publisher may be asking for a shorter index still. The space available may require an index only 80 per cent as long as the draft so far prepared. This task is more difficult. Some entries might be merged and the least important ones omitted. If the book is to have 16 printed sections of 16 pages each, it is not a practical option to add a couple of extra pages to accommodate a long index. Discuss a realistic final length with your publisher.

Finally the index is ready; now it must be formatted for delivery. Like the main manuscript, it should be delivered not looking like an index when typeset, but as a double-spaced printout ready for copyediting and design mark-up, together with a word processor disk if you have created one. Check that you have consistent rules of alphabetizing, using a style guide when in doubt. Check that you are consistent in abbreviations (St. Jerome or St Jerome, Saint Jerome or Jerome, St.) and in capitalization. See that the presentation of numbers is consistent: whether you use 124–28 or 124–8, be consistent. Deliver a clean, careful index to your publisher and the book can move to its final stage.

One problem often occurs in indexing. An author may pick up inconsistencies in style and spelling which had remained unnoticed throughout the earlier writing, editing, typesetting and proofreading stages. When you are compiling the index it suddenly becomes apparent that "Maupassant" and "de Maupassant" are both used in the text in surname-only allusions. The indexing solution is simple—list all entries together under one form, with a cross-reference from the other form. But is the main text to be corrected at this stage? That is a decision on which you should make a recommendation, but the publisher's editor may finally decide. If something is really an error—if, say, you have misspelled a name several times—then it is better to make the correction at this later stage than in a reprint. But if there are merely differences in style preference, it may be best to leave them.

The index copy will be copyedited, designed and typeset. You may be asked to check the proofs of the index—if you are, remember this is the very last stage of creating the book before it is ready for the printer. Speed is of the essence, and corrections must be restricted to those which are essential and not just cosmetic. And with the final check of the final proof of the index copy, you really can relax and wait for the book to appear.

Of course, from the viewpoint of the printer and the binder, the book is only just starting: nothing serious has happened at all so far. But that is not your worry.   *Yours truly, R.M.D.*

« 50 » *Jacket and cover design*

Dear Jack,

We are now organizing the design of the jacket (for the cased hardback edition) and the cover (for the limp paperback edition). To enhance identification and maximize impact, the front of the jacket and front cover will be identical, and the spine wording of the two editions will be similar. The back cover gives us limited space, which we shall use for a blurb. The jacket has flaps, so we can use these for information on book and author, and use the back of the jacket as appropriate, perhaps to advertise other books on our list.

A while back you suggested that your sister-in-law be asked to design the cover and jacket; she is an up-and-coming visual artist with strong painting and drawing skills, and you feel she could represent the spirit of your book. I am afraid we are going to say No to this offer.

The cover is not a decorative item. It is a marketing tool. It has specific needs, even in the most specialized of scholarly books. If the cover

was not needed to sell the book, we could save the considerable effort
and expense that go into designing, originating and printing it.

For that reason, marketing decisions should influence the visual decision. That does not mean flash, unrealistic, garish and unsubtle design. It does not guarantee some substantial budget for dressing up the
work. It does mean appropriate and purposeful design.

The cover serves to identify a book—to make it recognizable in a
library, in a bookshop, in a catalogue or on the owner's shelves. This
requires clearly readable title and author's name on the spine and the
front, and an identifiable image in form and colour—whether this
image consists of letters and colour only, or uses a graphic design or an
illustration.

The cover also conveys something of the tone of a book. Too flashy
and commercial a cover may give the wrong message—that a scholarly
book is not meant to be read by peer professionals but only by an untrained general audience. Brightest is not always best.

But where a book is to appeal across disciplines, to students or to
some lay readers, and especially where bookstores are expected to
stock it, a bright and lively cover may be appropriate, perhaps with a
full-colour illustration. The tone of the cover suggests the tone of the
book; the cover should be neither too upbeat nor too downbeat for the
actual contents, level and market of the book.

The subject matter itself also guides cover design. A book on Sudden
Infant Death Syndrome—however general its audience—should not
get the jazzy design which might help to sell a book on the music of the
Swing Era. Authors are often concerned that a publisher will impose
some inappropriate illustration or design on a book. For this reason we
like to show our author the proposed design; but this is usually for
information and comment, to be changed only if we have made a major
error in judgement. Unlike the proofs, the cover is something we do not
ask our author to approve, modify or reject. The cover is like other
aspects of design and remains, under contract, our domain.

The use of an illustration on the jacket or cover is a common device;
but it is not essential. Often the illustrations in the book itself are there
for information, and may not have appropriate visual impact. A good
map or line drawing may look crude as a cover design. A photograph
powerful in impact within a book may have little meaning on the cover.
In my view, a cover illustration must have an immediate impact, its
subject matter clear enough to convey the subject or tone of the book.
If it is "informational," and meaningful only to someone who is already
reading the book, it will fail to serve the purpose of a cover picture.

On the other hand, a work of art (an artistic photograph, a drawing or
painting, a cartoon or a fabric design) is created for its visual impact.
While it will not usually *depict* the subject matter of the book, it may well

symbolize it in a more valid way. There is a vast wealth of visual material to choose from, and those who hold such material (artists, commercial galleries, public collections, photo libraries, museums and general libraries) are usually willing to provide material for an agreed fee.

It is much more risky to commission a fresh piece of art to be incorporated in a cover design. The designer, author or publisher may not like it; the need to revise and rework may not fit the artist's normal way of working. It will usually be easier to choose an existing piece of artwork.

But that is not to argue that there should be an illustration on every jacket or cover. Many of the best book jackets are graphic designs, using abstract lines and shape, form and colour to create an identity, a feel and a visual impact for a book.

And back to basics: the words are most important: the title, the author's name and the publisher's name or logo on the spine; the author, title and subtitle on the front; descriptive text elsewhere on the book. Purely lettered front covers may prove most appropriate for many academic works.

The keynote is to consider the role the cover design is to play in each particular book. If the book will be promoted to libraries by fliers and catalogues, colour is less important than clarity of lettering. If the book will be sold to professionals at conferences, its visibility too is important. For bookshop sale and exposure, however, the cover or jacket must do more. It has to interest and attract, but also to inform. At the distance a customer stands from a book display, the cover should identify the author and title with clear lettering, and the visual image—graphic or illustration—must covey the level, the feel and if possible the subject matter of the book. A good test of any designer's rough for a cover is to put it at bookshop browser distance and ask, If I am the target purchaser of this book, does it convey the right message to me?

Having said this, let us face one brutal truth. Most design goes into the front cover of a book, with editorial effort focused on refining the copy on the back and the jacket flaps. For some—perhaps most—publishers, the spine is often an afterthought. Yet in the library, on the reader's library shelves, and even in the bookshop, only the spine is normally visible. Perhaps we pay too much attention to the rest of the jacket, too little to the spine.

In suggesting that we commission your sister-in-law to do the cover, I am afraid you fail to match our needs. As explained, we do not want to commission an illustration—we might not like the result or think it right for the cover's commercial role. Moreover, the cover must be designed by a trained and experienced graphic designer. We want to give the printer a piece of art in which a typographically informed decision has been made about every aspect of the lettering—font, size, spacing, arrangement, leading. We need an overall design which works visually, including the incorporated illustration. We need colour selection that makes visual sense, defined in colours a book printer can match. A good designer can often achieve the impact of a multicoloured jacket by the imaginative use of just two printing colours. Each printing colour should be presented to the cover origination house as a separate piece of artwork, with instructions about percentage tints, overlays and burn-outs. The thickness of the paper and the extent of the book define the spine width, and this information must be included in the cover artwork and design specification. This is all a technical graphic design task, not an artist's task alone.

Your request that a friend do the cover is a common one from authors. Our decision not to accept this is a common one from publishers.

Yours truly, R.M.D.

« 51 » *Printing*

Dear Dr. Pressman,

The final page image of your book has been sent to the printer, and the next thing you will see will be a bound and finished copy!

We checked the final revised proof in house, to ensure that all corrections had been made and that all late changes to text (including the index and last-minute adjustments to the front matter and to the pagination) had been made accurately and without the introduction of further errors.

Our production manager arranged for the covers and jackets to be printed, and the die (chemac) supplied for stamping the spine of the case. We have had confirmation that the appropriate materials are available—the text paper, the jacket paper, the material used for the cover.

The first task before printing is to generate transparent film carrying the image for printing, with the pages "imposed"—set up in the right relationship to ensure the correct page order after printing and folding the printed sheets. This film may be generated by the printer, or it may be done by a separate production house, especially if colour separations are required.

This film is exposed to a strong constant light source over a light-sensitive paper, which is processed into a printer's proof (ozalid, blue, dyeline). This proof may be sent to the publisher to check. The publisher's production staff will examine the proof for layout, position and quality. There may be a similar editorial check that photographs or other elements added at the printer or film maker have been put in their correct position, with the correct orientation and correct face uppermost. Authors are not normally expected to check the blues/ozalids.

Once all is confirmed as correct, the printer will make printing plates from the film and, after appropriate preparation, will print the book. After all the effort of research, writing, editing, typesetting and creating the final image for the book, the actual machine time for a scholarly book with a modest print run can be disconcertingly short! After printing come the many stages of the binding process: folding and gathering of the sheets; sewing or other method of holding the pages together; and finally the addition of the cover or the case and jacket. The books are cartoned and shipped to the publisher's warehouse.

We shall inspect advance copies of uncased book blocks and of bound stock; if these are approved for release, be assured that as author you will receive an advance copy before the whole complex operation of distribution begins. We hope it gives you pleasure, as well as relief, to hold the book in your hands at last.   *Yours truly, R.M.D.*

« 52 » *Errata slips*

Dear Mia,

I am glad you were pleased with the first pre-publication advance copies of your book, and I will pass on your remarks to our designer and production manager, and to the printer.

It is disturbing that in reading through the text again at this stage you have identified some errors. Text errors should have been picked up earlier: the editing and proofing stages we have been through have given plenty of opportunities to check the text.

We realize, of course, that some errors creep in at the very last moment. Sometimes these are serious errors at the printer's, which we have failed to pick up at ozalid (blues) stage. A picture may end up in the wrong place or may be transposed; a section might be repeated; or some other rare disaster may occur. There may also be problems in the printing itself. If our advance copies were to show poor or smudged inking, faulty binding or other technical problems in the manufacturing stage, we would question and probably reject the stock.

But in this case you are noting corrections which you admit should have been identified before, and you ask us to print and include an errata slip. We are very reluctant to do so.

One reason is cost. The mechanization of printing has made hand work very expensive. If an errata slip were to be inserted, each packet of the books would have to be opened, each book opened and each slip glued into position (as your book will have continuing and library use, we could not insert a loose sheet). The cost would be substantial, apart from the delay in publication.

But we are also hostile to errata slips in principle. They look sloppy, they suggest amateurishness in the preparation of the book, and they draw attention to errors which, to be honest, readers might otherwise never notice or need to notice.

If you will send us a list of corrections, we shall guarantee to make the changes on the printing film so that they will be included in the reprint. Most reprints slip in a few typographical or other corrections; for that rare book with a great many errors, the reprint might even be labelled on the title page "reprinted with corrections, 19XX."

Our only concession to errata slips would be an error so great that it misleads readers. If a textbook or a professional book has errors in figures which will mislead in practical effect (and not just in the logic of an argument), or presents data which will be reused and may mislead, then conscience dictates that action is needed. The publisher may well decide to go the whole way and either reprint the affected pages, to be inserted by hand in place of the offending text, or else print corrections to be pasted on to the relevant pages. To include actual errata slips would draw attention to the error so blatantly as to cast the value of the whole book into doubt.

Either way, you can expect to see few if any errata slips in books. Please send us your list of corrections. We shall look at them carefully and urgently; but unless there is an error so misleading as to endanger the users of the book, the changes will probably be held over for the next printing.   *Yours truly, R.M.D.*

« 53 » *Don't assume all is well*

Dear Professor Griff,

This is a letter of apology—and of thanks for chasing us on progress of your book. I am alarmed and disturbed at what has happened.

While I am glad you wrote to ask about progress, I wish you had done so six months ago. You had submitted your contracted manuscript, and it was sent out for freelance copyediting. You answered the copyediting queries, and the copyeditor returned the text to us for production; her invoice was submitted to our accounts department and paid before she went overseas.

Unfortunately, meanwhile, our in-house editor had left the company—having been offered another job by the former member of our staff who had signed you up as an author. When your copyedited manuscript came into the office, there was no one waiting for it. It was put on a shelf awaiting attention and never resurfaced; it was not yet in design or typesetting, and no one spotted that it had fallen into a black hole in our organization. I can only express our sincere regrets that this has happened. I do acknowledge, as you say, that you had not contacted us before because you assumed that all was going well, even though you had not heard from us. This faith in publishers is admirable but is sometimes misplaced: all institutions have their problems.

To be wise after the event, it would have been best for you to probe occasionally to see how progress on your book was going; we could quickly have identified the problem if it had come to our attention. Even when a book is going through editing and production, and afterwards while it is being marketed, the occasional courteous enquiry may be productive. It will keep us on our toes.

The publication of a book is a joint endeavour between author and publisher, with the cooperation of outside parties. Neither should be so distant that we cannot talk about problems, nor should the author assume that the publisher is some anonymously efficient machine. Again our apologies. Be assured that appropriate action on your book is now our priority: it is now on an accelerated schedule, and all our departments have been briefed for action. Next time please hope, but do not assume, that all is OK. Keep in touch.   *Yours truly, R.M.D.*

« 54 » *The cost of books*

Dear Percy Mannie,

I am sorry you feel that the price we are charging for your latest book is too high. You are right that, even allowing for inflation, we set a price higher than your last book for us. But when you suggest that we have deliberately priced it to avoid selling any copies, is that quite fair? And when you claim that all your students and colleagues would buy a copy if it was one-third the price, are you sure? If only it were true!

Publishers get many complaints about the price of books, but with experience they discover that they get these complaints, basically, no matter what prices they put on their books. So they tend to judge the right price not by what people say but by what people do—that is, by the real sales patterns.

I lost faith in anecdotal pricing research while covering a huge international academic conference in a lavish big-city hotel. We had a large display of books of every kind. People asked why the expensive hardback books weren't cheaper; they asked why the cheaper hardback books weren't in paperback, and why the paperbacks weren't cheaper. For the cheap paperbacks they asked whether they could have a free copy to consider "for a class," and, failing this, whether they could have a discount. Upon receiving the good news that our inexpensive paperbacks attracted a 25 per cent conference discount, we were asked if we wouldn't be selling our exhibition copies at knock-down prices on the last day and said they would come back then.

The difficulty is that more books are available than academics, professionals, serious students and interested amateurs are able to buy, whatever the price. Fine; blame us for publishing too much. So a publisher has to decide what sales of an individual book will realistically be achievable at different price levels, and decide which combination of real sales and price will recover the book's costs.

For a specialist monograph of importance, the number of libraries likely to buy a library edition may be relatively easy to estimate, on the basis of sales of similar books published in the last couple of years.

For a basic student textbook, which the publisher knows is just right for an identified course, the price is not too much of a problem; and if the initial print run is an underestimate, the book can easily be reprinted.

The problem comes in the middle, with a book which may attract discretionary sales. Though it is not yet a student text, nevertheless there is a market beyond the specialist libraries. But how large is this sale, and what combination of real sales and possible price will work?

This is not just a question of maximizing the publisher's margins and the author's royalties. With scholarly books the larger part of the costs are fixed whatever the print run. There is a block of costs in initial editorial work on the book, in copyediting, designing, typesetting and proofreading it, and in creating the cover or jacket, together with any fees for permissions, picture research or artwork. These editorial, production and promotion overheads are fixed irrespective of the print run and sales. And even at the printer and binder there is a significant block of initial costs (making ready the printing machines or the bindery production line, origination of illustrations, cost overheads) which are fixed whatever the size of the print run. It does not cost much more to print 2000 copies of a book than 1000. It does make a difference if sales are 1000 on a book costed over a projected 2000.

So the publisher is deciding whether to try and recover the costs (the larger part of the costs) over sales of 1000 or 10,000, and whether to spread them over a hardback edition, a paperback, or both. These are questions of judgement as well as enthusiasm. Whatever the decision, the sales have to reach the level over which the book was costed. Too often, they do not.

As an author, you naturally feel optimistic. We feel optimistic, too; otherwise we would not have published your book, would we? But we are comparing it with other books, at different price points, to gauge where we can price it.

Your last book was on a broad general theme in your discipline. At the time, you were writing and lecturing very widely around this topic, which was certainly a live issue. We set quite an optimistic print run and spread the fixed costs over that run, so in your eyes (and the readers') the selling price was quite modest. The book was not adopted as a textbook for student purchase, despite your hopes at the time. But it was bought by a large number of your academic colleagues, and by eager postgraduate students who were on the same wavelength as your ideas. There was also a good international following for the book, as anticipated. The book did actually sell a little more slowly than we hoped (which is why it never reprinted), but we were happy with the sales and therefore, in retrospect, with the price.

Your new book is no less excellent in content, but it is on a narrower theme and is less international in appeal. We are sure it will be widely bought by libraries, and used and read in library copies. But it does not correspond to the kind of book which many individuals will purchase for their own use—whatever your friends, whom you quote, politely tell you! So we have costed it over a smaller print run, thereby in effect pricing it up.

You say that pricing an edition solely for library sales is effectively self-fulfilling, because it is placed beyond the reach of individual purses. That is true. Unfortunately, it is emphatically not true that pricing down to the individual pocket is equally self-fulfilling. Only a portion of the academic books published each year, out of the tens of thousands of new books, have the potential to attract significant individual sales. Even if every book were heavily subsidized in price, scientists, scholars or professionals would not have the time to buy and read everything in their discipline. For every high-priced book whose author thinks it would have sold well at one-third the price, there are several low-priced books which did badly in commercial terms—and publishers (university presses among them) who have disappeared as a result of too many bad judgements.

So it makes sense for scholars, as rational economic actors, to buy those books they can afford and both need and want to have. It will also remain true that students buy what books they must, influenced not only by costs but also by other perceived priorities for their cash. And if second-hand copies of books are available, or if they can share a book for a course with fellow students, that too will have a heavy impact on sales.

It therefore serves little purpose for you—or a reviewer—to say of a high-priced hardback edition of a specialist academic monograph, "How are individual scholars and students expected to buy this book at this price?" They aren't. They are expected to order it for the library. There is a fond assumption among scholarly publishers that the real specialists in a particular topic may have to buy their individual copies. But these very individuals seem to be the ones who end up getting their free copies for review in the academic journals!

If the publisher is wrong and assumes too many sales with too low a price, they have to take the loss. Fortunately, if we make the opposite mistake there is a fail-safe. If a book builds up a high reputation through reviews and word of mouth, and speedy sales show we printed too few copies, we can always reprint. And since we have recovered most of our fixed costs on the first printing, we may be able to reprint in a smaller quantity than the first printing without increasing the retail price of the book. If we originally published in hardback for libraries,

we can reprint into paperback at a significantly lower price—if we decide that there really is a market for a paperback among sufficient individual purchasers.

At the end of the day, we are pricing to make the best achievable
sales; and if we make the right decision often enough, we shall survive
long enough to publish your next book!   *Yours truly, R.M.D.*

« 55 » *Pricing a book*

Dear Mr. Count,

You are like many authors in being puzzled and, perhaps, disturbed
as to how we calculate the price we put on your book. You are right
that, for each additional copy of your book we print, the cost will be
only a few dollars, and the overall total of invoiced costs for producing
your book represents only a small fraction of the selling price. So where
do publishers generate their selling price? Do they, as you suggest, just
invent the highest price they think they can get away with, and hope
for the best?

Publishers are often reluctant to explain their costing, since authors
and others can be misled by a brief explanation. So here is a lengthy
one. I hope I can explain the relationships between costs, prices, and
the incomes of author, publisher, printer and bookseller.

There is a basic formula which dominates all book pricing, whether
publishers use it formally or intuitively. When the royalty is set *as a
percentage of the selling price*, to achieve a given gross margin the selling
price needs to be set in line with the following formula:

$$\frac{C}{Q - F} \div \left[\left(\frac{100 - D}{100} \times \frac{100 - G}{100} \right) - \frac{R}{100} \right]$$

where C = total production Cost
        Q = print Quantity
        F = Free copies
        D = Discount (per cent)
        G = Gross margin (per cent)
        R = Royalty (per cent) on selling price

In practice, the publisher will use spreadsheets—or trial and error—
to reach an acceptable balance between price, cost and margin.

The formula is simpler—and the variables easier to discuss—when the royalty is recalculated *as a percentage of the publisher's receipts* rather than of the selling price:

$$\frac{C}{Q - F} \times \frac{100}{100 - D} \times \frac{100}{100 - G - R}$$

where R = Royalty (per cent) on publisher's receipts

It is easier to explain this with actual figures, and easier still to make these figures simple. So please don't quote the actual figures back to us or to other publishers—they are examples only, even though the formula holds good for all titles.

Using the basic formula, we may have a situation where the price is:

$$\frac{\$10,000}{1200 - 200} \times \frac{100}{100 - 33.3} \times \frac{100}{100 - 60 - 10}$$

which calculates as a price of $50. Let us examine this further, using these simple figures, and see why a production cost of $10,000 for printing 1200 copies translates into a selling price of $50.

First, the discount. To sell the book, the publisher needs to offer the bookseller, wholesaler or library supplier enough of a discount to attract and (in their own view) retain these customers' business. If no discount is given (as sometimes happens with the sale of private institutions' publications), the resellers must impose their own markup. The discount varies by territory and supplier, and by category of book. A textbook with firm adoption prospects may attract a low discount; a general trade book, ordered in quantity, may attract a very high discount. The publisher needs to price according to the average discount, and for this calculation we will assume a modest one-third discount—33.3%. The publisher receives, then, only two-thirds of the price paid by the final buyer; or, to put it more harshly, the reseller marks the book up by 50%—a significantly larger share of the selling price than the author will ever receive.

This gives us the first element in our formula, cash actually received.

The figure of $\dfrac{100}{100 - D}$ becomes $\dfrac{100}{100 - 33.3} = 1.5$

The publishers may expect to sell some of the copies (even most of the copies of some titles) by direct mail, whether to libraries or to individuals reached through mailing lists or advertising in specialist outlets. If they offer such direct-mail copies at a discount to the customer, what they are doing is to absorb some of the costs that would otherwise be met by the bookseller, in order to retain some of the income that would otherwise be retained by the bookseller. The cost of supplying single copies is high: soliciting orders, handling the receipt of orders, handling payment for those orders, and packing and despatching single copies. Such sales have the effect of lowering the average discount, but that saving is likely to be balanced by an increase in the overhead costs of marketing and distribution.

This is the next calculation. The overheads of the publisher are substantial. For a large publisher they will match those of any service organization; for a small publisher they will represent an even larger percentage of income. University presses have high overheads, as do commercial publishers, although the smaller university presses may be subsidized in ways which help them to stay operative. A realistic assessment of overhead costs is needed in pricing books if a publisher is to continue in business.

Of course some of the costs are constant no matter how many books are published: buildings, administration, depreciation on computers and other equipment, and so on. Some costs relate more directly to the number of titles: the costs of the editorial department, the production department and the marketing department. Only a modest part of the publisher's overhead costs will vary with the number of copies sold: essentially the distribution costs. And one final cost—warehousing—relates largely to the number of copies not sold; happy is the publisher with an empty warehouse, however he may boast of the groaning shelves to admiring visitors.

Good business management will keep tight control on overheads, but some drop in overhead costs may be unwelcome. A drop in distribution costs might reflect a drop in sales. A drop in marketing expenditure might lead to a drop in sales. But, alas, a cut in the overhead costs of editorial and production departments is rarely other than beneficial to the cash flow of a publisher, private or institutional.

By convention most publishers allocate a fixed percentage of income to overhead costs in calculating prices. It would be equally valid to allocate a mixture of variable and fixed costs: for instance, to say that 20 per cent of the income of any new publication will be spent as the cost of generating that income—advertising, sales representation, distribution—plus $10,000 for fixed overheads, however many copies we sell and however much income we make. Some publishers do calculate prices and margins this way; but most adopt a general percentage. They might say that all overheads together will cost 50 per cent of the invoiced value of sales, the income from their books. Their costing formula must take this fully into account.

But if publishers recover only their overheads and the money they pay out to authors and for production, they will have no cash resources to expand their publishing, fund inflation or fund failures; they will have no resources to repay bank loans, pay their taxes or support their sponsoring institution. Most important, if they are a private publisher, they will have no profits; and if they have no profits they will cease to employ staff and hence to operate. All publishers—university presses, institutional imprints, public companies or privately owned publishing houses—need to make a profit. The targets may differ, as may the degree of risk the publisher takes in seeking that profit, and university presses may speak of a net margin rather than a net profit; but it is there in the price workings.

The private imprint must make enough profit to pay shareholders or owners, pay tax on that profit, and still have cash to reinvest in the business. A university press may be exempt from taxation, but it may also find itself taking on some financially riskier projects, and to reassure its host university and maintain its campus profile it needs to be generating as much of its own funds as possible. To the overheads must be added the required net margin. The gross profit or gross margin target combines the overheads and this surplus. An overall target for the net surplus might be 15 per cent of turnover before tax; that might go down to 5 per cent if expectations are modest. Let us assume a target 10 per cent net margin in our model; added to the 50 per cent overheads, this gives a 60 per cent gross margin which we must recover from the selling price.

We give ourselves 5, 10 or 15 per cent as publishers; we pay the author a comparable amount as royalty. Whether this is calculated as a percentage of the selling price or of the sum we actually receive from our customers, it must be included in the pricing formula. Let us assume, for simplicity, a figure of 10 per cent of these receipts as the author's royalty—the same figure we are seeking as our own net margin.

Then the third part of our pricing formula involves the relationship of the different partners:

$$\frac{100}{100 - G - R}$$

which gives, in our example,

$$\frac{100}{100 - 60 - 10} = 3.33$$

If we are paying our author an advance on royalties, that does not affect this calculation, although it does affect the cash flow of the book. If we are paying a flat fee to the author instead, we include it in the production costs.

So we are now left with the production cost—the total of all costs allocated to the production budget, from the first invoice (perhaps a refund of costs for a photograph obtained by the author) to the last invoices from the shipper of bound stock. A large part of the costs are present whether you sell 500 copies or 5000. These costs—copyediting, design, illustration, typesetting, proofreading, jacket or cover origination, and other incidentals—are the publisher's fixed costs in production. For a best-selling popular paperback novel, the fixed costs may be modest compared with the costs of printing 100,000 copies and a glittering cover. But for your scholarly work, unfortunately, the printing costs are a smaller proportion of the budget.

The variable costs do vary with the number of copies printed, and so this number is a crucial decision in the planning of the book. Too few copies and the book may be too expensive for its market, or it may sell out quickly and require an uneconomic reprint. Too many copies and the book may clog up the warehouse for years, never recovering its production, marketing or overhead costs.

Printing and binding costs are not all, strictly, variable costs. They include a variable amount per copy, but they also include a basic amount for undertaking the job, making printing film, doing camera work on illustrations, making plates and making ready the printing machines, together with the make-ready time at the bindery. The visitor to a printing plant that specializes in small-print-run academic work will be surprised how much time is spent with the presses not running; and when they do run, the time spent actually printing off 1500 copies is not so very different from the time spent for 2000. Certainly the paper may cost less if the print run is cut, but the planning and preparation time does not. So the costs of printing and binding actually include the invariable cost of the first printed and bound copy and the truly variable cost of the next so-many thousands. The publisher has to play with these costs to decide how many to print.

But the real key figure is costing over sales, not print run. It may be appropriate to print a few extra copies against unexpected success. It is always necessary to print extra copies—sometimes an alarming number of extra copies—as "frees" which will earn no income at all. These include copies given to the author, copies for national or state legal deposit libraries, and especially review copies for journals. For a book which may be used as a student text, inspection copies for teaching staff are usually unpaid frees. Additionally, there will be a number of copies damaged in the warehouse or in transit, or returned from booksellers or exhibits in unsaleable condition. These have to be added to the total print run; they must be subtracted from the total print run in assessing income.

So in our model formula we have decided we need 1000 hardback copies to sell and another 200 copies for frees. These generate a production cost of $4000 in fixed costs and $6000 in printing and binding costs (the latter is made up of $1200 in startup costs, which do not change with the size of the print run, and a per-copy manufacturing cost of $4, which amounts to $4800 for our order of 1200 copies), bringing our total production cost to $10,000. This is $8.33 for each unit produced, but $10 for each book we expect to sell.

We now have the third part of our formula:

$$\frac{C}{Q - F} = \frac{\$10,000}{1200 - 200} = \$10$$

The whole formula comes together:

$$\frac{C}{Q - F} \times \frac{100}{100 - D} \times \frac{100}{100 - G - R}$$

or

$$\frac{\$10,000}{1200 - 200} \times \frac{100}{100 - 33.3} \times \frac{100}{100 - 60 - 10}$$

so:

$$P = \$10 \times 1.5 \times 3.33 = \$50$$

where P = selling Price

Thus we have constructed a price. The $4 invoiced production cost of each new book becomes $8.33 for each book produced, but $10 for each book we sell. To achieve a net margin of 10 per cent we need to receive $33.33 per copy. Of this, $3.33 will go to you as the author, and $20 will come to the publisher as gross margin—$16.66 as overheads, $3.33 as pre-tax profit or surplus. And in this example, for every $33.33 we receive, the bookseller or other intermediary will receive an average of $16.67 as their gross margin.

So the move from $4 to $50 has been quite simple, unnervingly so. Just to cheer you up, we will cut the price to $49.95, which sounds more acceptable.

Who gains and who loses in such costing? Those external suppliers involved in production gain most. They will be paid in full, without question, even before the book is published and regardless of the success or otherwise of the book. Certainly the bookseller seems to gain a great deal—assuming they will sell the copies they buy within a reasonable time. They have some credit period in which to pay us, and if they sell the book within that period they will have incurred no risk and no cash outlay. If they fail to sell the book, they often have the right to return the book to the publisher for full credit.

As author, you have to wait for sales: your royalties are earned on every copy sold, and you should expect to receive them even if a bookseller defaults on payment (though not if the books are returned to us for credit). Sales may be less than you hope or more than you expect, but you will receive some income on the book whether the book is, from the publisher's perspective, a success or not.

The publisher apparently stands to gain most, with a target gross margin, in our model, of 60 per cent of receipts (40 per cent of the selling price). In fact, this gross margin will be achieved only if the book sells all the copies that have been budgeted—in this case, 1000 copies at $50. We have to sell 334 just to recover the production costs and pay your royalties on those copies—a "weak break-even." After 750 are sold, we have a "strong break-even"—we have no net profit on the project but are now poised to begin making one. This is a little illusory: if we had costed our overheads as a cash sum instead of a percentage of income, we would be making no net margin until the sale of the 900th copy. Only at the sale of the 1000th copy do we achieve the proposed 10 per cent of receipts as our margin. And what shall we do with that? Well, if your book has been selling particularly well we shall expect to reprint it or paperback it, or go into a new edition, in which case that 10 per cent surplus and more will be ploughed back into the project. If the book has completed its saleable life, a publisher will use the surplus for other publishing and the other demands on profit; if the sales are below expectations, that is a risk we shall be taking. After all, risk is what publishers are for.   *Yours truly, R.M.D.*

« 56 » *Changing the pricing variables*

Dear Mr. Count,

I am pleased that you found useful my explanation of how a publisher makes pricing decisions, and of why your particular hardback book might end up priced at $50—a multiple (quite modest for the publishing industry) of five times the production cost. You asked if there were any changes we could make in this instance to achieve a different price.

That is a reasonable question to ask, and to answer it we can use the same costing model as before. Which of these factors can we change? The basic formula to generate the price was:

$$\frac{C}{Q - F} \times \frac{100}{100 - D} \times \frac{100}{100 - G - R}$$

So we appear to have six variables to play with!

The best way to change the discount is to declare a new set of standard discount terms, and you may be sure that we keep our discount terms under review, selecting the most appropriate discount terms for a particular category or even an individual book. While we may like to offer smaller discounts, we do not want to lose an important block of customers and sales. Equally, there will be some books which a major wholesaler, a book chain or even a book club might take in large quantities on a higher than standard discount, and this might be the best commercial route to take. So while the general principle of tight discounts is right, the price working must reflect our prediction about the likely reality.

As I mentioned in the last letter, direct sale is a way of reducing discounts. For those books which we sell direct, we might offer the purchaser a smaller discount than the bookseller receives; but our costs of handling these orders is higher. The costs of making a sale have to appear either in the discount or in our overheads; we cannot escape them.

The same is true of free copies: we can keep a tight rein on what use we make of free copies, but copies sent to the review editors of journals or to influential would-be reviewers, or presented as inspection copies for classes all represent a good investment—that is, as long as we cost these free copies as extras and not as sales.

You ask whether the gross margin we seek is realistic, or whether it can be lowered for scholarly books with modest sales. That question is put to university presses and institutional publishers more often than to private companies in the same markets. It is important for every organization to keep overheads under control and within budget, but their pricing should reflect the realities. And because it is essential to generate the cash that allows us to continue publishing new books, a surplus is usually required.

If we were always right in our sales predictions, we might occasionally allow ourselves to distinguish high-margin books from low-margin books, and consciously to cross-subsidize titles. In practice, there is unconscious cross-subsidy, as books which do better than we expected subsidize other books which do less well than we had hoped. But if some titles were priced at close to or below a break-even point, we would have to be sure of achieving all the expected sales both on those and on the more optimistically published titles.

Of course, the price cannot always reflect the ideal. If production costs have gone above budget, or if sales forecasts are revised downwards, it may be necessary to compromise and set a price acceptable to the readership and market which still leaves the publisher making little margin. That is a position of retreat, not of planning: an option for the least troubled solution to a troubled book. If we publish expecting a loss, there has to be a good reason why we do that, and a good strategy to keep the problem from recurring.

So what else can we change? Well, obviously, the royalty. In this respect the author's cooperation can make a big difference to the selling price—and the selling price can make a big difference to the book. Using our model, where a $10 production cost with a royalty of 10% of receipts generates a $50 price, the price is:

$$\frac{\$10,000}{1200 - 200} \times \frac{100}{100 - 33.3} \times \frac{100}{100 - 60 - 10}$$

which calculates as:

$$P = \frac{1500}{40 - R}$$

If the royalty is 15 per cent of receipts, the selling price goes up to $60 and sales will fall off accordingly. But if royalties are lowered to 5 per cent the price will drop to $42.86 (which the publisher would round off at $42.50) and sales will increase. If you forgo all royalties, at least on the first printing, the price can go down to $37.50 without any cut in production costs, average discount or gross margin. In fact, at this price the publisher might expect to sell more copies than at $50, in which case the print run could go up and the unit cost could come down, allowing the price to fall even further. So if you are keen to see a reduced price, consider lowering your royalties.

It is difficult for a publisher to suggest to an author a reduction in royalties after a book has been contracted, and you might find a publisher reluctant to make a commitment to a formal trade-off between author earnings and price. But there are occasions when an academic author specifically does not need or want royalties. They may say, "Don't give me royalties; pay them to my sponsoring institution instead." But they might do better to say, "Don't pay any royalties at all, and use the saving to ensure that the book comes out at a lower price."

The other variable is production cost. We have argued that only a proportion of this varies with the print run. To use our formula again, the cost was a multiple (in our model, 5) of the unit cost, defined as the total production cost divided by print run less frees. The fixed costs represent a significant part of this; if those fixed costs can be reduced, that makes a major difference to most academic books.

In the model book referred to in my previous letter, fixed costs of $4000 were added to the printer's costs of $1200 plus $4 per unit, printing 1200 costed over sales of 1000. If the fixed costs increase by just $1000 the selling price would necessarily increase by $5, and the publisher might decide that the print run looked too optimistic at that price. But if we could shave $1000 off the fixed costs, the $50 book could be priced at $45; the publisher might decide that at $45 the book could sell 1250 copies instead of 1000, and on that basis unit costs would be reduced further. With fixed costs now at $3000, and with printer's costs at $1200 plus 1250 copies (plus 200 frees) at $4, total costs will still be $10,000 but the unit cost per sale will be $8, and the multiplier of 5 gives us a $40 book—at which point we can reconsider sales potential and print run once again.

So the impact of a reduction in fixed production costs can be dramatic. How can you, as author, help to achieve this? A well-prepared manuscript, an accurate word processor disk, and art ready to use with permissions already secured can all help in this venture.

If a subsidy is available, the model above shows how dramatic an effect it can have. On a print run of 1200 less 200 frees, a subsidy of $1000 is like reducing the unit manufacturing cost by $1 per copy—which, by a simple multiplier, lowers the selling price by $5. The effect can be even greater if it encourages the publisher to embark on a more ambitious print run.

And I have not mentioned length! A reduced length helps lower both fixed costs and variable costs. A book that is 20 sections of 16 pages—

320 pages long—will find much better costs at 16 sections—256 pages. While the basic design, editorial planning, cover and binding will not be affected, this shorter book will cost a fifth less in all the other production costs which the publisher must take into account. A book which is a fifth shorter, and costs something approaching a fifth less to produce, can have a selling price almost a fifth lower, too. But the shorter book may generate higher sales potential, and that may allow the publisher to reinforce this costing trend by a higher run at a still lower price.

In fact, in discussion with publishers, most authors will suggest that a larger number be printed as a way to reduce the unit cost. And this is tempting for the publisher too. Most of those involved in scholarly and scientific publishing are enthusiasts, who would rather see 5000 users of a $10 book than 500 users of a $100 book. What are the problems here?

Given the model costing we have outlined ($4000 + $1200 + $4 per unit), what are the options open to a publisher? The factor of 5 times the unit cost will give the same margin regardless of whether the publisher expects to sell

> 500 copies at $80
> 750 copies at $60
> 1000 copies at $50
> 1200 copies at $45
> 1500 copies at $40
> 2000 copies at $35
> 3000 copies at $30
> 6000 copies at $25

We have to make such fine distinctions every day. It is an error of judgement for a publisher to project only 500 sales at $80 if the book could really sell more. But it is a greater error to cost a book over 2000 sales at $35 if there is no market of this size at this price, or indeed at any price. The publisher can judge how realistic the options are by looking at sales figures for similar books: too often, actual sales are below expectations, and stock has been wasted or warehoused for longer than was economically sensible.

Some books have little or no flexibility of demand: 600 libraries in the field will buy it, and that is the market. Other books have considerable flexibility of demand: a definitive biography or a medical reference book for the general reader may increase its sales significantly if the price is dropped. But between extremes most books have a modest elasticity of demand, which still requires a careful decision by the publisher. Looking at the figures above, the cautious editor may recognize that the book for which there are 2000 potential sales at $35 will have extra sales if it is priced at $30—but that those extra sales will not amount to as many as 1000 more copies, so that the risk is not worth taking on a first printing.

So, to answer your query, I am happy to think flexibly about options for the pricing of your book. I shall be influenced by ways in which we can help reduce production costs, and ways in which you can help us to do so. A tight control on length and the provision of illustration may be particularly helpful. If you can help us secure a subsidy or wish to accept lower royalties, we shall be happy to discuss those options.

Otherwise we shall be influenced by our assessment of the size of the potential market at different prices. We shall look at the recorded sales of similar titles, take advice from our marketing and sales colleagues and perhaps from their trade customers, and take the best decision we believe possible.   *Yours truly, R.M.D.*

« 57 » *Paperbacking*

Dear Mr. Count,

Your further queries on the pricing of the book raise the question why we are not issuing it from the start in paperback. We did your last book in paperback, and it sold considerably more copies than we are forecasting for the new publication.

Some books are obvious paperbacks. A title which will be used on higher-level courses as a required or recommended text may fit this role. Some books for the general reader may confidently be paper-backed from the start. There are different national traditions, too. In France many non-fiction books will appear only in paperback from the start. The USA continues the pattern of initial hardback publishing of general trade non-fiction and of many lower-level student textbooks. In Britain, Australia and New Zealand there are many who predict the end of the hardback original in general trade publishing, with hard-back textbooks as the exception.

But academic publishing is a little different. There is a core market of academic libraries, and these libraries still, customarily, are prepared to buy a hardback edition. They want a volume that will last on the shelves and in the hands of multiple users, who may consult it over a long period of time. A book may be on student reading lists and be in considerable demand. Most libraries, rather than have their own copies individually rebound in hard covers, are willing to pay the (smaller) cost which the publisher must add to the price for binding the entire print run.

A high-priced academic book—the traditional monograph—will sell to libraries and to those specialists in the field or sub-field who have to buy it. If there is a broader academic sale, or even some general sale, then a larger print run of the hardback at a lower price may be the best route for a publisher to take.

Issuing a book in paperback from the very start may convey one of several messages. It may say, "Here is a book for students"; it may say, "Here is a book for the more general bookstore to stock for non-specialist readers." But it may also say to academics, research workers and graduate students, "Here is a book for individual purchase, and not just for library reference." Such a book may reach deep into the discipline at all levels, and it may cross disciplines as well.

So the publisher's decision on issuing in paperback is based on a judgement—or a hunch—about the potential nature of the market and its potential size.

The issue is the same as with variable pricing in hardbacks. Issuing a paperback will not always result in significantly expanded sales, income and margin. An unwise decision to publish a paperback that has an insufficient market can undermine the financial viability of a book.

There is a basic problem underlying this issue. The paperback is perceived to be a low-cost, low-price item; yet in reality its cost is only slightly less than that of a hardback. It may cost a dollar or two less to produce, but it must be sold at half or even a third of the price of the hardback. Publishing in paperback from the start is therefore a strategic decision that the publisher employs to convey certain signals about the book.

Let us take again the model used in previous letters. We noted a unit cost of $4 after covering fixed costs. A paperback may cost, say, $1.50 less to manufacture. But that gives no saving on the other costs; and the paperback has to reach a wider range of outlets than the hardback, and for this a higher discount may be required.

Options for the hardback were:

    500 copies at $80
    750 copies at $60
    1000 copies at $50
    1200 copies at $45
    1500 copies at $40
    2000 copies at $35
    3000 copies at $30
    6000 copies at $25

If we were to publish only a paperback edition, saving $1.50 per unit, options would be:

> 1000 copies at $41
> 3000 copies at $22
> 3800 copies at $20
> 5700 copies at $17.50
> 11,450 copies at $15

So the sales forecast for a paperback-only edition, in a standard academic format, would have to be much higher to make it work.

For this reason, unless a title is a genuine adoption textbook or a general book with wide popular appeal, scholarly imprints tend to publish paperbacks from the start only if they are accompanied by a simultaneous hardback edition. While the public may see the paperback as the "main" edition, in practice the hardback is carrying a large proportion of the fixed costs. In such simultaneous editions, the purchasers of the hardback are, essentially, only libraries who wish to possess a bound copy. But not all libraries will pay the differential—some will be quite happy to buy a paperback copy.

Let us take the academic monograph which we costed as:

> 1000 copies at $50

If we publish this simultaneously in hardback and paperback, even holding the hardback at the same price, there may be 400 libraries and specialist purchasers who choose to buy the paperback, apart from all the new purchasers who would not have bought a hardback. Let us assume that 100 hardbacks and 100 paperbacks are set aside as frees, and that setting up the paperback entails a further $500 in fixed costs—it could be more.

The options, if we hold the $50 hardback price, are to cost a simultaneous paperback over sales of:

> 1850 at $20
> 2750 at $17.50
> 5500 at $15

if we are to achieve our 60 per cent gross margin. These figures work if we are certain that there is an individual sale of this size, together with libraries who will buy the paperback, and if we are certain that 600 libraries will still buy the hardback edition. If a significant number of those libraries opt for the lower-priced paperback—an increasing trend—we need to sell proportionally more paperback copies.

The difficulties of this model show why many publishers have conventionally preferred to issue a hardback-only edition first, using it to recover all the fixed costs. When the hardback has recovered all its costs and provided the required net margin, a reprint into paperback can be costed. Under this model and costing, with all the fixed costs recovered, a paperback reprint can return a similar gross margin with sales of only 1500 at $15. This is a safer route.

However—again contrary to many authors' expectations—a paperback reissue does not always pay dividends. A book may be, in reality, a specialist book that has found its niche in libraries, with those individuals who must have it buying it in hardback. If there is no significant additional market for a book from individual sales, it does not matter how cheap a paperback edition is: the sale will not be there to justify it. Most publishers can identify books which should never have been reprinted in paperback, academic books whose paperback reissue sold fewer copies than the high-priced hardback original.

We share with authors an enthusiasm to see our books in inexpensive editions, widely bought and widely read. Unfortunately, we are aware that not every book suits this format. We shall hope to make the right decision for each book.   *Yours truly, R.M.D.*

« 58 » *Help with marketing*

Dear Venda,

With your book under way in production, let me reassure you that our attention will soon turn to marketing, and that we shall welcome your input and advice in this. Marketing a book is a partnership. The author must recognize that the publisher has not only professionalism and resources in marketing, but also experience of other comparable titles. These comparisons will show which forms of marketing effort will work—and which will not.

By marketing we mean identifying the real potential readers and users of the book, the best ways to make them aware of the book, giving them enough information to make a decision on ordering or purchasing it, and an easy means of doing so. In academic publishing, marketing is not a matter of hyping a book for unrealistic expectations of general appeal; but if there is a potential general appeal we shall seek to maximize it. Marketing effort is needed for the specialist research monograph, as well as for the book of broad intellectual significance and interest. We must concentrate on publicity, carefully moulded to seize the attention of the potential readership, and sales effort to convert need into fulfilment.

The resources which we publishers put into marketing a book vary, of course, depending on the size of the publisher and the diversity of their list. A small publisher may have one marketing executive to do everything. A large publisher may have specialist staff for a wide range of different functions—media, space advertising, conferences, library information, direct mail, bookshop sales and so on. But more important, a publisher can gauge from previous experience which forms of effort pay off—what kinds of publicity and sales endeavours produce the results required for particular categories of books. And, in turn, the market will respect and recognize a consistent approach from a publisher, valuing the quality and accuracy and relevance of information received.

But you, as author, can guide us in the right direction. You can give us information which will help us make decisions, so that our resources are used in the most productive way. The success of this partnership depends on your realism and our professionalism and enthusiasm. The more accurate, reliable information you can give us, the more we shall trust and use it. Write to us. Many publishers have standard information forms on which they ask their authors to advise on marketing: their questions should be considered and answered conscientiously and carefully.

It will help our marketing and sales people for you to say where you think your book belongs. Identify the level—is it a specialist book, a professional handbook, a student text (at what level), a book for general readers (again, at what level)? Specify the subject area—if it is of interest to more than one discipline, identify the different disciplines with precision. Publishers may send targeted mailings to readers in many different disciplines; what they do not have is a list of "other miscellaneous." The more definite you can be, the better. If you say your book is of interest to marine microbiologists, you are nominating a category to whom we may be able to mail and advertise; if you just say "biologists," we may decide that is too large a category to try and reach by either mailings or space advertising.

Help may also be valuable concerning special regional interest. If your book has identifiable potential markets—even small ones—in different countries, tell us. If there is a particular very local or regional market which might not be adequately reached by our normal marketing routines, that too is useful.

We value your advice on all the real audiences for your book—and your help in reaching them. We may know how to write and design a good advertisement, but when we are deciding where to place such advertisements you will have a better idea of the relative strength of the specialist journals in your field. You can give us your suggestions for review journals, exhibits, media promotion and so on, together with details on book awards in your field.

Some publishers like you to look at a list of journals to which they propose to send review copies. Our list is enclosed: please annotate it with your comments, although the final decision on priorities for review copies has to lie with us. If the list includes any journals which no longer review books, please delete them. Equally, if there are any whose reviews routinely appear years after publication—whether because they delay sending books off for review, have dilatory contributors or just stockpile completed reviews awaiting publication—delete them.

On a more positive note, please add in any new or forthcoming journals which we may have missed, and any journals which may be in specialized areas or not in the mainstream listings we rely on for journal addresses. If you can supply up-to-date addresses for the journals you add, the publisher will be appreciative.

If you have contacts with influential reviewers to whom we might send a book in the hope that they would place a review, let us have your ideas.

We also need your help in supplying some copy about the book—a draft blurb. We shall edit and rewrite this, but your first pointers are useful to us. Yes, I know, constant demands to summarize your work are unwelcome. We kept you to a tight length in writing the book, and asked you to write a short introduction and conclusion to summarize it. Now we want a draft blurb in just a couple of hundred words, which we can edit for the book jacket; and even this will be summarized and revised again for our catalogues, and for the one sentence in which we sum up all your years of writing in a space advertisement.

So for the blurb please think of the points that will draw the attention of your potential readers. Don't try to emulate advertising copywriters (if necessary, we will do that). Give a brief, clearly written account of what the book says, what are some major points of importance and who will find it of interest.

We may want your help and contacts in securing some quotable quotes to use on the book jacket or in advertising. If there are fellow authors and scholars whose names are well known, at least in their field, perhaps we can show them a manuscript or a first proof and invite them to make some quotable comment on it. Your contacts will be invaluable here.

All the information you give us will be considered and used in our marketing plan. You may be disappointed that we do not take up all your ideas. Experience will show us which routes will work and which will not. So please do not be surprised if we do not follow up your suggestion to send a copy of the book to every politician with a supposed interest in science, or if we miss out on an exhibit at a specialist seminar in Guam, or if we fail to advertise in *Time* magazine. I am sure that between us we shall be able to market your book most cost-effectively, and ensure that those for whom it is appropriate will hear about it, acquire enough information to make a purchasing or ordering decision, and be given an easy enough route to acquire the book.

Yours truly, R.M.D.

« 59 » *The book launch*

Dear Prof. Ersnacz,

This response is going to disappoint you, but we are not planning a formal launch for your book. Please don't take this personally. We do just occasionally mark the publication of a book with a celebration, but it is not our normal pattern.

The reasons should, I hope, be clear. We publish a large number of books; and academic and scientific and professional publishers as a group publish tens of thousands of new titles annually. If each new book were accompanied by a ceremonial social event, such festivities would monopolize academic life and dissipate the energies and budgets of the publisher's staff.

We know that for you, as author, the publication of your book is a major landmark. And so it should be. We take its publication equally seriously. But for us, publication means an opportunity to promote and publicize it, market it and achieve real and continuing sales. Unfortunately, among all the marketing ploys competing for attention, the formal launch or informal party rarely achieves a useful marketing advantage. Or, to phrase it differently, the time and effort and money spent on a launch could be used in more productive ways to promote the book.

Books have a particular problem, among the creative arts, in lacking a rite of passage. Theatres have a first night, films have a premiere, art exhibitions have an opening. In academic life, the public lecture and the seminar or conference paper are less dramatic versions of the same kind of "first performance." Even printed magazines have a date when they officially reach the newsstands. But most books sort of slide out into the world. After all the effort of research, writing and production, the publication day of a book is in some ways an anticlimax.

When is a book actually published? The author may relax when the last proofs are returned; the editor may celebrate when the camera-ready copy or film goes off to the printer. For the production department the key date is the delivery of stock into the warehouse, and as author you will see advance copies around that time. But there are dates for sending out review copies, for showing samples round the bookshops, and for shipping orders from the warehouse. The most formal occasion, especially for general trade books, is the official publication date when reviews in the weeklies are hoped for, and when bookshops are supposed to release the book (though too often they ignore this). This publication date may pass without notice.

The yearning for some launch to mark the real "publication" of the book is a natural one. But, to be honest, this is often for the author's benefit rather than for the book's. The author can assemble long-sceptical colleagues and long-suffering family and friends and say: Look, here it is, done and finished. Like courtiers gathering in the queen's bedchamber to witness the birth of an heir to the throne, the crowds of invitees can gather to see the book being "born," transformed from a work-in-progress to a part of the material world.

But the chances are that a modest launch party by private invitation will have no noticeable effect on the success of the book. If some dignitary turns up, that might attract some of the media, but the media might equally question your celebrity guest about some other matter of public interest. In general, media interest in your launch will be modest (perhaps your university newspaper will report it, perhaps not). The likelihood that busy scholars will leave their work to travel to see a book launched is slim. There will be a complimentary speech from someone, you will give a courteous reply, your publisher will say a few words ("This has been a wonderful experience of collaboration," or "We take any major credit card"), and then the crowd dissolves into the traffic after cocktails or coffee.

Yes, I know, you point out that you have been to some excellent launches and assumed it was the normal procedure. Perhaps it is, for some publishers; but for most it will be the exception.

When is a launch worth having? There are of course general trade books by major authors which will get media attention from some heavily publicized event. And some such general books are written by card-carrying academics. But, with respect, I do not think you would categorize your book at this level.

There are also books linked to an individual—a festschrift or a volume dedicated to a particular scholar or a collection of their essays. Such a book is, in itself, the celebration of a life and work, and it is natural to extend the celebration with a social event. But this is more a

person launch than a book launch, and when such an event is appropriate it is more suitably mounted by the honoree's institution or colleagues than by the publisher.

Finally, there are occasions when the specialists in a field are already
gathered together—especially at a major conference. They do not have
to be summoned from all corners for a launch event; they are together
already. A publisher may be exhibiting at the conference, or may be
scouting for new authors. An event to launch a book at the conference
may be a means of announcing the publisher's presence, to establish an
identity or confirm a commitment to publishing in a particular field of
study. Here the book is the excuse for the event; one is almost celebrat-
ing a publisher, not a book. Is there an imminent conference in your
field at which all your peers will be present, and where we might consider mounting an exhibit of many books and also hosting an event to
signal yours?

But we should be flexible in marking the book's publication. Instead
of a complimentary speech and drinks, why not mark it in a more academic way? Could you launch it yourself, with a public lecture on the
theme of the book, which we could use to publicize it? Or should we
explore a seminar on its theme, held as part of a scholarly conference?
We could distribute copies of the proofs to the panelists in advance. Let
us have your ideas. But as for a simple out-of-the-blue launch party,
please accept our apologies, but the answer must be No.

Yours truly, R.M.D.

« 60 » *Getting reviews and publishing reviews*

Dear Prof. Feil,

Sorry to hear you are frustrated over the lack of published reviews of
your book, which we launched last year. After a couple of early newspaper and magazine reviews, the peer assessment in the academic journals—and the resultant publicity and sales—has been very slow in
coming. This is, unfortunately, a common experience.

Be assured that we did send off copies of your book, with price and
publication details, to a range of potential review media (and details,
with the offer of a review copy, to others). Although yours is a scholarly rather than a general trade book, we thought it would generate
some discussion in the more general media, so we sent copies to the
book pages of key daily papers as well as to the more intellectual weeklies and monthlies, and to a couple of influential specialist writers who

review or write for the press. A larger number of review copies were sent to the academic and professional journals in your field and in related disciplines—those on the list we worked out with you, except for a couple you had mentioned which do not, as a matter of policy, publish book reviews.

Details of your book will also have reached the wider group of journals to which we send a catalogue of our forthcoming publications, with an invitation to them to ask for copies of books which they would like to review. We did receive some requests for your book by this route.

All told, then, a large number of copies of your book went out for review. As you say, to date not many reviews have come back. But from experience, we can assure you that this is not a reflection on the scholarly worth of your book; it is, rather, a reflection on the efficiency of your peers who handle these journals.

I know you were encouraged by the initial media response. *Choice* in the USA produced an early, concise and informative review of your book which identified its strengths and its market—just what is needed by librarians and other central book buyers, who are the primary readers of that useful publication. We were pleased that one of the major weekly review sections included your book in a composite survey of three titles on the subject, and that one of the few remaining intellectual monthlies ran a full-length review of it. The review in your local university newspaper and the feature article in the local newspaper were useful, and the specialist radio programme which combined a review with an interview probably reached a large number of people.

For a book by an academic author one can expect only modest coverage in the general media, if any; your rate of success has been quite good. The book review editors of newspapers are protective of their limited space. They have to be very selective in what reviews they commission, and their primary responsibility is not to authors or publishers but to their readers, whose diverse interests must be reflected. The reviews in the general media must be for entertainment and interest more than as a text of record. No matter how strong a newspaper review, it will have vanished into the bin within a few days.

The general literary, intellectual or current affairs magazine has served authors well in the past. But this is an endangered species, and those few that survive—and the even smaller number that are being launched—can give only modest space to books. They often prefer, not unreasonably, to use a new publication as the excuse for an article around the topic. At least your book gets a mention, including price and publisher, even if your work becomes the starting point for a discussion of a general topic. You may find the same happens in the local and international book review magazines—but at least your chance of being covered is greater in a publication devoted entirely to charting the literary and publishing landscape.

Occasionally a scholar's or scientist's book may be taken up by a specialist writer for a newspaper, rather than on the book review pages. We always assume we have to send such a writer their own review copy—their chance of acquiring the book editor's copy is far too slim. But coverage in an article by the science writer, the economics editor or the social welfare correspondent is as welcome publicity as the formal review.

But to be realistic, all this is icing on the cake. By far the majority of reviews will be those by your peers in academic and professional journals. And here are to be found frustrations.

Authors are concerned to see reviews in order to have their work assessed and evaluated. It is therefore, to a large extent, a matter of professional status and, to be blunt, of personal gain to see a positive review of one's work in a major journal. But, to be equally blunt, this is of no interest to the publisher. We know your work is good—otherwise we would not have published it. We want to make the potential readership aware of the book so that they will buy it, or require their library to buy it, or advise their students to buy it. Reviews are, from the publisher's viewpoint, tools of sales and not of evaluation.

Academic books (and general books) have an increasingly intensive selling period. A book makes most of its sales during a period from the time it is announced until, say, six or nine months after publication. After a year it will have been a success or a failure—either it will have established itself as a book with a future (perhaps more sales, a hardback reprint, a paperback edition, textbook adoptions) or it will have finished its useful life in the publisher's inventory, although its useful life on the library shelves may be long and rich.

The published review, to be of value to a publisher's sales, must come within this first year, and preferably within the first six months. The review assessment then links in to the advertisements, mailing pieces and conference exhibitions by which the publisher is promoting the book. It may still be in the academic, specialist and up-market bookshops after a year or more, but perhaps by then it has already been moved to the backlist (though not into the ghetto of special orders or out of the computer catalogue). But the window of opportunity for establishing it has been a very narrow one. Just as bookshops are deciding whether to stock a book right around the time it is published, rather than later, so libraries are increasingly making their decision to acquire a book in the first year of its life. In the second year they have many other books which are competing for the budget.

The publisher's hope—it should be the author's hope too—is that all the potential purchasers of a book are made aware of its availability, and of its price, its subject, its level, its quality and its importance, as early as possible. While advertising can accomplish this to a limited extent, a peer review is far more convincing. Publishers often feel that any review, even a critical review, is welcome coverage: even a bad review at least informs readers that a book is available, suggests that it is worth arguing about, and inspires them to consider making up their own minds or ordering it for the library as a contribution to a debate.

Authors, on the other hand, understandably prefer good reviews. And that leads to the main problem with academic reviews: the academics. For it is they who manage most of the journals, and write and edit the reviews; and it is they who all too often undermine the whole process.

There are exceptions. There are good professional and academic journals which come out frequently and publish reviews promptly. There are journals which come out only in one, two or three issues a year, but which still ensure that their review pages cover new books, with reviews commissioned to tight deadlines and published without delay. But these often seem the exception.

You can, I am sure, easily name journals in your field which routinely publish reviews of books which have already been out for three or more years. Often, such journals also have a backlog of reviews written but waiting to be published. They have a backlog of reviewers who are sitting on review copies of books without delivering their reviews. Or, worse still, the journal has a backlog of books which have not even been sent out for review. Such journals do a disservice to the whole academic community, and it is the authors, not just the publishers, who should be complaining.

These late reviews are damaging in several ways. First, they may be intellectually dishonest, because they review yesterday's work in the light of today's insights. They report as new a title whose impact has already been made or failed—so the review may be wise after the event. They are announcing a book which might even be out of print; if not, the book will no longer be stocked by bookshops or shown at conference exhibits, because it is considered backlist by now. The price will very possibly have been subject to an increase, and the book, if successful as a hardback, may already have been reprinted as a paperback. A late review is of value primarily as an item of historical record; and publishers' priority is the present, not the past.

Because some journals can manage their reviews promptly, those which do not must search for excuses. Perhaps one answer is for a journal cursed with a backlog to make a clean sweep—issue brief notices instead of all the overdue reviews, and start again with a more rigorous schedule. They could firmly establish new procedures for despatching books for review, following up reviewers, and publishing review copy without exception in the next journal issue after receipt.

Review copies can be obtained early—in fact, to help a journal meet its copy date a publisher will almost always be willing to release a pre-publication proof for review on request. A review copy provides a reviewer with a free copy of a book they might otherwise be expected to buy; it is not unreasonable to make a prompt review a condition of this. After all, publishers impose tight deadlines for peer review of manuscripts, and these do not even see the glory of print. If it takes a few days to read and review a book, these few days could be spent next month or nine months hence; why not insist on now? And once a book review is submitted, it should invariably appear in the next journal issue. The space is already allocated for reviews: if it is filled up with reviews of old books, the one-time clean-out strategy should be enough.

The academic is author but is also at times a reviewer; the scholar is a reader of reviews but may also be on the editorial board of a journal. It is in the interest of the whole scientific and scholarly community, and of the health of publishing and writing, for a sharp tightening of review procedures. In this information age, the review pages whose books are not the latest publications should be an object of ridicule.

Yours truly, R.M.D.

« 61 » *Newspapers and magazines*

Dear Rita,

We are as keen as you to see coverage of your book in magazines and newspapers, but we should look at realistic options.

As you know, we shall send out review copies to magazines and newspapers which we think might include a book review, and our catalogues go to the book review editors of a wider range of publications. Since we consider your book as having unusually wide potential, we also plan to send out a press release with the offer of a copy of the book to specialist magazine and newspaper writers in your area. We shall need to give them your contact numbers in case they decide to follow this up. Your suggestions on any magazines we may have missed will be invaluable.

A specialist writer—freelance or staff—may build an interesting feature article around the work of a particular academic author. The book will be the handle, but the article may go on in other directions, related to the theme of your work. We hope the resulting article will at least mention accurately the title of your book and, ideally, give full bibliographical details.

The writer may want to interview you, so we need to keep informed of your whereabouts and movements. Such an interview might be to give the writer background information, or an edited version of the interview itself might even appear in print.

We would urge you to decide, before such an interview, just what main points you wish to emphasize. It will help the feature writer if you are prepared in advance to detail points of interest both in your argument itself and in the background to your research. The interviewer can decide which are important to their particular audience. But do not assume that a journalist—even a specialist journalist—will ask the questions you want to hear or lead the discussion in the directions which seem to you most relevant.

But why not go beyond this passive approach to magazines and newspapers? They depend for their survival on a supply of good copy; why not provide them with some? With your help, we could approach suitable publications to see if they would like to publish edited extracts from your book. We have some ideas but would like your suggestions for what would be good material to extract: something which can be read, understood and found interesting on its own, and which will then lead the reader to acquire the whole book.

In many cases, though, an extract can be unsuitable or difficult to define. Better still, could you write an article or two related to the theme of your book, to be published around the time the book appears? Many magazines take articles from outside contributors. The up-market weekly, monthly and quarterly journals of science or letters welcome well-written pieces by academic authors. If you contribute something to appear when your book is published, that is an advantage to you and us (it publicizes the book) and to the magazine (it gives a timely angle for the appearance of the piece).

It is worth making approaches early to suitable magazines, with an outline of what you would write. There is much to gain from a well-considered article by you, in a magazine of influence read by those who might be interested in your book. For most academic authors it is a more realistic project than generating a staff journalist's interest in writing a feature article, and it is more likely to reflect accurately the emphasis and line of your argument.   *Yours truly, R.M.D.*

« 62 » *Radio and television coverage*

Dear Gloria,

We may be in the age of electronic media, but I suggest we must be realistic about what we can expect in the way of coverage of your book on television and radio. Even if there were a distinguished scholarly author talking about their book on a late-night chat show every night of the year, some tens of thousands of scholarly authors would still never be mentioned on the airwaves.

But let us not be pessimistic. There are scholarly books which can benefit from exposure on radio or television, and can reach or broaden their market by this means. And a good author can use the media to advantage. There may not be much time given to book programmes as such, but there are many other contexts in which a book or an author can be mentioned or an academic can be interviewed about their work.

Sending off books in the same way we do journal review copies is not the answer. There are a few book programmes which may act like magazine book review sections, but they are rare—and overworked. Instead, we shall probably send the media a press release with some key details about you as author and about the book itself. We need to indicate your availability, in case a programme wishes to interview you. Their decision will often be at short notice, so we need to be sure where you will be and when. In fact, if we believe your book may be taken up quickly because of some controversial or current-affairs interest, we must be sure to publish at a time when you can guarantee your availability.

We should hope to have some coverage of you on your university radio station or perhaps on local radio. While the audience may be narrower than your aspirations, the medium is the same—the technique of presenting your argument and defending it. Be aware of who your audience is, and plan your remarks for them.

Perhaps the book will achieve coverage on some specialist programme in public broadcasting. Although the programme may be geared to a particular theme—science or religion or history—the audience will be wider, and perhaps less knowledgeable and less attentive than you are used to in other surroundings. Be tolerant; be communicative; avoid the temptation to lecture.

But you may be that one academic in a thousand whose book attracts general and national attention. At short notice, perhaps, you will find yourself on a national chat show (of course, we cannot promise you that). Such interest may emerge not because of the intrinsic merits of your writing or because of the carefully crafted press release we sent out, but because some other part of the media has already picked up on your work. Media people tend to feed on one another—the best chance for something to be a feature or a news item is that someone else has made it a feature or a news item.

There are many strange experiences to be had in this realm. The media seem to work on short deadlines and foster a sense of urgency. Your book may have been out for six months; you may have finished it eighteen months ago. But a researcher suddenly latches on to it in some connection—perhaps a current issue, perhaps just some new interest or new awareness. They phone—they have to have a copy of the book by courier for two o'clock; can the author be ready for an interview at eight o'clock? The author, who has been happily engaged on other matters for a year and a half, is asked to justify in thirty seconds some statement she cannot remember writing; or he must sum up the argument of the book in one sentence.

It is well worth preparing for the short grabs habitual with the media. You have had ever-increasing difficulty first in reducing your book to 100,000 words for the publisher, then in creating an 8000-word introduction, and finally in getting the draft blurb down to 300 words. Now you must summarize your project in one sentence and defend it in another. There is no time for academic reservations, for weighing the probabilities and limiting the conclusions. It is best to decide on the one-line summary in advance and prepare three things you want to say about the book. Try to say them no matter what question you are asked: study a political interview if you are doubtful about the technique.

We know who you are, you know who you are, and the staff researcher who brought you on to the broadcast programme by now knows who you are. Be prepared for the fact that the producer, other staffers and perhaps the interviewer or programme host have no idea who you are. If it is difficult enough summarizing your book in two sentences, practise summarizing yourself in two sentences. "Associate Professor of Physiology at the University of X" may not be what they are after. May we beg you, just this once, not to be modest? Try and identify some key facts about yourself that will interest the media and their audience—achievements in research, unusual career aspects, or whatever. "A major new discovery in creating safe drinking water, by a former plumber turned college professor"—that kind of thing.

Time is against you; broadcasting is measured in seconds, not minutes or pages. If you identify the key points and deliver those early, you may still have time for subsidiary and additional angles. But if you start with some minor detail, you may never have time to convey the main thrust of your work.

In discussion programmes, be prepared for the adversarial approach that is so beloved of the media. In fact, if your interviewer is not too clear what you are about, they may organize the programme for you to debate with someone who thinks they know what you are about but thinks you are wrong. The debate is for television or radio, not the academic common room or the university seminar, and body language and tone of voice play as big a part in your argument as the carefully chosen words and eminent reasonableness with which you will doubtless greet any hostile questions or remarks.

One other point about broadcast interviews: make sure you mention the title of the book at least once, preferably several times. No one in the audience is recording your words and can recheck this essential information afterwards. And get the programme to announce full information about the book—your name, the title, the publisher and (if it bears repeating) the price—and confirm its availability.

There are other ways of using radio and television to announce and promote your scholarly book. For instance, some authors work with university or other colleagues to prepare a video. But the video that works well for educational purposes, in the classroom, may suddenly seem inadequate when considered by a television company, where production standards are high. Be realistic.

It will be better—though it is rarer—if you can persuade a television producer to make a documentary film about your work. If that happens we should discuss ways in which we can make the most of the opportunity. The screening of such a programme and the publication of the book should coincide. The visual memory is a short one. If a programme on your scientific breakthrough is broadcast too far in advance, your audience may have forgotten about it before publication. But a broadcast too long after publication may find that the book is already perceived by bookshops, libraries and library suppliers as a backlist item.

Radio and television can, in their own particular ways, help promote certain books where the authors are prepared to fit in with their special demands. Let us explore the possibilities. *Yours truly, R.M.D.*

« 63 » *Bookshop sales*

Dear Sally,

With our publicity plans in place, we can look forward to what is, to us, of primary importance—selling your book. Of course, you will be pleased to have it in print; you will be glad to see reviews of it published, and to hear it talked about. But our concern moves on to making sales. Without good sales we cannot continue as a publisher of other books. With good sales you will earn the royalties you certainly merit; and with fortune the book may continue to sell for some years, as the hardback reprints in paperback, a new edition follows the old edition, and the book's growing reputation leads to subsidiary rights, translations and more.

To the general public, books are objects in bookshops and in libraries. The academic community knows that the picture is more complicated. The pattern differs by level of book, by subject and by state and country.

So it is impossible to generalize on the means by which a particular book will sell. But there are some general trends in the sale of scholarly books which apply throughout the English-speaking academic world, and there are as many differences.

For many scholarly books, sales made by a publisher's trade representative to individual bookshops may be a minority of sales for that particular title. General shopping-centre bookshops—both chains and independents—are in business to survive and make a profit. If they have too few titles in stock they will not attract a clientele; but if they have too many titles these may sell slowly, too much cash may be tied up in stock which must be paid for, and the business may collapse.

So in deciding what to stock, any bookshop manager or owner must make a balanced selection based on the perceived needs of their own particular customers. For backlist titles—anything other than new books—the decision is easy. Most booksellers will look at what has sold, and consider reordering it. If a particular novel or dictionary sells regularly, it will remain in stock. If a book sold well initially but now sits for months on the shelf, it will not be reordered. Most bookshops—other than those specializing in remainders and discounted items—will relate backlist orders to sales experience.

This means that, if a bookshop has not chosen to stock a title in the first months of its existence, it may be difficult to persuade them to stock it later. There will be too many new books on offer from publishers and their representatives: they are choosing from these, not from items they overlooked last year.

There may be exceptions. A book may have established itself so successfully elsewhere that the publisher's representative can convince the bookseller of the error of their ways. But such second thoughts are more likely, I suggest, to come from customers' asking for some book that is not in stock.

Commercially, some booksellers find it is more profitable to stock a small number of titles, bought in large quantities with a correspondingly high discount. But for more booksellers the ability to offer their customers a wide range of choice is a source of strength and pride.

These general trends apply beyond the high-street community bookstore. The same decision must be made by academic and professional and specialist bookstores: they cannot stock titles which will not sell or will sell only slowly. A shop specializing in books on indigenous peoples or professional architecture or science monographs faces the same constraints. A good multi-disciplinary academic bookshop near a university campus needs to stock books it knows it will sell, not books for which there is only one potential purchaser on the entire university teaching staff.

The general bookstore may stock only those books from the academy which have succeeded in breaking beyond the confines of scholarly writing. A publisher with a record of quality academic writing which sells will be convincing; a well-known author helps. The jacket or cover design is important. The price to the public and the discount to the bookseller will play an even greater role.

Specialist educational suppliers and college textbook stores also have their own priorities. Their textbook shelves will be influenced not directly by the publisher's representatives but by the teaching staff of the institution.

So do not be surprised, alarmed or despondent if your own academic book is not visible on many bookshop shelves. If it is a textbook it will appear in the text stores in due course. Otherwise, a priority is to ensure that it appears in specialist bookshops, those to which readers in your field will turn. There may not be many such shops which serve your subject, but we shall aim to reach them.

Some such specialist outlets also operate a mail-order business, and the inclusion of your book in their catalogues may be more important than its visibility on their shelves. We shall cooperate with the shops in providing information, and perhaps even mailing pieces, to help them sell your book.

Fortunately, most bookshops will sell items they do not have in stock. A review or an advertisement or word of mouth leads to a potential purchase; the bookshop places a special order which the publisher is happy to fill. Unlike most retail outlets, a bookstore can display only the tip of the iceberg of available material. Behind it lie the hundreds of thousands of titles in print, and a mechanism by which the small local neighbourhood store can get publication details and fulfil a customer's request.

So when your sister complains she cannot find your book in her local bookshop, ask her to order it from them. Who knows? They might be sufficiently impressed to order two, and make it a stock item from now on.   *Yours truly, R.M.D.*

« 64 » *Library sales*

Dear Billy Teak,

The annual sales and royalty statement for your book shows what you describe as a "minimal" sale of your book, and you are clearly alarmed. We, the publishers, ought to be alarmed by poor sales, too; but in fact we feel quite satisfied with the position.

All the advice we took on your manuscript confirmed that it was an important contribution to the field, which would be consulted by students and professionals and would be a valuable work of reference for years to come. The initial published reviews confirm this view of the book's quality.

The content, length and format do, however, clearly mark it out as a specialist work of scholarship. It was never going to be bought by students as a textbook, nor by the general public. Specialists in your field would certainly want to have a copy available, but it is not the kind of book which they are likely to buy for personal use.

It is, then, a model of the kind of book which is going to sell to libraries in universities and research institutions. There are several hundred libraries which collect in this field, and we printed the book in a quantity to match this potential market. Inevitably that led to a fairly steep price, but we do not think the price has deterred the potential audience.

To us the figures show that most of the academic and professional libraries with collections in your field have indeed bought it. We have indications that it is being widely read and referred to; we believe some libraries have it on special reserve for student use, and others have bought more than one copy. You will probably find that certain sections of the book, useful for reference, are photocopied frequently.

Our sales have matched expectations and we are happy. The critical response is good; the book is in constant use. If 800 libraries buy an expensive book, they do so in the expectation that it will be used by a number of readers. If an average of only five people read each copy, you still have more readers than a cheap paperback selling to 3000 individual readers—and that was never an option.

The influence of your book will therefore certainly be well out of proportion to the numbers of sales which you quote. We do not believe the number of purchasing libraries would have been significantly higher if the price had been lower. Nor do we believe individuals would have needed or bought their own copy. In fact, if we had issued a paperback edition instead of a library hardback, we might well have found libraries buying that instead of the hardback—few additional sales, but a drop in our (and your) revenue.

Publishers reach the potential library market by a variety of routes. We cooperate with established library suppliers, and of course some libraries purchase through a regular bookshop. We offer to supply libraries direct, and give them all the information they need in a format they can readily use and evaluate, whether purchasing decisions are made by library staff or on the recommendation of the academics or professionals we serve. The sales are made, by whatever route.

What we cannot combat is libraries' enthusiasm about sharing their resources. Libraries on different campuses of one university, or libraries at several neighbouring universities, or statewide and even broader library networks may share catalogue information and rationalize buying policy, so that fewer copies are actually out on the shelves but these copies are under heavier demand. Publishers who cut the print run to match this pattern must increase the selling price to compensate, so the libraries gain little. But the professionalism of libraries and of publishers' promotion to libraries remains strong; and you may assume that, as your publisher, we are maximizing the potential of your book for as wide an audience as possible, even if that audience is essentially using the resources of a library and not buying personal copies of the work.

Yours truly, R.M.D.

« 65 » *Direct sales*

Dear John Kermell,

As part of the plan for marketing your book we shall be undertaking direct mailings to selected lists. Enclosed you will find the details of your book to check. But we would also be happy to have your suggestions on appropriate mailing lists.

Scholarly publishers devote a lot of time and cash to sending out leaflets and catalogues to academics and professionals on a mailing list. The cost of writing, designing, typesetting and printing such pieces for all our different new books is quite high. The cost of creating or buying mailing lists, packing and mailing out is even higher. It is important, therefore, that both content and destination be carefully planned.

The main purpose of such mailings is to get the right kind of information out to people who will use it to place an order. We are not trying to mislead people into buying unsuitable books. It is better to give full and accurate information to a target audience than to spread extravagant advertising round a large and unselective mailing list.

Essentially, we want to tell people that your book is available; describe its contents and its level; say something about you as author; and give them the price. Readers come to value accurate information over hyperbole, and they are more likely to respond with a decision if they have enough hard information to judge the appropriateness of the book for their needs.

This may lead them to look for it in a bookshop, but for a large number of academic publications this search would be frustrating. They may wait to see it at a conference exhibit. Our hope, however, is that they will be able to take an immediate decision. That decision may be to recommend it for their institution's library, and such orders may come back to us through different routes—not necessarily linked to the particular direct-mail piece. Or a university teacher may consider it a possible textbook for a course, and may request an inspection copy.

We want to make it easy for the recipient to obtain the book. They might order it through a bookshop; but our mailing piece includes an order form to facilitate ordering direct from us. Many publishers will offer discounts to individual purchasers to encourage action (although not in Britain, where the Net Book Agreement ensures that most books are sold at full published price).

To publishers, direct selling of this kind offers a number of advantages. The response to information is a direct sale; the sale is usually made with direct payment, by cash or charge card without the need for credit. Responses to a mailing can be used to guide the next mailing and to build up more selective in-house mailing lists of customers. And the discounts to individual purchasers, if any, will always be less than the discounts to booksellers, who get long credit periods and sometimes have the right to return unsold books.

There are some disadvantages to direct sales. The cost of packing and despatching one or two books to an individual may be high compared to a bulk despatch to a bookshop. The use of direct sale, especially at discount, may discourage some bookshops from holding stock of a title and may therefore somewhat restrict the potential purchaser's opportunity to examine the book before buying.

For any mailing, we have to be aware of cost-effectiveness, so we are looking for lists of people to whom a book or group of books will have real relevance. That is where you might give us some guidance. If your book fits only a specific sub-field we do not want to mail to the much larger academic field as a whole. Equally, if you are writing for a particular target audience we do not want to miss some of them by mailing to a badly selected group.

If there is a professional association in the relevant sub-field, we can probably rent a mailing list from them. We may even ask your help in editing the list to maximize its effectiveness. It will be a great help if the rented list comes with mailing labels (or a computer disk to generate these), saving us the cost of retyping the list.

Alternatively, if there is a core journal, we may arrange to use their subscriber list or even to mail our flier with the journal. That has some disadvantages: the copies which go to libraries will often be discarded, not used for a purchasing decision.

To be realistic, we are unlikely to send anyone a mailing with details of your book alone. We shall probably mail details of a group of books, or mail a subject catalogue or a seasonal new books announcement, to spread the quite substantial printing and despatch costs of a mailing over a number of books. We expect readers interested in your book to be interested in others on our list, too.

Space advertising in a journal may be a better route than a loose insert. At least it will still be seen by those who read the journal in the library, long after the loose inserts have been discarded.

There is one further advantage of a mailing list over all other promotion: its international application. Books are international; so are mail and credit cards. If a publisher in one country has a mailing list that is international, the same books can be offered to readers wherever they may be, with a credit card or charge card number all that is required. To supply readers through bookshops, agents or distributors in thirty countries is a challenge for a small or medium publisher. It is no challenge to bill orders to a credit card company and drop orders into the international mails.

Bookshops, library suppliers and other routes for book supply will remain. But the internationalization of knowledge and of mailing and charging systems suggests that direct mail will play an expanding role in the future of academic publishing.   *Yours truly, R.M.D.*

« 66 » *Prizes*

Dear Winona,

As part of our collaboration to help promote your book, you have advised us on suitable journals for review copies, mailing lists for direct mail, and conferences for exhibits. We also need your advice on appropriate prizes for which we can enter your book.

We would like you to avoid being bashful. There are tens of thousands of books competing for readers' attention. We and you both know your book is outstanding. But your and our enthusiasm is not enough to convince the scholarly community, and reviews are very slow to appear. A prize for the best scholarly publication in one's field is a way of heralding a book's importance, and is invaluable in bringing it to the attention of potential readers, users and buyers. It constitutes a special kind of peer assessment.

This varies among disciplines and countries. Britain is reticent over awards; but the large US academic community has numerous forms of commendation, and for its size Australia is awash with prizes and awards. There is nothing cheap about having an award attached to your book—the larger scholarly publishers can be expected to have a few Nobel prizewinners scattered through their catalogue, so you will be in good company.

We cannot keep tabs on all the awards and prizes in each scientific and scholarly discipline, however, and that is where we need your help. We need details, not just at the time of publication but for two or three years afterwards. Sometimes prizes are for books just published, sometimes for books out in recent years. We shall be quite happy to submit the books in our name, if that is the accepted pattern for a given prize; but if a book must be nominated for the award, we again ask you not to be shy. Suggest to friends and colleagues that they put your book forward—it cannot win if it is not entered. And no one publicizes the unsuccessful candidates; there is no embarrassment if your book is not a winner.

If your work is shortlisted for a prize, we shall have a brief window of opportunity in which to advertise and promote it with vigour. Thereafter, if it is the actual winner, that tag will follow it for some years—perhaps stickered on stock in the warehouse, certainly added to the jacket or cover of a reprint, and featured in advertisements.

We also enter books for awards made by the publishing industry— for production, book design, indexing, even editing.

By helping us market your book you are helping your academic career, helping us sell your book and certainly helping to publish your next book.   *Yours truly, R.M.D.*

« 67 » *Subsidiary rights*

Dear Miss Naughton,

As you noted, the contract for publication of your book included provisions for various subsidiary rights apart from publication in book form. The contract makes clear who holds these rights, who will manage these rights, and how the financial proceeds will be divided.

Commonly it is the publisher who handles these rights, because they have experience and expertise; a publisher often has a separate department to deal with subsidiary rights. If an author has a professional literary agent, that agent may decide to retain certain subsidiary rights which are not prejudicial to the publisher's primary interest—the book itself. It is rare for an author to retain subsidiary rights, unless they have identified and can exploit particular additional uses of a text. If an author has already agreed to a translation or has plans to make a television series based on their work, or if a book is the hard-copy version of an electronic publication, these rights could be retained by the author in the contract—essentially by specifically deleting them from a standard subsidiary rights clause.

We believe that most publishers (or well-established agents) are better placed than authors not only to exploit subsidiary rights, but also to protect those rights. Legal action or the threat of legal action has to be invoked if copyright or publishing rights are infringed. Increasingly, too, there is the question—recognized in law in many countries—of moral rights. This is the right to be identified as the creator of the work, no matter how the legal copyright has been assigned, and it includes the creator's right to have their work presented whole and without manipulation or alteration.

Ideally a contract will cover all known rights. New issues emerge all the time with changing technologies, changing laws and precedents in intellectual property, changing research and educational needs. Some rights are traditional to trade publishing, while others are specific to scholarly communication.

One form of subsidiary rights is when we, the publisher, print and sell a special edition of the book to a third party. This may be an edition for another territory, sold to a publisher who has access to another major potential market for your book. We may run a cheap edition of a textbook or other title for use in the developing world. Such sales may be at a price which includes any royalty, and we shall then pay you at the royalty amount which our contract with you specifies for such sales. Alternatively, the sale may be of books only, and the secondary publisher pays us a royalty on actual sales. This income will be divided with you, again on terms defined in the contract.

We may also produce a book club edition, which provides welcome publicity. Publishers' consensus seems to be in favour of book club editions: they are thought to reach an additional market and enhance the visibility of a book. Indeed, if a scholar's book is taken up by a major book club—in history or science, say—that choice can be used in promoting the main edition. Sales to book clubs may be at a "royalty inclusive" price, which means that all the cash income due to you and to us is received up front; but sometimes they will be royalty-exclusive, and your income will depend on the book club's actual sales.

The most obvious other subsidiary right is the sale of book publishing rights to another imprint. After a scholarly publishing house launches a book and its wider appeal becomes apparent, a general trade publisher may wish to bring out a trade paperback edition. The new publisher will probably offer a royalty on sales, which will be divided between author and initial publisher. There may be advances on royalties, for division either immediately or at the next regular point of royalty payments to you, the author.

Alternatively, we may sell rights, rather than books, to a publisher in another country. They will normally obtain duplicate film of the pages from us, or they may photograph the book itself; in either case the fee for this use of the typesetting and origination comes to the publisher and not the author. But the royalty income which we receive from sales is then shared between author and publisher. Some rights agreements are for a fee rather than a royalty; but Western publishers prefer royalty arrangements, or a fee calculated on the whole projected royalty of an edition. And translation rights are a separate issue altogether.

Though certain other kinds of special edition are rarely exploited for academic books, they still have to be covered in a contract, even if each type is not specifically listed: talking books for the blind, large-print editions, braille editions and so on.

There are various kinds of non-book print rights. We may be able to arrange for an extract from your book in a newspaper or magazine. If so, it can yield significant financial compensation; but that is not very likely for a scholarly book. More often a publisher will see such extracts as good publicity; a modest sum changes hands for the actual extract, but the publicity generates much wider sales and therefore income. Indeed, in scholarly publishing it is not uncommon for an author to run one of the book chapters as an article in a specialist journal, without fee, but with due acknowledgement to the full book. A publisher is likely to give permission for such an arrangement, as cost-free publicity for the book, but is not likely to initiate it.

Quite different is the inclusion of an extract from your book in a "reader," an anthology of chapters from different sources, most often prepared for textbook use. This is a strictly commercial arrangement: we will negotiate an appropriate fee for this use, on terms which ensure the protection of your copyright and moral rights. Publishers are opposed to the free use of permissions in such anthologies: if you receive requests of this kind, you should pass them on to the publisher for handling. But we would be unlikely to refuse a reasonable proposal for anthology use: it will introduce a new group of readers to your book and may lead them to acquire it.

The traditional anthology, produced by a publisher, is giving way in many institutions to the locally produced anthology, perhaps produced within the teaching department itself. The same issues of protecting rights and copyright apply.

Multiple photocopying of your writing is a different matter. There is a race between publishers and users over this. Formal licensing and copyright clearance agencies have helped smooth the path. But the technologies always seem one step ahead of legal and administrative controls. Photocopiers evolve from making single copies to making multiple copies, then to collating and stapling two-sided multiple copies. They may even be used to scan documents to be stored in memory and printed out on demand. The scanned images can be networked to other photocopiers on campus, or to other campuses. As publishers attempt to improve their protection of copyright, the technology to erode this protection also improves.

Nevertheless, we shall make every practical and cost-effective effort to license multiple photocopying for the appropriate fees, and this protection of your rights will also generate some income for you. The legal restraints on individuals' photocopying part of your work are looser, and you would probably not object to individual colleagues and students copying sections of your writing for their private use. Where these copying services are provided commercially, however, subsidiary rights issues are again raised. Document delivery services providing journal articles or book chapters, whether in hard copy or electronically, are subject to negotiated limitation and fees for use.

Electronic means of reproducing your work are in flux, and we cannot be clear what rights we shall need to protect, and be able to sell, in the future. It is a challenge to note the ease with which a manuscript can be scanned into a computer file and distributed across academic networks. We need to collaborate with scholars, both as authors and as users, to deal with the implications of this technology. We expect to license formally all rights which impinge on intellectual property, and to signal this licence with a cash sum. This applies to the use of your material on CD-ROM, or scanned into a text or illustration file of any kind for distribution in an on-line data base. When we specify terms for electronic rights in your contract, we cannot be certain what this clause will have to cover in twenty-five years' time.

Other permissions for use are handled by ourselves: extracts of the text quoted at length in other books or elsewhere in print, reproduction of your illustrations, and so on. What we cannot and do not protect is the reuse of your ideas, your book title, short extracts from your book, or illustrations based on yours but completely redrawn.

It would be good to sell television serial rights to your academic monograph, but I trust you are not expecting this to happen. Just occasionally, though, an academic book may lead to a film or video or television or radio spin-off: these final subsidiary rights therefore need protection and control and so are best included in the contract.

In sum, then, you should find that your publisher is acting to protect all rights in your book. Active exploitation of these rights will take the form mainly of negotiating other book editions (translations, co-editions with other publishers, book club deals) and also of controlling permissions for the use of material selected from your work. A book is more than a package of chapters; it represents a package of intellectual property whose use and protection will continue to expand and vary with changing demands and changing technologies.

Yours truly, R.M.D.

« 68 » *Translations*

Dear Prof. Orlang,

Thanks for sending on the letters from the two overseas scholars who expressed interest in translating your book. You also passed us the name and address of a professional translator you met at a conference, who expressed enthusiasm for your book and wishes to translate it for a local publisher.

Sorry to disappoint you, but most of the time it just does not work like that. It is gratifying that your book, which we published last year to nationwide acclaim, has found an audience internationally. We certainly agree it would find an even larger audience in editions in other languages. But the problem is not to find a translator—it is to find a publisher for a translation.

Translation arrangements are normally made publisher-to-publisher; the foreign-language publisher would then expect to appoint their own translator. We do not ourselves publish in languages other than English, nor do we commission translators for our books. We seek overseas publishers to take foreign-language rights, and it is not our role to suggest what translator they should use.

Perhaps your colleagues could suggest your book to local publishers in their country? It is possible—just possible—that their interest might be followed by an invitation to be responsible for that edition. But in most countries it is unlikely.

We too consider approaches to translate and publish English-language editions of books first issued in another language. Occasionally we are approached by authors, and if we are interested we would follow up by approaching the publisher. More often we are approached by the overseas publisher, and they assume we would select our own translator. When we are approached by a translator who asks, "May I translate this excellent book for you?" our reply has to be, "You do not hold the publishing rights—you have nothing to sell."

The internationalization of scholarship means that ideas and books in most subjects cross national frontiers. But the internationalization of English means that our own editions will sell into markets in many countries where English is not academics' first language. For many academic books in many subjects, the English-language edition will serve international needs very adequately.

There remain, however, a significant number of English-language books by scholarly authors which do sell in foreign-language editions.

The landmark books in an international discipline—whether philosophy or theoretical physics—may attract publishers who can issue an edition in their own language—Spanish, Japanese or whatever. Furthermore, a book with real potential as a textbook may merit translation into many different languages, so that Dutch, German, Bahasa, Portuguese and Arabic editions gradually emerge. And of course many of these editions are published for use in more than one country.

If you, as an author, have existing contacts with a non-English-language publisher, we are keen to pursue these. You may have had an earlier work translated, or have been a commissioned contributor to such a work. Similarly, if you are known in a particular country, that is an additional strength for us in approaching local publishers there. If we can say you have been a visiting professor in Germany, or have long-term research consultancies in Japan, or contribute regularly to the scientific media in Brazil, that will help us advance translation deals. Otherwise we shall be sending details of your book and the offer of a copy to appropriate publishers. We shall see them at book fairs; they may come to see us.

Each publisher will have to compare the books we offer against their own list, market and priorities, just as they would with an unsolicited proposal in their own territory. They will need to assess not only the cost of publication, but the additional costs of translation and the complexities of editing and adapting a work prepared for a different market. Their cut-off point of viability will therefore be different—a book will have to be stronger than a local title for them to decide to take on translation rights. Length affects translation costs directly—a long book is less likely to be translated than a short one, unless it is the definitive textbook in a field or a universal reference work that no one can do without.

So be assured that we are pursuing possible publishers (not translators) to see if foreign-language editions of your book are possible. If there are no bites, do not be despondent. The worldwide use of the English language in scholarly communication means that your book will certainly be used in most countries of the world. Translation would be a bonus, though a welcome bonus.   *Yours truly, R.M.D.*

« 69 » *Getting your book into the developing world*

Dear Donna,

I admire the concern of yourself and your co-authors that your book should reach an audience beyond the rich Western countries, and should serve the needs of readers in a range of poorer developing countries. You believe the contents of your work are particularly important for the Third World; and you have asked us, as your publishers, what we will do to ensure the book reaches these markets, and what you can do to assist in this effort.

As you say, several of your authors, when undertaking visiting lectureships and research trips to developing countries in which they are particularly interested, have expressed concern at the inadequate availability of book and journal material there. They report research institutions and university libraries with cancelled journal subscriptions, out-of-date reference works and minimal access to new books in the field for research workers, teachers or students to use. The libraries have no cash to pay international document delivery services for journal articles. Your colleagues are also distressed about the limited range of books available in local bookstores for students to buy. So you want to try and reach some of this audience with your book.

There is certainly a book hunger—indeed, a book famine—in many of the poorer countries of the world. That extends not just to the so-called Third World, but now to several countries of eastern and central Europe too. The shortage of printed matter is of concern to all, for books are a keynote to education and training, and education is the foundation of real social and political as well as economic development. As world citizens—not just as authors or publishers—we share your concern over the global book hunger.

Unfortunately, no easy solution to this emerges. It would be good to see the movement of knowledge by electronic means if print proved too problematic. If the global electronic revolution were being driven by needs (and not by resources), we might see inexpensive on-line services for research workers worldwide. Underfunded libraries might download print material for student needs, generate inexpensive reproductions of educational materials from an electronic data base, under licence, and see an information and resource explosion by means of new technologies. But, alas, those who are wealthiest in print media also have the best access to the electronic media; those who are poorest in resources for books and journals are also those who can least afford electronic access to resources.

You and your co-authors have one major advantage in wishing to communicate worldwide: your use of the English language. A book in English can, in theory, communicate not just to the 300 million mother-tongue users of English, but to the 300 million for whom it is a second language, and who are often the more educated or educationally ambitious in their societies. Another 100 million are fluent speakers of English as a foreign language, and many more have some level of reading knowledge of English. So you have an advantage over the scholar who writes and publishes in Swedish, or Igbo, or Gujarati. And the most buoyant area of educational publishing worldwide is English Language Teaching materials.

Language may reduce the barriers, but the real world raises them by limiting opportunities for trade, since the movement of books and of copyrights is a movement in traded goods.

You are aware, as authors, that your book says things which readers in developing countries need to hear. But there is some distance between what they need (as you perceive it) and what they want to read. An author may believe he can identify a local "need" for a book on community participation in modernizing rice production. This perception may come from several years' research work in different communities, along with a study of the roles of local and national government there. But what that country may *want* in terms of readers, buyers and markets for books may not be this study at all but an appropriate first-year textbook in marketing, with an emphasis on manufactured goods and the urban sector. The demand rather than the need determines the book market—and in many developing countries the strong demand is for textbooks.

Visitors to developing countries sometimes despair at the relative abundance of cheap, trashy, seemingly irrelevant imported novels rather than educational books. But those books are the ones that encourage literacy, including literacy in English—they make the reading habit a more attractive and accessible, less elitist activity, and the willingness of booksellers to spend sparse foreign-currency allocations on importing mass-market novels is a reinforcement, not a denial, of the power of reading and the hunger for it.

Beyond what a market wants is the question of what a market can afford. This is an even more difficult question, but it is less abstract than that of need. There is a definable market level, in a local currency, at which a book will find a sale—whether as a schoolbook bought by government or the school itself, or as a textbook bought by a college student, or as a general book bought and read for entertainment.

And over and above what the local market can afford in local currency, there is the broader question of what the country can afford in foreign currency. This places severe limits on the provision of imported material, and is the main concern facing authors and publishers in the developed world.

Such international publishers find it extremely difficult to promote their books into many developing countries. It is harder than in their usual markets to physically ship the books to their end destination—distribution remains a major challenge. But this is not so hard as the challenge of actually getting paid for what is delivered. And getting paid in convertible currency, which can be fed back to pay an offshore author and reinvest in new publishing, may prove hardest of all. There are many countries which have moved, in a short period of time, from importing vast quantities of books from overseas publishers to being supplied with none at all.

These issues have led to the discussion of a number of different strategies, but some have unwelcome side effects—as, indeed, do other activities of the aid industry.

In scholarly and scientific books and journals, some of the best schemes have been partnerships between an institution in a developed country and the library of a university or other institution in a developing country. The latter may be provided with a limited number of journals on a continuing basis, or it may request books carefully selected to meet local needs. The end users decide what is required, and the partnership ensures continuity.

More dramatic in cash, but more stressful to all, is the one-off grant from the World Bank or a similar body. A number of countries have had substantial improvements to their university and other library systems from large one-off grants. These allow the importation of a large block of books and journals to prop up an impoverished system: books and journals which would not have been imported by the ordinary routes, and books which would not have been published by local imprints. Such an injection of cash inspires enthusiasm (even greed) from competing local libraries and competing overseas publishers or book suppliers—with, inevitably, the occasional suspicion of impropriety somewhere. Such an exercise, while valuable, is very like famine relief compared with sustainable development strategies. It injects knowledge resources artificially at a point in time, freezing the state of knowledge at the moment of the grant. For journals, especially, it is disruptive, bringing in back numbers but not giving local research workers the security of being brought continuously up to date with their field through current journals. And a dependency outlook must follow from the all-or-nothing approach. But, that being said, no publisher or library is going to decline the offer of World Bank or similar bulk purchases.

Textbook provision has followed different routes. International aid donors have invested cash in textbook development as they have in other forms of development aid. But non-local textbooks have arrived by other means. The Cold War spawned a great industry of cheap textbooks, most sponsored from government sources or sources sympathetic to one side or the other of the global rivalry. Artificially inexpensive books were flooding developing countries from the USA or the Soviet Union, and from other nations too, as part of the propaganda value of exporting knowledge with an image of a way of life. The rationale and the funding for these Cold War exercises have come to an end, though the new Cold Warriors now arriving—evangelical religious groups—have many of the same characteristics.

But there are still commercial pressures to dump textbooks. A Western publisher wishing to offload unsaleable stock (perhaps a now superseded edition of a textbook) cannot reputably do so on the home market. It is too tempting to dump it, at nominal cost, on a developing-world market—the books are removed from the metropolitan markets, an expressed market need is met, some cash changes hands, and the educational system of the recipient country is left still one step (at least, one edition) behind the Western producer.

Such dumping may be formal—offloading the whole stock of the last edition. But there is also the effective dumping practised by a number of textbook publishers over the years. The run-on cost of a few more copies of a text is very low. If a local bookstore with a shaky credit rating will take them, there is some chance that they will pay, even if the chance is small. The cost outlay on these books may be modest, and the income is welcome if it comes; so the exercise takes place for marginal gain.

What is wrong with this, if it fulfils a need? Why should we, as publishers, not offload unsaleable stock at cost, if we can find a market? Why should you, as concerned authors, not be happy to see your books head off into otherwise inaccessible markets by any means possible?

The major reason is that this kind of dumping—whether cynical commerce or well-meaning aid—acts directly to the detriment of the development and the health of a local publishing industry. And it is a direct disincentive to home-grown authors, whether they publish in their own country or overseas, to find their more relevant books driven out of the market by non-relevant dumped stock from overseas sources. In this sense intellectual production is no different from import substitution in other areas, no different from cash-crop strategies. An airlift of grain may help in a single bad harvest, but a nation needs to build its agricultural infrastructure, productivity and distribution—not rely on short-term aid—if it is to survive.

Local authors, publishers, printers, wholesalers and booksellers must be sensitive to the real needs and changes in their markets. They must accommodate to changing syllabuses in schools and changing patterns in popular recreational reading. They need to know what the priorities are for institutional libraries, and how students' use of textbooks is changing. They need to gauge the right balance between permanent and disposable books, between print and non-print; the price levels which are tolerable and the trade-off which users are prepared to face between quality of production and cash price.

How does this impact on writers and publishers from outside the developing world, from the advanced Western nations? It may well mean that an author could decide to publish inside the country of main concern, not outside. But if an author does publish outside the Third World, how to access those countries legitimately?

One option remains the honourable cheap edition. The $50 book is not likely to sell into country X; but if copies can be run on and sold legitimately into the local book trade, on sound commercial principles, at a lower price to meet a real need (visible from a defined market), that can be explored. It is not the same as the aid agency's giving them away, or the publisher's dumping them.

An alternative would be a local reprint. If a book's main Western edition really does pay for itself in the non–Third World market, then a local reprint for one territory may suit all parties. This too must be a straight commercial arrangement, not least to honour the principles of intellectual copyright. If it is not, the exercise is again helping to undermine the local publishing scene. The most productive approach to local development may be the licensing of a local edition to another publisher. Cash must be available to compensate the initial publisher and the author. Such local licences can help an author reach their market; they can help the local publishing industry develop. They can help the "Western" publisher, who can attract authors by showing their willingness to be flexible—and who can reach different markets with different licensing agreements.

Some countries have now legislated for themselves the principle of compulsory licences for textbooks. Under such laws, if an overseas publisher is approached but does not enter into negotiation for a local edition within some specified time, then a legal local edition (with due payment) may be authorized. Most publishers would wish to avoid this. Publishers' other fear is that a cheap local edition or reprint licensed for one territory may migrate into other territories and compete with legitimate editions there.

It is, then, possible to have arrangements which meet the real needs of different markets, honour international agreements on intellectual copyright, maintain the cash flow of publishers in metropolitan countries, and support rather than undermine the development of indigenous publishing.

But in reality this is likely to apply to textbooks, needed by students, more than to academic books, even if you believe students ought to want to read and buy your work. However important a specialist book should be to a developing nation, it is more likely that existing resources will go elsewhere. Given a choice as to how to use their resources, especially their foreign-currency resources, local publishers, wholesalers and booksellers will reflect the commercial realities and prefer textbooks to specialist books, books with a certain market in a defined context to books which have a message to a less well-defined audience or to an audience which is not really a book market. If we publish your book as we plan, it will be for the audience and market that we can reach. Unfortunately, apart from the occasional copy which goes to a Third World university or government library through regular purchase or aid donation, that means you are writing for our local audience and for export to those countries which have enough convertible foreign currency to spend on scholarly work in English.

Yours truly, R.M.D.

« 70 » *Reprints and new editions*

Dear Peter,

I am sorry you have seen so few copies of your book in the bookshops and at conference exhibits recently. You wondered if this shows that it is going out of stock and is in need of a reprint. I wish this were so, but the majority of academic books only ever see one printing, and yours is no exception. After some years of sales and critical success, the book seems to have reached the end of its natural selling life.

This does not mean the book has ceased to be useful. But the libraries which need it have now acquired their copies, perhaps multiple copies if the book is assigned for student reading. The individuals who work in your field have had plenty of opportunity to buy it, or to decide not to. It has not established itself as a core text for a large number of regular courses which are repeated each year, and you would agree with us that the book is not a general read for the trade buyer. We have almost sold out the stock on hand, and we plan to let your book go out of print.

The annual selling pattern now is a few "top-up" copies for libraries, a few sales to individuals and libraries newly acquiring in your field, and the occasional textbook use for small senior-level courses here and there. Unfortunately these numbers are not sufficient to support a normal reprint. If we reprint just the small numbers suggested by this pattern of sale, the cost to us of each book would be very high, it would not be possible to sell them at anything like the current price, and we would price the book out of its small remaining market.

On the other hand, if we reprinted a larger quantity to reduce the unit cost, we would be building up stocks to last us many, many years—stocks which we would probably never sell. This would help to add to the existing pressure on our warehouse. Books which are not selling cost money every year to warehouse, to inventory and to move around as warehouse space is readjusted. Perhaps more important to us as commercial sellers of books, an uneconomic reprint would tie up all the financial gain from your book, and more, in additional stock which would not return the cash to us. We would rather use these financial resources to publish new material, or reprint books with a proven continuing demand. All books reach the end of their useful warehouse life, the point where they have to go out of print, and sometimes do so quite quickly.

There is now an alternative to this decision to put out of print a book which is selling in modest numbers. Publishers have the option, if they wish, to bypass conventional printing and go for a no-frills, low-print-run reprint using xerographic or similar technology. This is reproduced not from printer's film or publisher's camera-ready copy, but direct from copies of the book, from which printing plates are made for each page. These are used to print single pages, which can be bound up into an unsewn volume. The quality of the binding is below that of the conventional library edition; it is unusual to pay for a jacket to be reprinted. The quality of the text remains, in general, very acceptable, but illustrations, and especially photographic illustrations in half-tone, will not retain their quality in the current state of this technique.

The appeal of this technology to publishers varies with the book. Many publishers will in conscience be happy to sell out the latest printing of one title, breathe a contented sigh, and draw a line under it; it has earned its audience and its cash return. Other titles, if low-priced or paperback, may still be too expensive to reprint in this format if the selling price is to be maintained.

These special short-run technologies probably come into their own with the hardback library monograph or specialist title. It is often difficult to get the numbers right for these. The publisher may—often—overestimate the demand from the libraries and specialists for a casebound edition. But they may also underestimate it. If a book is continuing to sell modestly and a "normal" reprint is uneconomic, it may make excellent academic and commercial sense to reprint a small number—50 or 100 or 150—unjacketed, casebound, unsewn, but of high enough quality to fill the remaining demand and keep the book in print. Publishers' views and experience of this approach will vary, but the issue will remain an active one.

When publishers undertake a normal reprint, they routinely strip into the front matter (prelims) a line giving the reprint date. They will usually take the opportunity to make essential corrections to the text. Errors may have been noted in published reviews, or by readers of the book who have advised the publisher or the author. The author should inform the publisher at any time of errors which require correction, and should certainly do so promptly if a reprint is in the air.

Correction is costly at this point—it must be made to film already finalized and stored by printer or publisher. Real errors should be corrected, but minor improvements cannot be accepted. With present technology, it is also sometimes difficult to match the type precisely and make a correction unobtrusively. Typesetters change their equipment and their typesetting systems, and other typesetters may find it difficult to match existing setting because of the great range of setting options which exist.

A book which continues to sell well—especially a book which has a textbook use in course adoptions—will require a new edition from time to time to keep it up to date in content, and attractive in competition with other textbooks in the field. A publisher will discuss with the author the needs, priorities and limitations for such new editions. An author may be tempted to add to the book, while the publisher may think the current length and therefore price are right and may want changes within the existing length. The costs of a full new edition can be substantial: new text needs editing and typesetting, and if the whole book must be typeset and proofread again it will incur much of the cost of a new book. Textbook authors have to realize that the decision on the timing for a new edition may be difficult to take yet, once taken, requires quite urgent action. The old edition must sell out during a given academic year, and the new edition must be released for the next academic year. It is not a feasible option to be a few months late with the revised text.

Authors sometimes propose a new edition themselves, because the book is now out of date in its content: data, ideas, bibliography. But the decision on a new edition is primarily an economic one, and only the publisher can make that judgement. If the sales of a book have fallen off and a simple reprint is uneconomic, the release of a completely new edition may not be enough to revive its flagging fortunes. The author says a new edition is needed because the book's sales are failing; the publisher says a new edition is needed because a book's sales continue to stay high.

For your book, we do not feel a new edition is appropriate, and unfortunately we do not think a reprint is viable. But how about a new book from you—that is something we would really welcome discussing. Call in and let us have a talk!   *Yours truly, R.M.D.*

« 71 » *Keeping in touch*

Dear Greta,

You are right, I am ashamed to say. I looked in our files and it is a couple of years since we were in touch. You saw details of our marketing plan for your book, it was published, and we have not been in contact since. Of course you have had royalties and royalty statements and copies of some reviews we received—but that is all.

That is a common pattern with a publication. After all the excitement of the courtship, the engagement and the wedding ceremony, the publisher-author relationship settles rapidly into the apparent anomie of suburban routine.

Once a book is published and the author has made a contribution to marketing plans and ideas, contact between the author and the publishing house may come to an end except for annual royalty statements. Once the initial thrust of the promotion and marketing of a new book is under way, the publisher's involvement with that book may also drop back to a routine level. Increasingly, the thrust of promotion is around the time of publication and soon after. In the following months and years the book will appear in subject leaflets, will be seen at conferences and exhibits, and may be listed in a "best of the backlist" section of a publisher's catalogues, but it will not receive much additional special attention. Indeed, it may continue to sell well—inspection copies for courses might be sent off, orders filled, requests for review copies met, reviews received and circulated, royalties calculated and paid—without its being central to anyone's consciousness after the flurry of the pre- and post-publication period.

It is worth while keeping in touch. There may be new opportunities to re-promote the book—a different conference, a prize award, some new courses. We welcome information which is supplementary to what you originally gave us for our marketing campaign.

What is understandable, but not particularly welcome to the publisher, is a succession of author complaints. The book was not at X bookshop; this journal never reviewed it; why was it not advertised for the second and third years in a conference programme? If the author believes there has been an error or omission it is best dealt with at publication, when the marketing of the book is in focus, not two years later when the opportunity is lost.

Yet there are other good reasons for author and publisher to keep in touch. An author may pick up some errors—the typesetter's or the author's own—which should be notified to the publisher for use in any reprint. The author may have hard evidence that a new market niche has emerged. Perhaps a paperback of a book initially published in hardback would suit a series of new courses. For some books which sell well and find a real niche, the question of a new edition should be discussed: the author does not want to get a sudden request to prepare a new edition in two months.

Finally, there is the point when a book goes out of print. When that happens you, the author, need to know.

Some authors ask for the publishing rights to be returned to them when a book goes out of print. This is worth some caution. Your original publisher may be planning to leave it out of print for a while with the possibility of revising it. If not, perhaps you can find another publisher who would take it on, in a different format for a different market. Check to see if your publisher would have any objection to that in principle; get them to confirm in writing a willingness to let publishing rights revert to you. But until you have such a new publisher, it is probably best to leave the rights with the original publisher. They can protect the copyright and deal with subsidiary rights; and in reality, permission fees for photocopying and quotation and other subsidiary rights are far more likely for most academic books than a new edition from a second publisher.

So let us keep in touch, and exchange thoughts and notes. Most of all, let us keep in touch about your writing plans and our publishing needs. Once a relationship is forged between an author and a publisher (or publisher's editor), that should lead to further ideas, projects and collaboration. It should be a long-term reflection of the bond that ties together all who are partners in the fascinating world of scholarly publishing.

Yours truly, R.M.D.

≋ ≋ ≋ ≋ ≋ ≋ ≋ ≋ ≋ ≋ ≋ ≋

« 72 » *Research grants—inputs and outputs*

Dear Professor Desmay,

I do wish you and your team had approached us four years ago, when you were preparing your grant application. I realize that scholarship is pure, and the paths followed by research are mysterious. But if, as you suggest, you always had a book in mind, could you not have discussed it with a publisher at an earlier stage? Or even with colleagues who were street-wise about the troubled world of scholarly and scientific publishing?

Your application to a major funding body for a research grant was successful. You were kind enough to show me the text of your original proposal, from which it is clear that you already had plans for how you would write up this work. The three volumes you planned included one lengthy and detailed presentation for the broad scholarly readership, of 250,000 words, together with two volumes of apparatus and data, for specialist use but essential to the understanding of your research results.

It is impressive that you received public funding to such a high level from a granting body, and that your project received renewals of this funding because of the success of your research. There is no doubt that you have contributed to the field, as your note in *Science* shows and the lengthy conference paper delivered in Riga confirms.

I am sure, too, that the funds were very helpful in supporting and encouraging young research workers. Not only were you able to provide a research assistant with a part-time salary, but by funding substitution for your teaching for a period you were able to give another academic some lecturing experience. And, as your acknowledgements show, two secretaries were kept in employment at different times on the manuscript itself.

The irony is that, after all this effort and all this public funding, your manuscript is unpublishable. We do not say that lightly, because we recognize the importance, or the potential importance, of the work you have undertaken. Indeed, we can see a good book and some other forms of publication lurking within your existing draft—it is just a pity that you have completed the writing in such a problematic format. It would take perhaps twelve to eighteen months' more work to write something which could be published. But, as you say, the research grant is finished, the staff are all laid off, and after the long research period you are now committed to three years as head of department with no further time for research and writing above and beyond your teaching, administration, and work on the Academy's committees.

You showed us the very positive comments made on your grant application by the research committee's referees. We do not dissent from their assessment of your reputation, your energy and your imaginative approach to methodology. But they were asked about the quality of the proposed input: your talent, your research design, the infrastructure for completing it. They were not asked to comment on your proposed output: an unpublishable book designed neither for publishers nor for libraries nor for colleagues—unviable and unappealing.

Research Councils, foundations and other grant-giving bodies are the seductive Latin lovers of the academic world, with smart, expensive suits and silver tongues, wooing with the offer of gifts to the favoured ones, gifts that seem to promise the researcher a new lifestyle, perhaps even with cash to spend on a few little luxuries. It is hard not to flirt with these handsome seducers. They shower praise and gifts, and indicate that you are, if not the only one, at least one of the select few. But afterwards, when they are gone and only the scent of aftershave lingers, the pregnancy becomes someone else's problem.

Many scholars do not see their funded project through to full term. But for those who do, the publisher may well be called in at best as midwife, at worst as the reluctant recipient of a large unwanted bundle on the doorstep. How do we make sure that every child sired by moments of Research Council tenderness and sweet nothings will find a place in a loving home?

Most academics would be reluctant to see even more power given to the central bodies of Research Councils. They accept that grants may be less forthcoming to those who failed to produce last time. But they would not want research funding to be limited to those projects whose outcome was totally determined from the start. Research can, after all, lead in unexpected directions, take new paths, have new emphases and uncover unpredictable fields for enquiry; it can also fail to match the researcher's hopes, or fall apart for other reasons. It would be wrong— most scientists and scholars would agree—to make a research grant entirely conditional upon a particular output.

But surely it is not unreasonable for a research design to have an expected or an intended output as well as research questions, methodology and budget? If referees must assess the quality of the researcher, the importance of the topic, the soundness of the methodology and the realism of the budget, could they not also assess the value of the proposed output? Or just be sure that the researcher *has* a proposed output?

Publishers would not suggest this output should always be "a book." They would not want it always to be a book. It might be one or more papers in specialist journals. It might be an archive of manuscript records, or a computerized data bank. It could be a video or an audio output; it could be a multimedia course. The proposed output from a research project could be a technical report, with a specified distribution or even for an institution's internal use; or it could be a full and formally published book. The point is, surely, to have some form of projected output.

Applicants for research grants will commonly have taken advice on the cost elements of their budget and on time lines for their project, and will discuss with colleagues the formulation of research questions and research methodologies. Many will also discuss possible outputs with colleagues, and with publishers or other gatekeepers to the available media for communicating the results of thinking and working in the scholarly environment. But others, clearly, consider everything except the form of the outcome: and so, all too often, a piece of funded research, using cash, time, institutional resources and commitment, leads to a result which does not fit possible media forms or which is limited by some avoidable features of format.

If a research grant application does include a clear concept of the proposed outcome—book, article, tape or whatever—then the creation of this output can be included in the research design. It can be included in the time line—so that writing up the findings falls within the funded research period—and in the cash budget. For print publication, that means funds to create the illustrations to a final and publishable format, to finalize the tables and graphical presentation of these (not just the unmassaged data), and to prepare a typescript or word processor file which a publisher can work with. This may be a basic manuscript with accompanying disk; or it may be camera-ready copy to an agreed design. Certain scientific journals impose page charges, and these may have to be costed into the grant as well. The earlier the options are explored, the more productive the use of time and money.

If these elements are omitted from the budget in the research grant application, the project may well reach the end of its period with neither time, people nor cash available to produce any visible output at all.

It may happen that a research project fails to produce research results at the desired level, and the proposed output is abandoned. The format of the output may well change from original expectations—the book might become three journal articles, the microfilmed archive might become a single deposit, the on-line data base might become a distributed printout. If the funding has allowed for the most ambitious of realistic options, no harm is done by trimming back.

Is this interference in scholarly priorities? Would it be further evidence of the intrusion of the state into academic freedom? Or would it be a reminder of the real-world realities which are at the heart of—not external to—the scholarly and scientific community?

The major funders of research publish lists of their successful grant applications; the browser can add an imaginary sentence at the end of each. In some cases this sentence would say: The research is intended to produce a book 100,000 words long on X, designed for international publication by a reputable scholarly press. In other cases the sentence might well read: In my discipline, research like this often leads to one short but extremely valuable paper in a journal, a stepping stone to knowledge. And occasionally the sentence will read: On the whole, to be honest, and just between you and me, I don't suppose anything tangible will come from all this, though it is a jolly interesting research area and I'll probably give a seminar paper on it somewhere.

But there is a final sentence which is unsaid in some successful applications. This reads: My team and I will work extremely hard through the research grant period and will produce at the end one or more typescript reports which will sum up the results of the work in a format that will prove unpublishable. We will then feel frustrated and disappointed, and will wish we had concentrated more on the intended format and content of our output before our research design was completed and our research grant application was finalized.

So if we say No to your book proposal in the form offered, can we discuss realistic alternatives which you can produce? And next time, can we gently suggest that you plan the outputs along with the inputs?

Yours truly, R.M.D.

« 73 » *Who sets the agenda?*

Dear Dr. Korniston,

Your letter was certainly stylistically refreshing, in its almost messianic tone of denunciation. You have quite built up our self-confidence by your assertion of the power ("strangulating grip," I think you wrote) exercised by publishers and other corporate controllers of the cultural and intellectual life of the nation.

If I can précis parts of your argument, you feel that publishers have a narrow, reified and deeply conservative view of the generation of ideas, bounded especially by the concept of the discipline—the traditional academic field. You feel that we are locked into this suffocating framework, which defines what we consider publishable. We are limited by our concept of the academy, of the subject area, and of the book. In our entrepreneurial role as publishers, limited by economic factors, we subvert the expansion of true knowledge and communication among scholars. I take your point that you are responding not only to the puzzled and negative response which one of my colleagues gave to an idea of yours some time back, but to the similar difficulties faced by a number of your friends and associates.

Ironically, last week I was bearded at a conference by a long-established senior author of ours, who attacked me through the whole coffee break with accusations effectively saying the opposite. Our author accused us of blowing with the wind, or giving over parts of our list to the trendy, temporary and intellectually lightweight. He had noticed new categories in our list, categories which did not represent departments established in his own university. I had to argue that in some cases these were regroupings, or new descriptions, of subject areas with which he was well familiar. But in some cases they were genuine new intellectual developments. He might not like these trends, he might not respect the practitioners in these new subject areas, but they were established, producing good research work and writing which found an audience, and attracting student numbers. I do not think we convinced him that we are not slaves to fashion. Ironically, when we published his own pioneering first book twenty-five years ago, the reviews then accused him and us of lightweight neophiliac and superficial tendencies. Now it is the cornerstone of his field.

Individual commissioning editors will, inevitably, have personal fads, enthusiasms and interests, which will influence what books and subjects they run with and what they leave to one side. Collectively, a publishing imprint tries to balance the innovative with the tried and tested. A good publisher will have work that sits safely and solidly in the established framework of discourse, but will also be proactive and reflect new trends. These might be new lines of enquiry or discourse within a field; they may be reassessments or new ways of packaging a field; they may be newly emerging fields. A judgement must be made about which new trends have staying power, meriting a book or a series or a programme, and which new trends will be forgotten or mocked by next year.

The publisher whose list stays only with the tried and tested will keep a loyal but diminishing readership, and in time will fade completely. The publisher whose publishing programme tackles only the latest fads will have equal difficulty in achieving stability and survival, although they may have more fun while going under. Ideally, we strive for a balance.

To some extent this regulates itself. In traditional areas of enquiry and teaching, we have a healthy backlist, some regular authors, and the continuing publication of new projects in some established series. With regular watering and occasional weeding this part of our garden will stay fertile. But for future growth we should also be digging new flower-beds—here we need to be more active and more thoughtful.

This does not mean we can throw money, time and resources at every self-declared trend. We should probably be progressing in measured steps towards new paradigms, splinter fields, adjacent academic areas of merger and schism. We are not going to be taken too seriously if we publish only in radioastronomy and semiotics, or if we suddenly graft gender studies onto a list in medical science.

We may enter new fields cautiously: raise a flag, wave it and see what the response is. Whatever we publish, there will be some who praise and some who condemn. The best yardstick may still prove to be sales.

If we publish in a new area, we need the reassurance of selling what we publish. Similarly, if we continue to publish in an area long established on our list, sales of books give us some objective evidence that that area continues to have a market. If a subject area is on the rise, sales in that area should increase year by year; if it is fading, we will see the reverse.

New subject areas and new approaches also force us to confront our own limitations. We are publishers of certain types of material; we create particular artefacts—the book, the journal, perhaps also microforms or electronic media. We are what we are. Not every new academic field sees the book as of primary importance. To some, the immediate exchange of information by electronic mail is central. To others, regular workshops and conferences are defining the field and are seen as adequate forms of communication, superseding the formal and slower business of book and journal publication. Still other fields, established or emerging in the universities, have the core of their existence in practice—in action—not in print.

As publishers we are here not to document or reflect every field but to contribute products. For most of us, that means primarily printed works—in those contexts where they can serve a real and continuing need.

Perhaps, in response to your complaints, we should ask if there really is a need and a market for the kind of product we might create in a new field, or whether some of your colleagues might see the book as itself a symbol of just the kind of narrowness they are trying to erode.

And what of our distinguished author who harangued me last week? We can assure him that we shall continue to reprint and sell the existing books in his field as long as there is a demand for them. We shall publish new work of importance in that field on the same basis. But this will not inhibit our moving, expanding into new areas of academic life in our publishing, subject to the criteria outlined above. Publishing must be innovative. The agenda is largely set by the academic community itself; a good publisher is guided by that agenda, testing it against measurable standards of what is feasible; and the publisher who does not adapt to changing academic interests is quickly replaced by the publisher who does.   *Yours truly, R.M.D.*

« 74 » *Books and the appointments committee*

Dear Dean Ng,

We do, of course, know Dr. Optimus, to whom you refer in your confidential letter. As you say, he has a manuscript with us, which we are considering for publication in our academic publishing programme. We had seen an earlier draft of his proposal, which we thought looked promising and could fit the list we are developing. We were pleased to receive his manuscript so that we could make our final publishing decision.

In your letter you make, in formal terms, a disturbing and—to be frank—unwelcome request. You note that Dr. Optimus's current temporary appointment comes up for review shortly and that he will be under consideration at a meeting in two weeks' time for a permanent and tenured position. The weight given to his publications record in this meeting will, you suggest, be a major or even determining factor in the appointment. So you are asking us to report on our position and ask if we are likely to make a firm decision within two weeks.

In fact, we knew of this already. Your polite letter suggested that the information we could provide in confidence would be helpful to your committee in allowing them to evaluate . . . etc., etc. Dr. Optimus was blunter. He rang us last week, in some panic, to say that his review meeting had been brought forward, his job was on the line, and a decision on his book manuscript now was essential to save him.

Not surprisingly, publishers object to this kind of pressure. It comes quite often; we think it unfair on all parties. And it does not get any better higher up the academic ladder. Decisions on appointment, tenure and promotion all seem to put undue weight on the judgements publishers make, and publishers come under great pressure quite distinct from the normal commercial demands of the literary marketplace.

Of course, universities and colleges use certain criteria in assessing candidates for appointment and for promotion. Research capabilities and productivity are, inevitably, among these criteria; discussions will long continue about the weight given to research publications as against other measures of academic achievement.

Academics undertake research as part of their career goals, their job descriptions and their inclinations. As we all know, in some fields research may lead to one major technical paper every couple of years; in other fields a monograph and many articles each year or two are not unusual. Individuals vary in style—some scholars prefer to work away on the single major monograph for many years, to make a lasting contribution to their field, while others in the same field may turn out a continuous flow of short articles, often with overlap, across the range of outlets from conference proceedings and informally published so-called grey literature to semi-popular and scholarly journals.

It is up to the academic community to evolve valid means of assessing unlike against unlike in scholarly output. But, undeniably, The Book has taken on a leading role in the process. We all hear phrases like "You have got to have a book to get tenure" or "For promotion your books are what count."

This puts the publisher in an unwelcome position of power and responsibility. For the publisher—even the scientific, professional or academic publisher—is not seeking to follow the same criteria as the academic committee. We realize that an outstanding scholarly book published by an outstanding scholarly imprint may be a feather in an author's cap. But the publisher's decision on a book proposal rests on different criteria from the purely academic.

A publisher ought to take on a book because it has a potential market: because it will sell, and help the publisher to remain in business. So an adequate but not brilliant book in a large subject may well be published in preference to an outstanding book in a small subject. Related to this, a publisher will take books in particular subject areas where they are active. Subjects with fewer active publishers may find it more difficult to secure publication—and in such areas, where publishers have less competition, it is possible that the decision to publish may be taken on a slightly different basis.

The rules of the marketplace apply to all publishers. Even those who are in receipt of university subsidies, or who are effectively a department of a government body, have to decide their priorities in allocating their resources. So, in essence, even the most academic of academic publishers is taking an essentially commercial decision and not an academic decision alone. "Merit" is not enough for acceptance. To be published, a book needs to be in a subject area, on a level, and for territories in which the publisher is active and knowledgeable. It needs to have a market.

It must also reach criteria of length, scope, style and presentation which are not, in themselves, related directly to the academic worth of a manuscript. Occasionally this will mean that a publisher takes on something saleable which does not have all the hallmarks of academic brilliance. More often, it means that an academic or scientific or professional publisher will turn down a manuscript which does have all the signs of academic qualities, but which cannot be published for a range of practical, financial and commercial reasons.

So how does that affect your committee, meeting to consider the fate of our potential author? It certainly does not mean that if we say No to this book we are making a judgement on the quality of the work that should influence your appointments committee.

If we turn it down, we shall not give you our reasons, which are confidential. We may give the author our reasons; at least we will give the author *some* of our reasons. If there are helpful, constructive reports from our readers, about problems in the book which could be put right with further effort, we shall discuss those with the author. But those are confidential to ourselves, our advisers and the author. We are unlikely to tell your committee whether we said No because a manuscript was sheer drivel or because it was so brilliantly ahead of its time that we feared the subject would take ten years to reach the point where the book was saleable.

If we do accept the book for publication, and our author is then given an appointment or promotion, we should probably feel pride that our author is also recognized by the academic community. We like to feel we are picking winners, identifying rising scholars of merit, and choosing books whose importance will be widely appreciated. But, equally, a publisher is unlikely to confess to those rare occasions when they take on what they secretly think is a junk book in a junk subject—but at least a growth junk subject, which might bring in some cash at a hard-pressed stage in the recession.

As for timing, we do understand the author's anxiety for a quick decision. We do not resent the (occasional) reminder from an author that a decision is still awaited, and an enquiry about the progress of a review. In general, a book that is of no interest will get its (negative) decision quite quickly. A decision on a book that has potential may take longer. The publisher needs to be convinced of the merits of the book, commonly by peer review, and of its saleable qualities. We usually have to go through various internal consultations and procedures before an editor's enthusiasm can be turned into a contract, which implies a substantial forward commitment of our time, money and personnel in production, marketing and warehousing. Good publishers who survive are those who take the right decisions; they do not tarry to take the right decisions, or rush and take the wrong decisions. The peer review may be the longest part of this process; some members of that same academic promotions committee (or even our author!) who are pressing for a quick decision on one book may also be serving as reviewers and delaying a decision on another book from another publisher.

Finally, we should I suppose feel honoured by your reference to the weight you give to "the serious academic work" which might come from "a distinguished publisher of scholarly reputation." But, curiously, I do not feel that way. First, a book is a book. Its merits do not relate directly to the merits, apparent or real, of its publisher. For good reasons, an author may go to (or be approached by) a promising small, local, specialized or unknown press; an author may have good reasons for choosing between a local and a distant publisher, or between publishers of one genre or another. No false snob appeal about the name of the publisher should be attached to a book, nor should it be automatically assumed, in assessing an academic's output, that the name or type of publisher is what really matters. Not least, that puts even more unrealistic pressure on the publishers whose name is believed to mean more than just a publishing decision.

Worse, though, is the notion that a narrow academic monograph must, necessarily, count for more than a book of wider appeal. What do universities and promotion committees have against books that sell? Where does the idea originate that there is an inverse correlation between appeal and value? The well-conceived textbook that influences a generation of students may draw wide respect for the work and approach of a university department, and do as much to put the department on the map as its members' production of specialist scholarly monographs for their peers. The book written to reach an audience across all disciplines, and appearing with a publisher's slightly too vulgar promotion, may have all the merit of an academic book—or more. If there remains a prejudice in assessing scholars' worth by the type and level of their writing, is it not time for this to go?

So even if we do make our publishing decision before your meeting, we dislike the implications of your letter and the moral pressure it puts on us. We must have the freedom to make decisions on what we shall and shall not publish on our own criteria. It is unpleasant enough when we have to say a final No to a manuscript in which we have shown interest. We do not want the additional knowledge that we have put a blot on an academic's career. But publishers' editors also feel unnerved when they learn that their decision to add a particular book to their programme has been the catalyst in gaining some senior academic a step up the career ladder. They may be pleased for their author, but they do not believe that the formality of a publisher's commercial decision should exert a disproportionate influence on a scholar's career path. We would like the academic community to remember that the criteria for academic excellence and the criteria for publishing decisions cannot be identical.

And we would like authors to remember it, too. We like to know why an author has written a book. If it is to communicate with an audience, great. If it is to contribute to a field of study, fine. If it is written to make a significant contribution to a field of knowledge, well, we can explore that further. But if it has been written as a dully dutiful step, a necessary requirement in an academic career, then it will probably read like that, and we really won't have much common ground.

Yours truly, R.M.D.

« 75 » *Subsidies*

Dear Prof. Urkasz,

After you heard of our decision not to offer publication of your book, because we felt it was on too specialized a topic, you advised us of the possibility of a subsidy to help publish it. The contribution from your university is—as you note—modest, but in this financially pressed academic world it is still generous, and it does show support for your work.

The possibility of some more substantial institutional underwriting is even more significant, though it is not surprising that the institution wants a publisher's commitment before it considers funding the project. It also wants a statement on how the money will be used, and a commitment on several items, including price, print run, royalty and format.

We have thought hard about the invitation to publish this book with a subsidy but, in the end, have taken the decision not to proceed on that basis. I know you will consider this disappointing; you may also consider it surprising, since we have occasionally accepted subsidies for books, and may do so in the future.

Subsidy publishing is a sensitive area, and one about which there is no consensus shared by all publishers, and no view shared by all universities. And a variety of meanings are subsumed under the phrase "publishing subsidy."

At one extreme are the institutions which are freed from the normal constraints of the market by a subsidy applied to the whole publishing programme. This is true of some university presses, notably in North America, and especially the small ones. The bigger ones have reached a stage where they can stand alone: in general, the bigger the press, the smaller the subsidy. There is an argument that university presses should, in most cases, receive some form of subsidy from their host universities, to free them from the special problems associated with scholarly publishing. (Of course, that argument is less strong if their publishing is less scholarly!) If not a cash grant, then indirect subsidy such as the use of campus buildings free or at reduced cost, or the availability of finance at low rates of interest, would seem to many academics a reasonable use of university funds.

Other publicly funded institutions also frequently have subsidized publishing programmes. If this makes publications of importance available to the public at prices that would otherwise be prohibitive, most of us would regard this as funds well spent. If it results in the employment of three people where commercial or university publishers have to make do with one, we can only wish them good luck and hope that the auditors and cost-cutters do not find out too soon. To be sure, if government departments bring out material identical to that of the commercial publishers, but with taxpayers' funds undercutting the market price, there will be a much livelier debate. But most would agree that there are meritorious publications through publicly funded institutions which would not appear at all through commercial and self-funding imprints.

At the other extreme of subsidy, there is the author who offers to underwrite his or her own book with personal funds. Scholarly imprints usually avoid such arrangements. This sails too close for comfort to the "vanity publishing" that authors are warned against—where a packaging house produces a small number of printed copies at a writer's expense and pretends to have "published" them by holding them in the warehouse for a while.

Yet between these extremes other forms of subsidy arise. It is common enough for an author to help pay for the publication of a paper in a scientific journal; but for any respectable journal this follows full peer evaluation of the quality of the paper. The cost of helping to finance publication will have been a modest amount compared with the cost of the research project itself.

The same principle can be extended to the publication of complex technical material. A book with an unusual number of complicated tables, a monograph in (say) geology or archaeology which must include graphic data and illustrations, or a multilingual (and multi-font) dic-

tionary may be impossible to cost as a "normal" book if the publisher
has to pay for this specialist level of typesetting. But if the subsidy is to
restore such a book to a more normal level of costs and price, it may be
easier to apply the subsidy directly to pay for specialized typesetting—
whether it is done within the author's institution or by a typesetter
appointed by the publisher—produced as camera-ready copy. There
can then be no disagreement on how the subsidy has been applied.

If a book requires colour plates or fold-out charts, or has other extra-
ordinary production costs, a subsidy could also be allocated to pay for
these without misunderstanding or suspicion of irregularity.

Sometimes the same argument applies to an unusually long book—
that a subsidy will allow a more "normal" pricing. But in such a case
we might ask whether the extreme length is appropriate, or only self-
indulgent. The definitive grammar of a vanishing language may merit
500 pages and may need a subsidy to be publishable at a reasonable
cost and price. But is that historical monograph, or that literary reas-
sessment, really worth a subsidy to allow its 500 pages to be published
uncut? Does that readership really want an abnormal book at a normal
price? Or would they prefer a book of a more appropriate length, less
taxing on their time and attention? It would be better to subsidize the
author to spend time abridging the book!

But finally we have the book of reasonable length, and of no great
technical complexity, which the publisher might decide to decline because the market is insufficient, or because the scholarship is worthy
but not sufficiently exciting to attract a readership. Such books may
come with the offer of a subsidy from the author's institution, or from
a supporting donor. Why does the honest publisher not snap them up
and publish at less risk, or none?

The basic reason is that you can subsidize a book, but you can't really
bribe an audience. Publishers should be using their time and resources,
their name and reputation, to publish books of worth to readers as well
as of value to the author. In many subject areas, if a book does not have
a real or adequate market, injecting a few thousand dollars into its budget, and so dropping its cover price by a few dollars, is not going to
generate a readership which does not exist. If no one wants to read
your book, a bribe to the publisher may look all very fine, but when
translated into a bribe to the public it too often seems pointless.

There is a good alternative. Publishers will often suggest not a cash
subsidy, but a guaranteed purchase of so many copies. The sponsoring
institution will often have access to an audience which is not that of the
normal book trade—staff members, customers (for a company history), official bodies associated with an organization, overseas recipi-
ents. Having a large part of the print run pre-sold allows the "normal"

publishing ratios to operate on the rest, and signals the donor's gener-
osity far more effectively than an acknowledgement on page iv of the
front matter.

The other obstacle to subsidy publishing lies with misconceptions,
perceptions which are not shared. Publishers consider themselves the
best judges of print runs, prices, format and design. They have plenty
of data for comparison, in the performance of other titles. If they get
these judgements wrong too often, they will go out of business (or the
publishing trade papers quietly announce that their senior staff are
leaving to establish a consultancy), so the question will no longer arise.

A publisher may see the offer of a subsidy as a way of publishing,
under a normal combination of format, price and print run, a book
which could not otherwise be published at all. The body granting a
subsidy (or the author obtaining a subsidy) may see it quite differently:
as giving them the right to insist on a low price, or a large print run, or
a paperback edition, or a full-colour cover. This is intruding on the
commercial judgement of the publisher, and it opens the door to dis-
agreements and arguments. And sometimes a subsidy is tied to a particularly high royalty rate, so that the apparent publishing subsidy is,
in fact, a subsidy to the author and not to the publication at all.

Some subsidizing bodies raise difficulties by requiring a publisher to
make a formal commitment on price, print run and other details when
applying for a grant, all very long before the date when these have to
be faced in reality. Other institutions, defending the public purse they
control, invite publishers to "tender" for a subsidized work and are—
or perhaps are not—disappointed when the mainstream publishing
houses stay clear and the funds go to an unknown firm willing to make
some acceptable promises. So for all these reasons, publishers are cautious about accepting the offer of a subsidy.

Now, this may all sound very pious. If we say No to your book,
despite the generous offer of a subsidy, you should just vent your feel-
ings and then try elsewhere. In due course you will quite possibly find
a suitable publisher. They may even do what you hoped and expected
would be the results of your subsidy. But there remain publishers who
will always ask of any book: Is there an audience, a market? Who is the
book for? In much of the humanities and social sciences, a book which
cannot survive on its own may not merit underwriting, but may better
reach its audience in another form (in-house publication? journal articles?). Pre-purchase for a special audience the publisher cannot reach is
much more acceptable.

If the book has special costs in origination—technical typesetting,
colour art, lengthy appendices of essential data—and the subsidy can
clearly be applied to these to make the book more normally costed,

then the subsidy may be much more welcome. But the author, the publisher and the provider of the subsidy must all agree that they are turning a problematic publication into a normal one, that abnormal costs are being covered in an abnormal way, and that this does not immediately nullify the other variables of normal publishing strategy. In the end, it is the punters who decide—the purchasers, whether they are individual professionals, or a special interest group, or the acquisitions librarians of international academic and scientific libraries.

Yours truly, R.M.D.

« 76 » *Book exhibits and the academic conference*

Dear Conference Committee,

Conference organizers know that an exhibit of books or other professional tools is a familiar feature of the annual disciplinary conference. But the analytical skills that are central to the discipline do not always extend to analysing the role, nature and social behaviour related to the book exhibit.

You were kind enough to consult us and other publishers in advance about the exhibit for your forthcoming conference. It sounds an important conference, in a large and important subject. You expect a good number of people to attend, and we would like to join with you in making the exhibit a part of the conference. If we can avoid the common—the usual—mistakes, we should both benefit from it.

Most academics think they know what the annual conference is for. It is the one and only opportunity each year to achieve a whole range of professional goals. Those academics may be separated in far distant cities, and cannot drop in on each other's departments and seminars. The annual conference gives the opportunity to present a formal paper on current research and ideas. It is a chance to catch up on colleagues' research and ideas, perhaps to plan a stage of a collaborative research programme, or at the very least agree on an exchange of data and informal reports. It is also an opportunity for job candidates and employers to meet. The social side of the conference has to be the main purpose or the main memory for many—again, the annual meeting overcomes the tyranny of distance and the mobility of academic careers.

And then there is the book exhibit.

Street-wise academics plan to spend a significant time at the conference book exhibit, and they do this not just to escape from boring papers or hide from colleagues they wish to avoid. They attend the book exhibit (usually several times during the conference) for three specific and planned purposes.

First, it is the one annual opportunity to look at the new publications in the field, to make a selection, and to purchase them at a discount. Academics realize there is minimal chance of finding a good range of books in one's specialist field in any local bookshop. Unless all purchases are to be taken on trust from publishers' catalogues, or delayed until the academic reviews come out, a conference exhibit should provide the best if not the only opportunity to examine and buy the year's publications. It suits both publishers and readers to place cash or credit card orders at specially discounted conference prices, prices which disappear after the conference ends. So the academic arrives at the book exhibit with a credit card and a list of some titles to look at alongside the unknown new books. The publisher arrives with a checklist of discounted prices, a good exhibit of new and recent books, and a credit card machine.

Second, the conference exhibit is the best opportunity to select possible textbooks for next year's course. So the seasoned conference-goer arrives at the annual meeting with a note of the courses they will be teaching next year and a list of the textbooks currently in use (if it is not a new course), and checks at each exhibitor's booth what new textbooks are available or forthcoming. The publisher arrives with a well-briefed sales representative, an information sheet to give away on each textbook title, and a form for the academic to complete requesting early despatch of an inspection copy of the textbook.

Third, the determined academic arrives at the annual conference with a book proposal—maybe two. For the street-smart, this will be in the required format—two or at most three pages of description of topic, subject area, level, market, timetable for completion, and competition; and a two- or three-page structural outline with word count. A one-page summary of all this may also be useful, as a lead-in. An enthusiastic author may have arranged in advance a meeting with the publisher's editor. If not, the one page can act as a lead-in to secure an appointment. The street-wise conference-goer may check the conference exhibits for publishers who look likely to consider the book, and either leave an outline with sales staff to pass on to the editorial department, or arrange a meeting if the editor is attending the exhibit in person—a meeting which might never happen if it had to be fitted into office hours.

The unwelcome strategy pursued by less experienced authors is to bring the whole manuscript in a single copy to the conference and describe it in great detail to one sales representative after another at every exhibit booth. If a publisher is attracted by an outline, a useful conversation can take place; if the publisher wants to see the manuscript, it can be mailed later. However enthusiastic, they may not want to carry it home from the conference with the luggage.

How does this affect the conference organizing committee? Professional attitudes at a book exhibit are to the advantage of academic readers, academic teachers, academic writers and publishers alike. But things do not always work so smoothly—and one reason for that is the failure of conference organizers to plan the exhibits wisely and efficiently.

The first misjudgement is lack of information. The conference committee may have only one conference to organize, but publishers have to choose from many. Early and adequate information on place, dates, size and costs is important to secure proper publisher representation.

A second problem is location within the conference. For a small conference it is valuable to ensure that registration—late as well as early— and all tea and coffee breaks are held in the book exhibit room. Because time is crucial to a successful conference, it will not be worth while for book publishers, booksellers and other product exhibitors to attend the conference unless the delegates are brought to their location at every available opportunity between lectures—the registration and the tea and coffee breaks are the minimum. There is a break-even point in conference size—probably a four-figure registration—which makes it viable to locate the book exhibit in a separate room.

Some phrases from organizers of small conferences that are sure to keep publishers away are:

"Your books will be quite safe; we are putting you in a room off the library."

"We will tell everyone at the first session where they can find you."

"For security you'll have to pack up every night during the last lecture."

"You are welcome to move the books over to the other building on Thursday and Friday for the plenary session."

The book exhibit has to be set up in a space which is secure for overnight storage, so the conference organizers must plan to have their registration and tea and coffee in such a room.

On the positive side, a conference can impose a charge on exhibitors—at the very least, the equivalent of an additional conference registration fee, and perhaps more. But the charge has to be reasonable. The publisher must pay a considerable cost to ship and staff a conference exhibit; direct or indirect sales, or the value of manuscript acquisitions, have to exceed this cost if the conference is to work. A small additional charge to exhibitors is fine if the location meets the requirements noted above. If the conference organizers decide to make no charge, they may attract enough exhibits, especially from informal and institutional imprints, to make the whole event a positive and major part of the conference, to the advantage of all participants.

But sometimes, alas, balance goes out the window. Some academic conferences have been placed in the hands of conference organizing companies, who are experienced in the professional-level whizz-bang meeting and who propose exhibit fees accordingly. Where fees are set to suit, say, the suppliers of hospital equipment or engineering hardware, few if any publishers are likely to consider the return worth their while. There have been major academic conferences where exhibitors' fees have been so inflated that book publishers have kept their distance, to the complaints of the delegates and authors alike.

Publishers can help conference organizers by contributing to a conference in other ways. Perhaps the publisher, as a promotional move, will give support towards bringing one of their authors to the conference as a distinguished guest speaker. And if there is to be a cocktail party early in the conference, the organizers should certainly ask if a publisher would like to turn it into a launch party for an appropriate book or series of theirs—and subsidize the cost of the affair. Academic publishers are—rightly—sceptical about the value of the book launch out of context, but a conference is a good place to present a new project to its intended audience. And if the conference wants further support from publishers, why not ask the leading publisher in the field (or, better still, their nearest rival) to supply the conference holdalls?

At the end of the day, all the lessons learned from a conference, both its successes and its failures, add to the collective knowledge of the conference organizing committee. And what do we do then? Typically, we appoint a brand-new committee with all new members to organize the next one, so they can make the same mistakes and learn the same lessons all over again.

Announcing the conference to publishers will have been rather an afterthought, and there are sure to be a series of misunderstandings about the cost. The book exhibit will be in a room down the hall and off the library, and for security it will be locked up before the end of the day's programme. Half the conference will be in another building altogether. The publishers' information sheets will be requested late, or left lying out on a table instead of being inserted in the delegates' folders. And the next year's committee will be mystified as to why the publishers refuse ever to attend again.

Good luck with this year's annual conference. See you there?

Yours truly, R.M.D.

« 77 » *Anthologies*

Dear Dr. Dunnin,

I am sorry the sales of your textbook have fallen off rather suddenly on this year's royalty account. After your three years' work in writing the book, including the period of leave you took from teaching, this must be very frustrating. It is not because students no longer find your arguments interesting, I am sure. The price of the book is close to the average for your field. And I don't think it is because academic staff no longer recommend your work.

But you already know one major reason for the decline, since you came in last term to show me the two "student readers" you had bought on other university campuses. I blame myself: I persuaded you that your book would be strengthened if you added one chapter summarizing the main argument of the book systematically. I suspected that some lecturers who did not want to adopt the whole book for their course might set that chapter only. What I had not anticipated was that their departments would—illegally—reproduce that one chapter in home-made readers to sell to their students.

So I can quite understand the surprise you felt when you picked up the two bound and stapled course "anthologies" on your travels and found the whole of your summary chapter reproduced. If I remember right, you were very angry on the telephone, and asked why we had given permission to have the eyes picked out of your book. We assured you we had not been asked for such permission, nor would we have given it.

I think you may be wrong in accusing your colleagues in other universities of a plot; instead, I suspect there is a basic misunderstanding. It is legal for an individual to make a single copy, for their own use, of a journal article or a modest section of a book. For purposes of making multiple copies of an article or pages of a book, institutions may apply for and be granted a licence from the copyright clearance organizations, but under strictly defined limitations.

The misunderstanding which so angered you as an author comes about when a university department creates a "book" that imitates a real publication, and this is a breach both of your intellectual copyright and of our publishing rights. Such a problem arises when, outside of formal permissions and legal limitations, several chapters or articles are bound together and distributed to a class of students. When they are sold for cash, even if the department claims it is done "at cost," the plot thickens. Who calculates which overheads are being recovered by that "cost"? And of course the copies you saw last year, at the university bookstore, must certainly have involved a markup by the campus store to cover their own overheads and a profit margin. You pointed out the irony that the resulting bound volume of illegally photocopied readings was actually more expensive than the typical paperback from which they had been taken. But the technology certainly now exists for a department of a university (or any other institution) to make and collate multiple copies of someone else's copyrighted work. The technology for copyright infringement will only get more sophisticated, with electrocopying into photocopier memory, scanning and manipulation of text, and advanced networking.

I doubt that much of this defrauding by lecturers of their colleagues, who have worked hard to write and produce useful material, is deliberate. Instead, I suspect it is naivety about the nature of intellectual property, and a misunderstanding about the "licence" that legalizes other forms of copying. It is also, in too many cases, a response to reduced funding for the teaching collections of campus libraries. This is not the authors' or the publishers' fault, any more than they can take the responsibility for students' decisions on how to allocate their cash as between reading matter and other options.

That charitable approach does not mollify the frustration you feel at seeing your own writing sold or distributed without permission by others. This problem needs a collective, collaborative response. There are many others in your position, in and beyond the university system, who feel their work is being misused. Perhaps you could lobby your professional representatives (does this mean your union? it probably means, in this case, the deans, principals, vice-chancellors) to act on your behalf to defend your scholarship, your writing, your copyright and your intellectual property.

While pressing this case, are you quite sure your own department is not infringing the work of others? It would be embarrassing for you to be caught on the other side. Formal permission is needed for all forms of reproduction in published form—from the distributed student reader or excerpt in a newspaper to a whole foreign-language edition. Authors and publishers will look sympathetically on a genuine request and will usually negotiate reasonable terms in light of who is applying and what their resources are. Most publishers are sympathetic, for instance, to an arrangement which provides single copies of articles or whole chapters to a distance-learning student who does not have access to a university or college library. But in no case can permission be taken for granted. I can certainly think of one elderly author of ours who might not like his work to appear in a student anthology of "examples of sexism in historical writing"; and most authors who would feel suspicious of abridgements without seeing how their work was abridged. In cases where a book does reproduce—with permission— the work of several writers, its compilers or publishers do not thereby acquire the right to license the further reuse of that material by others.

We had encouraged you to follow up your last book with a new guide for students to developments in your field. Now you ask, Why bother, if people are just going to photocopy, anthologize and sell your work behind your back? I can understand your reaction, but I would ask you to be patient. We are sure that the misunderstandings which have led these illegal anthologies to proliferate will soon be resolved. We are committed, as your publishers, to protecting your interest, as our author, by granting permissions only where appropriate, and only if properly requested in advance. It is in the interest of all of us in the academic community—writers, teachers, students, administrators, publishers, librarians, booksellers—to respect the property in which we trade, the exchange of ideas, copyright and intellectual property.

Yours truly, R.M.D.

« 78 » *Is too much published?*

Dear Dr. O'Farquhill,

The strained tones of your complaint sound a familiar note. As a reader, an academic and a member of your university's library committee, you wonder why we publishers continue to push ever upwards the numbers of titles being published in all academic and professional fields.

For every reader (or author) grateful to us for our publishing activity, there must be another reader or librarian groaning at the additional demands which the ever-increasing flow of published knowledge makes on their time and resources. To many, the knowledge explosion seems like an ignorance explosion: a widening gap between the literature which they ought to keep abreast of and the actual time they have for reading, or even skimming. Academic readers worry about how to keep up with the current literature in their field. Even more urgently, librarians worry about how to spread this year's frozen—or sometimes shrinking—budget across an ever wider range of needs.

New forms of communication ought to help by cutting back on the publication of new books and new journals. But the exponential growth of conferences, informal publications in print, and electronic communications only seems to add fuel to the runaway train of publishing. The surfeit of predictions about the paperless society and the end of the book are themselves merely adding to the print explosion.

It is true that the expansion of print seems undiminished. With perhaps a million books in English already available in print in North America, some 67,000 more titles are being added every year. Most academic libraries acquire English-language materials from a wide range of national publishers, as well as buying foreign-language materials. Their ability to acquire new books is also affected by the glut of serials: with 100,000 current serials to choose from, the emergence of new academic journals every week—every day!—seems like a blessing to very few.

Of course, not all these books and serials are scholarly or scientific. They include the very large number of general trade books and magazines for entertainment, information or enlightenment, ranging from popular novels to technical handbooks and specialist magazines for every hobby from amateur radio to zoology. And a significant part of the published output (and a more significant part of publishers' revenues) is in books for primary and secondary school use.

The largest number of journals and books, however, is probably in those academic, scientific, technical and professional fields in which training and research are dominated by the higher education sector: the universities and colleges. The print information explosion cannot be blamed entirely on self-published poets and community newsletters.

But nor can it be blamed solely on the publishers. It takes two (at least) to tango. Every grumble in the university staff club about the weight of new books in a field will be overheard by other academics whose books have just been turned down by a publisher, and who may have received some such explanation as "We are having to be very restrictive in what we take on . . ." or "Regrettably, in today's difficult publishing market . . ."

These prospective authors wish publishers would publish more, not less. An excellent book manuscript has just been turned down by one publisher; a proposal for another well-conceived volume has been declined by a second publisher. With a few colleagues, our scholar has developed an excellent idea for a new journal in a developing field, and they are finding it difficult to get a publisher: perhaps they will have to publish it on their own.

There are several reasons why so many new academic books and new journals are added to the pile each year. The best reason is the expansion of research and academic life worldwide. If the number of academics has multiplied tenfold, their output can be expected to multiply tenfold. Sub-fields develop and new disciplines emerge, and each needs its own corpus of syntheses, quality studies, technical monographs, journals of record and newsletters to exchange information. Even if their institutional libraries struggle to provide them with print resources, research scholars well perceive the need for a solid annual output in their sub-field.

More problematic is the pressure to publish for career reasons. Universities expect to see evidence of productivity to guide their decisions on appointments, tenure, promotion and even departmental evaluation. Research funding bodies expect to see outcomes from their inputs. The pressure to publish is not the same as the pressure to communicate. According to the widely used indices of citations published in the USA by the Institute for Scientific Information, the average scientific paper is referred to in some other scientific paper 6.65 times for US authors, slightly less frequently for British, Australian, Canadian or New Zealand authors. An awful lot of effort is going into researching, writing, publishing, distributing and acquiring those papers for a modest apparent use. And for every paper cited more than seven times, there is another paper with considerably less use. (These statistics cover over 2.5 million papers—a lot of thought and ink!)

We might argue that much of publishing is self-regulating. The publisher issues books and journals which meet a need. Titles which do not meet a need—which do not sell to libraries or individual readers—will not be models for further publishing; publishers who repeatedly misjudge the academic marketplace will cease to be publishers. If the large annual output did not find a sale, that output would not be repeated the next year; and journals without subscribers would fall by the wayside. To librarians who complain that too much is published, the reply might be: We publish it because you buy it.

But of course libraries have to be selective, and seek to share resources to spread their budget around. In professional, scientific and other academic areas, print runs shrink and prices go up accordingly. And to meet the challenge of fewer sales for each title, many academic publishers increase the number of their academic titles. In this way we, as academic publishers, do add to the problem. And shrinking markets are, in many ways, safe markets. There is less publishing risk in a print run of 600 copies of a book which will sell to specialist research libraries only than in one of 3500 copies of a book which has wide potential intellectual importance but which might fail to be recognized. A journal for a niche professional readership may be a sounder venture than a new magazine of innovative cultural perspectives.

If the marketplace were the only limiting factor in publishing output, we might all breathe more easily. There would be fewer books and journals if the numbers were limited to the demands of librarians and users, and to the judgements of commercial publishers and university presses on how to meet those demands. But we have seen many changes in forms of institutional and private self-publishing. Informal publication, the librarian's so-called grey literature, has become more formal. It has moved from the duplicated or photocopied paper for private distribution to the departmental monograph series, using the desktop publishing systems on personal computers, with laser and litho printers. Much of this output appears in annual bibliographical listings of new books and new journals. In fact, statistics reporting the output of publishers are heavily skewed, with many of the year's "new books" coming from an imprint that produces only one item or a handful of items.

The output of private or small institutional publishing has seen an improvement both in quality of product and in accessibility through formal bibliographic tools. The driving force, though, is at least as much the need to write and distribute as the needs of readers.

That might suggest an ever-continuing rise in publications, with ever-diminishing sales and distribution. The one possible barrier to this trend would be the replacement of the grey literature in print by a grey literature in electronic format. That is an issue of wider import. If communication within a small group of specialists changes over completely from small runs in print to electronic dissemination, then the regulatory mechanisms of market and publishers may reassert themselves; the output of new titles need not continue to increase and might shrink slightly. But if librarians merely shift their purchasing resources to include electronic publication and print publication, the impact on scholarly publishing is much harder to predict.

As publishers, we do not expect immediate change. So while we may continue to say No annually to hundreds of thousands of book proposals and manuscripts, we continue to say Yes to tens of thousands. Are we adding to the sum of human knowledge, or just making everyone feel more ignorant, and more desperate about the information flow? In either case, what we do is in the hands of you, as scholarly authors and scholarly readers.   *Yours truly, R.M.D.*

« 79 » *The electronic library and the end*
of the book

Dear Dr. Dimmage,

Sorry to hear you are losing heart over the major writing project. You sound as if you are wavering in your commitment to it. We are not wavering in our commitment to publish: we still very much want the work that you and we have agreed on.

Most authors go through a period of self-doubt before the final push. Most books demand a commitment which is bound to hit weak patches, a self-confidence (and support of others) which is certain to encounter occasional deflation. Can we meet over a drink and talk this through?

What concerns me about your letter is not the temporary doubt about the project, but the much more significant doubt about the value of full-scale book publication. Who put the idea into your head that the printed word was doomed, that the future lay entirely in the rosy world of the electronic media? It sounds like you have stumbled into the bar at some conference of tired librarians. You suggest that your colleagues are preaching doom and gloom, and that some of your students are mocking your print-based peers as dinosaurs confronting the age of higher mammals.

I assure you that print is not doomed as a means of scholarly communication. In saying that, I am not denying the potential of "electronic publishing." But let us not assume that the new must always displace the old; in most forms of the media, the new supplements the old.

Fact is difficult to distinguish from fiction—especially when it comes to predicting the near future. Unfortunately, there are some who achieve ecstasy from predicting the end of the world as we know it and the dawn of a golden age of on-line communication.

Some librarians (academic and professional librarians especially) cast themselves as the villains of the piece. They were once the custodians of the tools by which scholars worked and taught, a modest overhead on top of the expenditure on the tools themselves: the books and journals, and the cost of physically maintaining these; some shelving and desks; and an accurate and easily accessible catalogue. But the overheads started to grow, while the tools became fewer and were renewed and maintained less frequently. The warehouse staff became the gatekeepers of knowledge. This role of Cerberus to the research library is now accompanied by a love of whizz-bang tricks. New electronic hardware is the source of greatest pride to a vocal group of librarians, who devote an increasing share of their budgets to their Cerberitic pursuits, at the expense of the purchase of the tools themselves. Faced with the high costs of basic overheads and expensive hardware, libraries inevitably declare they are quite unable to purchase the books and journals demanded by their clientele. Transformed into information services managers, they will endeavour to make on-line data available in temporary electronic mode: if you want to take it away, you can run it off on the laser printer.

An exaggeration? Well, yes, perhaps so, but no more than the exaggerations of those who enthusiastically proclaim the end of the printed word in scholarly communication.

What can electronic media do? On the positive side, they can allow rapid dissemination of knowledge among the members of an invisible college, people from different institutions working in a shared research area. This is no different from the way geographically scattered branches of a business (even a publishing business) share information rapidly and accurately by electronic data exchange. This communication can be by electronic mail or bulletin board. It can be in an "electronic journal," without the problems and delays incurred by peer refereeing. It can even include the dissemination of research results as a formal paper, a pre-print copy of an article to be formally published in print, or a draft version.

In many cases that is enough. A field might be moving so fast that rapid exchange of information is crucial to the participants. In six months' time the field will have moved on and this information will be dated. Rapidly developing areas in certain of the sciences fit this profile.

So, too, do some applied fields. While economic theory may last, economic data changes rapidly and is needed quickly, as are the scholarly interpretations of data. Soon the interpretations will be too dated (or perhaps too embarrassing) to leave lying around in hard-copy form. Other applied areas are similarly built around current indicators.

Many disciplines have data sets, too, which require regular updating. On-line electronic communication was not pioneered for scholars; it developed because of the needs of the military, with government, academia and commerce coat-tailing it. By analogy, there are data sets in scientific and applied fields which must be updated regularly. Electronic publication has become irreplaceable here—the update on CD-ROM or distributed floppy disk, or, still more usefully, on a server accessed over a network from a lab or office computer terminal.

Perhaps the most useful of these electronic data bases, to the academic community, are—ironically—bibliographic data bases, guides to current print literature and to the holdings of books and journals in libraries. Of course, in many ways this bypasses the gatekeepers, although some of the access paths are obscure enough to demand an underworld guide. We need electronic catalogues to tell us where we can consult a hard-copy book or acquire a hard-copy version of a journal article; to tell us that the book acquired in January is still not catalogued or on the shelves; or to provide up-to-the-minute information that a yearbook has not been replaced for four years in a certain major public library . . .

It is no mystery that electronic forms of publishing should increase in range and in their value to international research. The mystery is why this development should be considered a threat to the printed word.

Historically, most forms of communication have been cumulative and complementary. Writing did not destroy the art of conversation. Papyrus did not destroy the art of monumental inscriptions. Monastic copyists did not make the writing of new books pointless. The publication of the proceedings of learned academies should have removed scholars' need to attend lectures—but it did not. Modern methods of communicating research results could have made the costly and cumbersome academic conference redundant, but such events become ever more, not less, frequent. Supplements to print—microfiche, microfilm, computer tapes and disks, CD-ROMs, on-line electronic journals, videos—have allowed the rapid dissemination of more and more information: yet each has added to the existing forms, not destroyed them. And among all these innovations one form, the printed and bound book, has had the greatest continuity and the widest use of all.

The book will continue. Not only are there more books published every year, but the greatest concentration of purchases of these books seems, in fact, to be in the most self-consciously "electronic" area of all—California, home of New Age librarianship. If California would only stop buying books and journals, we could believe more of this end-of-print evangelism. The places with least access to electronic media are, alas, those which have the greatest difficulty in acquiring print material.

The book may not disappear, but its contents may change. Scholarly publishers will have a new escape from the burden of printing enormous data sets to supplement an academic book: these can now be packaged with the book as a CD-ROM or a computer disk, or can be cited as being available in other electronic formats. Book publishers need not risk those publications (data yearbooks, for example) which date especially rapidly: they can happily leave these to the electronic publisher.

The impact of the electronic "revolution" may be even greater on journals. Not least, some academic journals (or, rather, their editors based in universities and research institutions) may take on board the challenge of the networks' greater immediacy and may speed up their procedures to move papers from submission through review to print. And more electronic journals may make the transition from bulletin boards and self-selected publishing to full peer review, giving the reader some assurance of quality. Most publishers would applaud a drop in the number of printed journals, but they would prefer this drop to be in someone else's list. The journal, which has had a shorter existence than the book, will perhaps change its plumage sooner.

But most research workers will want the results of their studies to be available in some readily accessible form, at a stage which can be labelled not "work in progress" or "draft" but "This is it, folks"—the definitive version. They want this to be available now, and still readily available in (according to discipline and topic) one or five or fifty years' time. They want it to be available—and easily located—in Miami and in Minsk, in Malvern and in Mildura. They want it to have an integrity which cannot be destroyed or manipulated by electronic means.

So I hope we can reassure you that the major definitive study and work of record on which you are engaged will not be wasted when we publish it in book form. And I know we can reassure you that you will not be regarded as a scientific fossil for having published in hard print. On the way to creating your book, you will certainly have read preprints on the electronic networks and exchanged e-mail with colleagues overseas about your work. You will have consulted peers by circulating lengthy drafts on the network and will have received data in electronic form from colleagues to use in your research. Of course you will be preparing your text and many of your illustrations on electronic files and will give us disks to assist in our editing and production of the book.

If you wish, we can discuss including a CD-ROM of data in a slipcase in the back of your book (though I suspect a CD-ROM will look even more old-fashioned and inaccessible than the book in a few years' time). We can advise readers where they can obtain the latest on-line update of the data bases which you and your colleagues have constructed, and on which much of the argument of your book is based. And we can be confident that on-line bibliographic and library accession data bases will make it easy for your fellow scientists to find and acquire your book.

If we are asked, and if you agree, we could release some of the material into electronic data banks, although journal articles lend themselves more to this treatment than do books or book chapters. And if an electronic publisher makes a reasonable proposal to make some of your material available on other electronic media—in a context which strictly protects your copyright and the other legal and moral rights in your intellectual property—we shall be happy to discuss any offers. We would do the same if offered television serialization or Bahasa translation deals.

So don't give up the book; keep writing the definitive, permanent version of your research, in a format which will make it widely accessible in many places and for many years. The permanence provided by the printed book is itself a guarantee that the book is here to stay as a mode of communication. Those who proclaim the imminent end of print in an electronic golden age may quite soon appear dated themselves.

Yours truly, R.M.D.

≋ ≋ ≋ ≋ ≋ ≋ ≋ ≋ ≋ ≋ ≋ ≋

« 80 » *Conclusion*

Dear Arthur,

Now that your book is successfully published, I am writing to thank you for a pleasant working relationship. I hope that you have found the experience of academic authorship less painful than you feared.

I suspect that we as publishers and you as author worked well together partly because we sought to understand each other's point of view, but mainly because we stayed in close communication. You told us, honestly and fully, what were your plans, your hopes, your intentions—and your timetable. We in turn sought to keep you in the picture on what we were doing, what stage we were at, what problems we were experiencing, and what questions we were resolving.

When we began to discuss your book, it was at a stage where our needs and yours could be compared. The plans for the book were adjusted to meet the requirements of the readership—the publisher's market—which we thought we could reach. Even before we could make a commitment to the book, we felt confident that the content, length, level and other aspects of the book were in a viable direction.

We agreed an appropriate time to show material for peer review; then we kept in touch over this painful process, and the unfortunate delays that prolonged it, before our formal acceptance and offer of a contract.

At contract stage we agreed, in writing, details which you and we both meant to adhere to: length, delivery date, advances and royalty payments. In finalizing the manuscript for delivery you followed our guidelines; we gave you answers to questions you raised, and you kept us in touch with progress.

You were patient during the stages of copyediting, design, typesetting, proofing, finalizing text and illustrations, and printing. But, quite reasonably, you kept a gentle pressure on us to make sure that the book kept moving and that there were no hidden problems. You were efficient in dealing with queries, proofs and so on, and we hope we were able to offer efficiency in return. When there were production delays—and there were several unanticipated problems between complete manuscript and final publication—you and we kept in touch and were both aware of where the problems lay.

We appreciated your input into the marketing process: your guidance in providing both ideas and information, and your willingness to respond to requests from our various marketing staff. We trust that we kept you informed of our plans, consulted you in key areas, and maintained a professional approach to launching your book towards the appropriate market.

The publishing relationship is between an author and the many different people in a publishing team. At times we may have seemed faceless to you; at times you may have been just a name to people on our team. But we hope that the right level of creative tension, cajoling and encouraging, informing and warning accompanied most of the stages of your book. You will judge how well we have done by the response to your book from its potential readers: their awareness of its publication, and their comments when they have read it. We shall judge your work—and our decision to publish it—both by reviews and by sales figures. But we shall probably judge the success of our author-publisher relationship, ultimately, by whether we find ourselves the publishers of your next book; by whether we pursue you for another title; and by whether your recommendations bring us work of quality from your colleagues.   *Yours truly, R.M.D.*

BIBLIOGRAPHY

≣ ≣ ≣ ≣ ≣ ≣ ≣ ≣ ≣ ≣ ≣ ≣

This book gives a perspective on scholarly publishing which covers broad general issues affecting the scholarly community, as well as technical guidance. While no other book covers the same ground for the same audience, there is much to be gained by perusing book and periodical literature.

Issues of concern to publishers and authors alike are aired in the excellent quarterly journal *Scholarly Publishing* (Toronto: University of Toronto Press) and more informally in the *IASP Newsletter* (Aarhus: International Association of Scholarly Publishers).

Of less interest to the scholarly author are the trade magazines: *Publishers Weekly* for the USA, *The Bookseller* for the UK, and *Australian Bookseller and Publisher* for Australia and New Zealand.

Publishers' addresses and current descriptions may be gleaned from *Literary Market Place* (New York: Bowker) for the USA and Canada, and *International Literary Market Place* (Bowker) including 175 other countries, together with *Writer's and Artist's Yearbook* (London: Black) for the UK. See also *Publishers, Distributors and Wholesalers of the United States* (Bowker). Often more useful, because it lists individual staff members with their particular responsibilities, is the directory of the Association of American University Presses (New York: Association of American University Presses).

Lists of books currently in print may be useful, not only to fill bibliographical gaps, but also to show whether your title has already been used. The publications by R. R. Bowker (USA), J. Whitaker & Sons (UK), D. W. Thorpe (Australia) and their associated companies provide most of the answers, in print versions or CD-ROM. See *Books in Print* (Bowker), *Whitakers Books in Print* (Whitaker), *Australian Books in Print* (Thorpe), and *International Books in Print* (Munich: Saur).

Among interesting accounts of scholarly publishing are Paul Parsons, *Getting Published: The Acquisition Process at University Presses* (Knoxville: University of Tennessee Press, 1989), and Walter W. Powell, *Getting into Print: The Decision Making Process in Scholarly Publishing* (Chicago: University of Chicago Press, 1985). There are many books to guide would-be fiction writers, and some for writers of general non-fiction, but these are of variable quality. The best should be used selectively by the academic author. There are some useful perspectives from an author-turned-editor in Beth Luey, *A Handbook for Academic Authors* (Cambridge: Cambridge University Press, 1990). Instructive insight on all aspects of academic writing, and a helpful annotated bibliography, can be found in R. E. Matkin & T. F. Riggar, *Persist and Publish* (Niwot: University of Colorado Press, 1991).

Style guides to writing abound, but style guides to preparing a manuscript for publication are fewer. Most widely used is the *Chicago Manual of Style* (Chicago: University of Chicago Press, 14th edition, 1993), which has periodic new editions. Authors can gain much from Judith Butcher, *Copyediting: The Cambridge Handbook for Editors, Authors and Publishers* (Cambridge: Cambridge University Press, revised edition, 1992). In Australia users are often referred to *The Style Manual for Authors, Editors and Printers* (Canberra: Australian Government Publishing Service, 5th edition, 1994). The *MLA Handbook for Writers of Research Papers* (New York: Modern Language Association, 4th edition, 1995) has a proven track record.

The *Chicago Guide to Preparing Electronic Manuscripts* (Chicago: University of Chicago Press, 1987) was a brave attempt to introduce authors to the complex coding of a manuscript, though it is now somewhat dated: but in any case, confer closely with your publisher before engaging in this level of preparation. On contracts, *Publishing Contracts: A Book of Precedents*, by Charles Clark (London: Butterworth, 4th edition, 1993) may help.

INDEX

References are to letters, not pages. Main references are in bold type.

abbreviations, 2, 40
academic books, *see* scholarly books
acceptances, 36, **37**
acknowledgements, 40
acquisitions editor, *see* commissioning editor
acronyms, 2, 40
advances, 20, 38
advertising, 58, 65
agent, literary, 20
anthologies, *see* photocopying
appendix, 3
appointments, academic, 74
artwork, *see* illustrations
audience, **1**, 18, 22, 58
awards, *see* grants; prizes

backlist, 63
bibliography, 3, 4, **10**, 40, 42, 49
binding, 51
bluelines (blues), 51
blurb, 50, 58
books published, number, 1, 78, 79
bookshop, 14, 30, 60, **63**, 65

camera-ready copy, **8**, **48**
captions, 11, 12, 40
career, academic, 74
CD-ROM, *see* electronic publishing
charts, 3
checklist: for manuscript delivery, **40**; for proposal, **17**
citations, *see* bibliography
clarity, *see* style
collected papers, **28**
colour, *see* illustrations
commissioning editor, 19, 31, 33, 34, 38, 39, 53, 70
comparative studies, 29
compositor, *see* typesetter
computer codes, 6, 7, 40, 46

computer files, *see* word processing
conference volume, **25**
conferences, 59, **76**
contents, 3
contract, 4, 12, 20, 35, 37, **38**, 39
copyeditor, 6, 8, 12, **42**, 53
corrections: to disk, 7, 42, **43**; to manuscript, 5; to published book, 52, 70, 71; to typesetting, **46**
costs, 12, 54, 55, 56, 57, 70, 75 (*see also* pricing)
cover, 12, **50**, 51, 63
cross-references, 42
curriculum vitae, 17

data, publication of, 3, 11, 23, 75, 79
decision, publishing, Introduction, 17, 18, 21, **34–37**, 73, 74
decline, *see* rejection
dedication, 40
delivery date, 38, **39**
delivery of manuscript, **40**
design, 6, 8, 12, **44**, 50
desktop publishing, **8**, 11, 14, 23, 25, 45, 48, 79
direct sales, **65**, 76
disciplines, 2, 29, 32, 73, 78
discounts, 54, 55, 56, 65
disk, *see* corrections; word processing
dissertation, 3, **24**
distribution, 55
dumping, 69
dyelines, 51

edited book, *see* multi-author book
editor: academic, 25, 26; publisher's, *see* commissioning editor; copyeditor
electronic manuscript, *see* word processing
electronic publishing, 67, 69, 78, **79**
endnotes, 5, 9, 40, 42
endpapers, 3, 12

errata slips, **52**
errors, *see* corrections
exhibits, **76**
export sales, 67

festschrift, **27**, 59
files, computer, *see* word processing
film, printing from, 51
footnotes, 5, 9, 40, 42
foreign languages, 68
format, *see* layout
free copies, 55, 56
front matter, 40, 42, 48
frontispiece, 12

galley proofs, 45, 46
gender-neutral language, 42
general books, 1, **30**, 39, 41, 63
grants, research, **72**
graphs, 12

half-tones, 12, 40, 44, 47
headings, 3, 5, 42, 45
headlines, 44, 45, 48
hot metal, 12, 45

illustrations, 6, **12**, 40, 44, 46, **47**, 50; colour, 12, 47
imposition, 51
index, 4, 44, 48, **49**
in-house publishing, 8, **14**, 23, 32
internationalism, Introduction, 31, 68, 69
introduction, 3, 22
irony, *see* patience and irony

jacket, 12, 50, 51, 63
jargon, 2
journals, 18, 24, 26, **32**, 58, 60, 61, 65, 69, 72, 75, 78
justification, 5, 6, 45

keyboarding, *see* typesetter; word processing

launch, 59
layout, **5**, 9, 10, 11, 40, 45, 48 (*see also* design)
length, **4**, 22, 38, 49, 56, 75
letterpress, 12, 45
level, *see* audience
library market, 1, 32, 57, **64**, 70, 78, 79

line drawings, 12, 44, 47
literary agent, **20**
litho, 12

magazines, 61, 67
mailings, 65
manuscript, 4–12, 16, 40
maps, 12, 47
margins, 5
marketing, 14, 55, **58**, 59, 60–62, 66, 75, 76
media coverage, **60–62**
multi-author book, 25, **26**, 27, 28, 49
multiple submissions, **15**

newspapers, 61, 67
non-academic author, **33**
notes, 5, **9**, 40, 42

organization, *see* structure
out of print, **70**, 71
outline, *see* proposal
ozalids, 51

page proofs, 45, 46
pageheads, 44, 45, 48
paper, 12, 51
paperbacks, **57**, 67
parts, 2
patience and irony, need for, 1–80
peer review, *see* review
permissions: granted, 67, 71; needed, 12, **40**
photocopying, 28, 64, 67, 77, 78
photographs, 12, 40, 44, **47**
preface, 40
prelims, 40, 42, 48
pricing, 4, 38, **54–56**, 57, 70
print run, 38, 54, 55, 56, 64, 70
printing, 12, **51**
printout, 5, 14, 16 (*see also* desktop publishing)
prizes, **66**
professional author, 33
profit, 55, 56, 57
proofs, 6, 45, **46**, 47
proposal, publishing, **16**, **17**, 26
publication date, 59
publicity, *see* marketing
publisher: choosing a, **13**; commercial, Introduction, 38, 55; reply from, 21, 34–37; visits to, 19, 76 (*see also* commissioning editor)

publishing decision, 16, **34–37**, 73
purchasers, *see* audience

quoted matter, 45

radio, **62**
readers, *see* photocopying
readers' reports, *see* review
readership, *see* audience
references, *see* bibliography; notes
rejection, Introduction, 22, 34, 35
reply, **21**, **34–37**
reprints, **70**, 71
research grants, **72**
résumé, 17
review, peer, 15, 16, 18, 34, 36, 39
reviews, published, 58, **60**, 61
revision of manuscript, 5, 35, 36
rights, **67**, 68, 69, 71
royalties, 33, 37, 38, 55, 67 (*see also* contract)
running heads, 44, 45, 48

sales, 14, 23, 30, 39, 54, 55, 56, 58, **63–65**, 75, 76 (*see also* export sales; library market)
scholarly books, 1, **22**, 23–29, 33, 60, 63, 65, 69 and passim
spacing, 5, 40, 48
sponsoring editor, *see* commissioning editor
structure, **3**, 8, 17, 22, 24, 42
students, 1, 31 (*see also* textbooks)

style, **2**, 9, 42, Bibliography
subediting, *see* copyeditor
subheadings, 3, 5, 42, 45
submission, Introduction, **13**, **15**, 16, **17**, 19, 20
subsidiary rights, **67**, 68, 69, 71
subsidy, 23, 56, **75**
subtitle, 41
synopsis, *see* proposal

tables, 3, **11**, 44, 48, 75
technical volume, **23**, 72, 75
television, **62**
tenure, 74
textbooks, 1, **31**, 39, 57, 63, 65, 77
thesis, 3, 24
time, production, 38, 39
title, **41**, Bibliography
trade books, 1, **30**, 39, 41, 63
translations, **68**
typescript, *see* manuscript
typesetter, 6, 8, 11, **45**
typewriter, 5

university presses, Introduction, 14, 16, 55, 75

video, 62

word processing, 5, **6**, **7**, 11, **40**, Bibliography

ROBIN DERRICOURT received a Ph.D. degree from the University of Cambridge and is the author of books and many scholarly papers in archaeology and history. Following an academic career, with research, teaching and administrative positions in archaeology, he moved into scholarly publishing in 1977. In his international publishing experience he has dealt with a substantial spread of authors and subject areas. His appointments, in both commercial and university press publishers, ranging from senior editor to managing director, have included twelve years as a publishing director for Cambridge University Press in both England and Australia.